Indigenous Knowledge and Human Development

About the Author

Dr. Indira Barua, MA, Ph.D. (1975) joined as a Faculty member in the Department of Anthropology, Dibrugarh University in 1976 and became a Professor in 1993. In 2011 she retired from her service and joined the Department as a UGC Emeritus Fellow. During her long academic carrier, she was actively engaged in academic and research activities. Her publication includes four books and more than eighty research papers both in national and international journals. Prof. Barua visited and presented paper in Chulalonkorn University, Bangkok (1984), School of Oriental and African Studies, London (1993), University of East London (2007). She was invited and financed by European Association of Modern South Asian Studies to deliver lecture in The 19th European Conference on Modern South Asian Studies (2006) in Leiden, the Netherlands.

Some of her works were collected as outstanding contribution in "Inventory of Marriage and Family Literatures", University of Minnesota, USA and Carolina Population Centre, USA. Prof. Barua devoted her research activities among the indigenous communities of Assam. Her research covers a broad area, e.g. ethnographic study, social demography, child care, indigenous knowledge, social process, women study, etc. She completed a number of research projects sponsored by ICSSR, UGC, etc. She is the life member of many professional bodies and is also a member of Advisory Body of the Anthropological Survey of India.

Indigenous Knowledge and Human Development

A STUDY IN NORTH EAST INDIA

Indira Barua

CONCEPT PUBLISHING COMPANY PVT. LTD.
NEW DELHI-110059

ISBN-13 : 978-93-5125-147-7

First Published 2015

Published and Printed by

Concept
Since 1974

Concept Publishing Company Pvt. Ltd.
A/15-16, Commercial Block, Mohan Garden
New Delhi-110059 (India)
T: 25351460, 25351794, *F*: 091-11-25357109
E: publishing@conceptpub.com, W: www.conceptpub.com
Editorial Office: H-13, Bali Nagar, New Delhi-110 015, India.

Cataloging in Publication Data—*Courtesy:* D.K. Agencies (P) Ltd. <docinfo@dkagencies.com>

Barua, Indira, author.
Indigenous knowledge and human development : a study in North East India / Indira Barua.
pages cm
Includes bibliographical references (pages) and index.
ISBN 9789351251477

1. Sonowal Kachari (Indic people)--Science--India--Assam. 2. Deori (Indic people)--Science--India--Assam. 3. Sonowal Kachari (Indic people)--Health and hygiene--India--Assam. 4. Deori (Indic people)--Health and hygiene--India--Assam. 5. Sonowal Kachari (Indic people)--Food--India--Assam. 6. Deori (Indic people)--Food--India--Assam. 7. Sonowal Kachari (Indic people)--Socialization--India--Assam. 8. Deori (Indic people)--Socialization--India--Assam. I. Title.

DDC 305.800954162 23

Preface and Acknowledgements

The present study deals with a topic which have much relevance in present day context, i.e. "Indigenous Knowledge and Human Development: A Study in North East India". Systematic exploration and study of indigenous knowledge have been globally regarded as a high priority research area. Moreover, such types of exploration in different regions enable us to understand the conditions and situations where the early human being lived. It also provides us a scope to know the developmental process. In many instances, such a study forced us to think about the folk wisdom of indigenous population.

Human society and culture evolved over time passing through various stages. Human beings in the 21st century are not the same as Man in 1871, when Taylor and Morgan for the first time defined and described culture and society. Then automatically a question comes to our mind: what was the life of early men? We, at this stage, naturally presume that life of the early men was not so congenial without having any technological infrastructure. But it is a pure misconception developed with the colonial mind-set of so-called civilized society. Civilization is vast; it is the condition or state of Mankind attained through ages of refinement in technology, intellectualization and intricacy of organizations among individuals and groups, and the spread of ideas over large areas of space. Evolutionary theorists emphasized the development of human society from simple to complex with many intermediary stages. If we minutely analyze we may trace that even the earliest man in the traditional environment utilized the natural resources to meet all their needs. They could, to a certain extant; deal with any condition with their limited technological knowledge and was able to turn the situation in their favour. That was the folk wisdom which taught the human being how to live with nature. This wisdom no doubt evolves from the empirical experience of generations over a period of time and which they orally passed on to the next generations. That was not a written document, and because of it in many cases such knowledge gets lost for ever. The tribal unmediated dependence on natural resources is closely related to their peerless ecological knowledge. There is no doubt that each community has their own simple indigenous knowledge, which is very much different from the knowledge acquired by the modern science. The indigenous knowledge dates back to more than 2 million years, when the prehistoric men started making their tools and interacting with nature. In certain sphere, they have evolved sophisticated technologies, such as the boomerang. Hundreds of years ago, a hungry Australian aboriginal threw a curved branch of tree to kill an emu chick. He missed the target but, to his surprise, the branch flew back to fall at his feet. He started to examine the stick and found that it was flat on one side and rounded on the other. He tried it again and again, and only after repeated practice, he could achieve the trick a second time. They understood the trick and tried carving a stick into the shape of a carved branch and found that it worked. Thus, the Australian boomerang was invented. It was a remarkable invention for the people who were so primitive that they could not count beyond the fingers of their two hands. It was mentioned that an expert can throw a boomerang to kill an animal 400 feet away (Stowell: 15). The invention of boomerang may be considered one of the typical examples of indigenous knowledge. They acquired the local wisdom simply observing the natural phenomena.

No human society is free from problems, and in the midst of problems they acquire knowledge due to necessity. Compared to modern life, the livelihood pattern of early men were different. It is true that gathering, hunting and fishing existed long before herding or cultivation. Despite their simplicity, food gathering and hunting economy have considerable technical competence. They not only require technical knowledge about the terrain, but most favourable times and conditions under which to obtain these foods. There are lots of examples recorded about the treatment of early men. It was referred how they applied ants and termites to check bacterial and fungal attack. Various secretions from ants and termites act as pheromones to check bacterial and fungal attack. Firth has referred how the indigenous populations substituted the vitamins, e.g. the

Bemba, who lived largely on millet, was strikingly deficient in fat and low in animal protein. Thus Bemba, who have little meat, eat caterpillars, locus and flying ants, the first being quite an important item of their diet, containing a high phosphorus and iron. He also mentioned about one of the most striking practices of eating earth. The Australians of the Daly River digging earth from underneath the slopes of the river bank and eat. They also eat the dry earth of the termite's ant hills. Edible earth contains a high proportion of mineral salt and the people obtain essential constituents for their health. This practice of eating earth is common in the countries, like Australia, South East Papua and Central America, Congo and in some parts of East Africa.

Impact of environment on health and disease has been stressed by many scholars. May (1960) mentioned that in China, before World War II, some of the villagers were seriously affected by heavy infestation of hookworm. Intensive study showed that hookworm patients were rice growers and others were engaged in silkworm farming. The rice cultivators' work in mud mixed with night soil, while the silkworm farmers spent their working days on ladders tending mulberry leaves. Here disease boundaries and cultural distinctions virtually coincided. Similarly, from Vedic age orchid was known for its beauty and medicinal values. Though orchids and plants are fast disappearing due to ecological imbalance, yet many of the orchids survived due to religious significance. It was reported that sacred blue orchids (*vandal coerulea),* although rare, have not become extinct since they are sustained by Wancho tribe in Tirap district of Arunachal Pradesh for use in worship and festivals. Beliefs, superstitions and prohibitions are always associated with the indigenous knowledge system. When people get some positive results, for any matters, be it plant or animals they try to preserve it, and put some restrictions and prohibitions so that it may not extinct. The early men did not understand about science behind every action. The anthropologists and social scientists who deal with the indigenous populations may ascribe scientific meanings into what may be referred as traditional wisdom. Due to this realization, meaningful research has been carried on among many indigenous population in different regions of the world. The human community in each stage of development has utilized any environmental situations to maintain sustainable living. In the days of rapid urbanization and industrialization, the indigenous knowledge may help us to find out alternative sustainable living.

Considering this backdrop, an effort has been made in the present study to focus the indigenous knowledge in two Scheduled Tribe communities of Assam. Sonowal Kacharis are one of the ancient scheduled tribe living within the geographical perimeter of Assam. Racially they are Mongoloid in origin and their language belongs to the Tibeto-Burman linguistic group. They are conscious about their identity and have Autonomous Council.

Deoris are also, one of the significant Scheduled Tribe, inhabiting the plains of Assam. Linguistically, they are affiliated to the great Tibeto-Burman group and racially belong to the great Mongoloid stock. Now, Deoris are recognized by the Constitution of India as one of the Scheduled Tribes of Assam. They too have Autonomous Council.

North East India is one of the most ethnically and linguistically diverse region in India. Culturally North East region is situated between the two great traditions of Indic Asia and Mongoloid Asia. This geographical-cultural condition of "in-betweenness" is one of the important factors for crisis of identity. This region provides shelter to numerous people of various ethnic affiliation having different social structure, cultural heritages and cultural linkage across the international borders. North East India is the home for more than 166 separate tribes speaking a wide range of languages. Various groups in different periods of time have migrated over the centuries from places as far as South East Asia; some as a conqueror and many in search of land. North East India is unique not only from the ethnic diversity, but also for the indigenous knowledge of these diverse tribes and communities that attract the researchers from time immemorial.

Assam, a land of blue hills and green valleys is situated in the heart of North East India, occupies a strategic importance since independence. It has become a museum of races being situated in one of the great migration routes of mankind. As per 2011 Census (Provisional), the total population of Assam is 31,169,272. The "Scheduled Tribes" account for a sizable proportion of the population of Assam and constitute an important segment of the social fabric of the state. As per the Scheduled Caste and Scheduled Tribe lists (modified under 1956), there are as many as 23 major tribal communities in Assam, of whom 9 are plain tribes and 14 are hill tribes. They are identified by the Constitution of India as socioeconomically backward section of people in the society. Among the notified Scheduled Tribe population in Assam the Bodos make half of the total population. The other significant Scheduled Tribe populations of Assam are Mishings, Karbis, Rabhas, Sonowal Kacharis: Tiwas, Dimasa, Deoris, etc. In Assam, they are living in the midst of rural communities of Assam and sometimes it is difficult to differentiate between them and as a result they have many common indigenous knowledge systems.

A study of indigenous knowledge system among the Sonowal Kacharis and the Deoris reveal that they have a rich tradition of indigenous knowledge, which they have accumulated in course of living in a particular region. The present study particularly deals with ethno medicine and the treatment of diseases. The analysis of data in two different settings, i.e. forest villages and revenue villages show slight differences. The study reveals that the numbers of ailments recorded in two forest villages inhabited by the Sonowal Kacharis are less in comparison to the revenue village. The Sonowal Kacharis also believe in supernatural causation of diseases. All throughout the year, they observe various religious rites and rituals to propitiate the specific god; responsible for a particular disease. More or less same picture is projected among the Deoris living in forest villages and revenue village. Due to long and permanent settlement pattern in revenue village, the villagers have rich tradition of indigenous knowledge. Most of the households have well maintained kitchen garden and the common jungles in the surrounding areas provide them the necessary herbs and shrubs for treatment. While forest villages in their rehabilitated situation, do not have much scope to accumulate the knowledge in the absence of elderly population permanently inhabited in a particular settlement. The Sonowal Kacharis and Deoris are both living in same environmental condition. They have their own methods of preparations and preservations of food items. Smoking, roasting and boiling are the ancient methods of cooking and is still followed by most of the tribal people. Hearth (fire place) plays an important role in smoking and roasting. The hanging platform above the heart is a must in the kitchen, but the number and size of platform varies in two communities. In their day-to-day life, they consciously/unconsciously prepare curry from herbs and shrubs which have medicinal value. Different varieties of fish and meat dishes are prepared by them. Besides the normal food items, they are very much fond of insects which are considered as delicacy having nutritious values. They also observe some prescriptions and prohibitions in their food items. In case of illness, they follow their indigenous beliefs and practices. Detailed analysis of ethnic food items may also reveal the migration history of a tribe, to a certain extent. In the present study an effort has been made to include various examples to focus such issues.

Indigenous knowledge/traditional knowledge are to be transmitted from one generation to the next. To understand the transmitting process, it is essential to consider various parameters, i.e. how the children are reared and socialized. Values, attitude and beliefs are associated with the child rearing and provide scope to understand the transmitting process. Effort has also been made to give an idea about the child rearing practices among these communities.

From early stage of civilization, the human being is to take measures and develop indigenous ways to deal with problems, both environmental and social. The study focuses that the knowledge system or precaution which the indigenous people emphasized is meant for longer social security. The sacred conservation practices, superstitions, religious taboos and prohibitions, no doubt, play an important role in protecting the natural resources, and thereby managing the eco-systems. Their knowledge about different aspects and elements from their traditional environment is also reflected in their folk literatures. It is the responsibility of social scientists and anthropologists to explore the indigenous process, because there rests the basic philosophy of survival mechanism of a society. Indigenous knowledge (I.K.) refers to the unique, traditional local knowledge existing within and developed in a particular geographical area. Indigenous knowledge as such refers not only to the knowledge of a particular community, but also to that of any other defined community of particular areas. Indigenous knowledge system delineates a cognitive structure in which theories and perceptions of nature and culture are conceptualized. Thus, to have a better understanding of indigenous knowledge system a thorough understanding of physical, natural, social and economic environment are prerequisites. The North East India is unique both from the ethnic diversity as well as indigenous knowledge of these diverse tribes and communities and there are still enough scope of exploring and interpreting these vast treasure houses of indigenous knowledge. It is hoped that this micro level study among two Scheduled Tribe communities in two different settings would project certain ideas about the indigenous knowledge systems in these areas.

The present study is the outcome of the project carried out as a UGC Emeritus Fellow for the session 2011 to 2013. I wish to take this opportunity to offer my thanks to the UGC for selecting me as an Emeritus Fellow to carry out the research in a topic, which has much relevance in the present day context.

I am also thankful to Dibrugarh University for giving me permission to carry out the research and providing me necessary infrastructural facilities.

I would like to thank all the villagers for their untiring help in providing the valuable information related to the topic.

I take this opportunity of acknowledging my thanks to all my colleagues, research scholars and office staff of the Department of Anthropology for their help and cooperation in completing the work. I shall be failing my duty if I do not thank to the field investigators for their help in collecting the data.

My grateful acknowledgements are due to my family members who are always a source of inspiration to me for pursuing my research activities.

For any unintentional factual error or any erroneous views which might have entered into the text is, however, entirely mine.

Dr. (Mrs.) Indira Barua

Contents

List of Tables

List of Maps

1
Introduction

The main emphasis of the study is to explore the indigenous knowledge and skills among certain indigenous communities of North East India and see to what extent it may be used for the developmental process.

The two terms—Indigenous Knowledge and Human Development, are closely related. The indigenous communities all over the world have their own indigenous knowledge and skills, on the basis of which the communities could survive and develop. In recent decades, the traditional communities worldwide are increasingly using their intimate knowledge of plant, soil, food and other resources for sustainable and holistic approach.

The term Development is a value based term, which cannot be defined ostensibly. It is used to distinguish the developed ones from the developing and under-developing ones or to uplift the weaker section and under-developed areas. According to Oxford English Dictionary "development" means: a "gradual unfolding". This concept of "gradual unfolding" works satisfactorily with two social processes, namely, the growth of knowledge and the growth of human control over the natural resources. A forward looking trend oriented concern is another feature of development. "Development by definition is the act or process of developing or growth evolution within the framework of available resources" (Desai, 1988). Different definitions are put forth by many social scientists, anthropologists and others. The term development is conceived as valuable for policy makers, planners, implementers, evaluators and beneficiaries.

Human development is desirable from both economic and social point of view. When we talk about human development, we should not simply focus on an aggregation of healthy and educated individuals. It covers the social aspects as well, which includes the social values, beliefs, customs, etc. A concept of human development that includes the social dimensions is wider than the concept of human development that focuses on humans as "resources". Health and education are crucial elements for human development, but do not constitute the whole of it.

Human society progressed because of man's ability to adjust and control over his environment. In the subsequent stages, various welfare and developmental measures were initiated by the Government in various plan periods for the progress and development of human society. Emphasis was given on economic development, eradication of poverty, illiteracy and family planning programme, etc. But development involves change and change involves adjustment in values, ideas and traditional socio-institutional system. Now, it is pertinent to see whether the indigenous and traditional knowledge may be manipulated for development or such beliefs simply act as a barrier of development.

An indigenous knowledge system encompasses the innovations, technologies, traditions, practices, wisdom and teaching, etc. of certain regional, indigenous or local communities. According to Warren (1991), "Indigenous knowledge is the local knowledge—knowledge that is unique to a given culture and society. Indigenous knowledge contrasts with the international knowledge system generated by the Universities, Research Intuitions and Private firms. It is the basis for local level decision making in agriculture, health care, food preparation, education, natural resource management and a host of other activities in rural communities" (Cited from Wikipaedia—the Internet Encyclopedia). It is surprising to learn that there are some highly evolved and sophisticated technologies of the indigenous people.

Indigenous knowledge may be considered as important natural resources that can facilitate the development process in cost effective, participatory and sustainable way. To ignore people's knowledge is almost to ensure failure in development (Brokensha, 1980). Since indigenous knowledge is essential to development, it is often suggested that it must be gathered and documented in a coherent and systematic fashion (Brokensha, 1980, Warren, 1995).

It is well known fact that the tribal people or indigenous people all over the world have accumulated knowledge over time, which in traditional set-up allowed them to live in balance with their environment and this helped them to adjust with natural resources for their livelihood. Knowledge and innovation derived from indigenous system cannot be credited to a single investor. They are community based and accumulated over time and generation. The indigenous knowledge system and skills and innovations are part and parcel of the day-to-day life of the people. The motivation derived from indigenous knowledge system is not for profit or individual gain, but for the welfare and common good of the entire community and future generation.

Indigenous Knowledge can be broadly defined as the knowledge which a (local) community accumulates over generation, living in a particular environment. This definition encompasses all forms of knowledge, know-how-skill, practices and beliefs that enable the community to achieve stable livelihood in their environment. In course of time, various belief systems emerge within the community, which on the one hand help in retaining their traditional knowledge system and on the other hand maintaining stable livelihood and mental/ psychological security. Thus, indigenous knowledge and belief system are interrelated.

Objectives of the Study

The entire focus of the present study is to give some ideas, regarding how indigenous knowledge and practices may be utilized in developmental process. The latent cultural and social dimensions need careful consideration for the success of any developmental schemes. Everywhere there are some deep seated cultural values, which prevent in adopting or accepting the new ideas. On the other hand some traits or beliefs may be identified whose inner aim is almost similar to those, which the policy makers are planning to introduce. Thus, cultural policy may be considered to be a means contributing to development, a goal of development and performance and a factor, which the programmer must keep in mind.

Thus, the two major objectives of the study are:

1. To explore and document the indigenous knowledge and belief system. Its domain includes areas like indigenous health care, reproductive health and child care, food preparation and preservation, natural resource

management and a host of other activities of the indigenous communities.

2. To find out to what extent such knowledge may be utilized in Developmental process.

To fulfil these objectives, the following areas have been identified.

Indigenous Health Practices

The practice of ethno-medicine by different ethnic groups to cure diseases and ailments bear a testimony to indigenous knowledge system. An effort has been made to explore ethno-medical knowledge, herbal medicine, magico-religious and spiritual practices that exist among the communities. Emphasis has been made to understand the concept of health, disease, etiology and traditional beliefs, customs and practices with regard to treatment.

It is also intends to find out different kinds of problems, diseases and ailments for which the services of the traditional medicine men and healers are sought.

It is also planned to describe ethno-medico-botanical description of different herbs and plants used as ethno-medicine for healing various diseases and ailments.

Emphasis has been given to assess scientific analysis and descriptions of magico-religious performances among the indigenous communities.

Finally, effort has been made to assess modern as well as traditional medical services.

Indigenous Knowledge Relating to Food

In the sphere of food habit, it is universally accepted that the women are by nature conserver and preserver of indigenous skills and knowledge. They arc also taking precaution of food and nutritional security.

An emphasis has been made to explore the indigenous ways of preparing and storage of ethnic food items.

An effort has been made to explore, analyze and document the entire food consumed by the indigenous communities and its associated dynamics to understand food consumption pattern and availability. It is also important to find out nutritional and medicinal values and to what extent the indigenous communities are aware about it.

It is also intended to locate various beliefs, socio-religious norms, traditional ecological knowledge systems which remain responsible for conservation of resources.

Indigenous Knowledge and Socialization Process

Indigenous knowledge, i.e. the local knowledge is transmitted from one generation to the next. So, it is considered necessary to understand the transmitting process, i.e. the socialization process. Indigenous knowledge and socialization process goes hand in hand. Various parameters are to be considered while dealing with the transmitting process. The role of different formal and informal institutions/agencies have been systematically studied and carefully recorded. Besides upbringing of the children; the effort taken by the family members to socialize/culturalize the children have also been recorded. The reproductive health care of the mothers has been well considered.

With regard to child care, emphasis have been made on the following points:

1. To find out the Indigenous health practices particularly in case of parturient mother and new born baby.
2. Effort has been made to find out the knowledge and beliefs associated with indigenous way of planning a family, gap between two issues, etc.
3. Care has been taken to have an idea of Indigenous knowledge pertaining to the treatment of women's disease.
4. Emphasis has been given to understand the child care practices, particularly to understand the nutritional and health status of children in the age group of 0 to 6 years.

Changing Scenario

Finally, it is also considered important to find out what is happening to indigenous knowledge system in the changing scenario.

Since, indigenous skills and knowledge are used in almost all walks of life of the people; it is humanly not possible to cover all the areas within the limited time frame. Therefore, certain limitations have to be made in this regard.

Hypothesis

On the basis of the above objectives and theoretical framework a few working hypothesis has been formulated.

1. Most of the indigenous beliefs and practices are pure fallacies.
2. There are scientific bases behind some of the indigenous beliefs and skills.
3. Indifferences to indigenous beliefs and skills adversely affect the developmental process.

Research Design and Methodology

Standard Anthropological method has been used either independently or in combination with others, i.e. (a) observation, (b) interview based on interview schedule, and (c) case study.

Explanatory research designs have been followed to carry out the research work. For studying indigenous skills, the qualitative approach has been adopted.

Following the purposive sampling method and degree of traditionalism, extent of forest cover and availability of traditional skills, the villages have been selected. The villages, where indicators of modern developments are negligible and people mostly rely on their own institutions and resources have been considered as remote socio-ecological system. And the villages which are situated near the urban centre have been considered, to find out the changes. From the selected villages, the respondents have been selected keeping the gender and age demotion in mind.

Depending on the nature of data, the techniques have been used either independently or in collaboration. For qualitative data, more emphasis has been put on techniques like, observation and collection of concrete cases, etc.

On the basis of pilot survey, both open and close ended schedule have been applied.

Selection of People and Area

In the present study, an emphasis been made to get a holistic understanding of the indigenous knowledge system among two

Scheduled Tribe communities, e.g. the Sonowal Kacharis, and the Deoris of Assam. Besides, the published data from the Tai Buddhist Communities have been incorporated. Racially all of them belong to the Great Mongoloid communities of North East India.

The entire region of North East India is a world of indigenous skill and knowledge. They are applied in different areas of problem solving, covering a wide range of day-to-day activities such as in health care, medical treatment, environmental protection, agriculture, food habits, etc. There is no written record of such practices, but they are guided by well established unwritten principles, which are transmitted from generation to generation. These are all time tested skills.

Assam, a land of the blue hills and green valleys which is situated in the north-east of India occupies a strategic importance since independence. It has become a museum of races, being situated in one of the great migration routes of mankind.

The Sonowal Kacharis

The Sonowal Kacharis are one of the most ancient Scheduled Tribes living within the geographical perimeter of Assam. Racially they are Mongoloid in origin and their language belongs to the Tibeto-Burman linguistic group. Endle (1911) describes the Sonowal Kachari as the earliest known inhabitants of Brahmaputra valley. They are conscious about their own identity and have Autonomous Council.

The Deoris

The Deori is a Scheduled Tribe inhabiting the plains of Assam. Linguistically, they are affiliated to the great Tibeto-Burman group and racially they belong to the Mongoloid stock. According to Brown, the Deoris are known as a branch of the Chutiyas, which belong to the great Bodo race. Now, the Deoris are recognized by the Constitution as one of the Scheduled Tribes of Assam. The headquarters of Deori Autonomous Council is in Narayanpur, Lakhimpur District.

Tai Ahom and Tai Buddhist communities constitute major communities of Assam who are rich in indigenous skill and knowledge. Efforts have been made to incorporate some of the published data in the present study. The aim is to give a meaningful scientific understanding of indigeno s knowledge and skills that exist among certain communities of North East India.

Rationale of the Study

The field of indigenous knowledge and technology that figured as the predominant area of contribution by the Indian Anthropologists in the 15th ICAES, 2003 still remains a major area of research. But this field is not a homogeneous field of inquiry under a single thematic boundary. It covers various dimensions and gradually the issues of tribal development are bound to link with the domain of indigenous knowledge and the two areas together become a significant field of research.

Lots of works has been done in relation to indigenous knowledge system among various communities of India. The North East India, with various ethnic groups, offers an excellent opportunity for studying indigenous knowledge. As people are habituated to live and survive with nature, the region is a treasure house of indigenous knowledge system pertaining to agriculture, food, medicine and natural resource management. But unfortunately, no systematic work has been done in this region covering diverse tribes and communities. Today many of the indigenous knowledge systems are at risk of becoming extinct because of rapidly changing natural environments and fast pacing economic, political and cultural changes on a global scale. The tragedy of the impending disappearance of indigenous knowledge is most obvious to those who have developed it and the implication for others can be detrimental as well, when skills, technologies, artifacts, problem solving strategies and expertise are lost.

So, it is a high time to record, preserve and resurrects all the indigenous knowledge systems and skills before this traditional knowledge are completely lost. It is hoped that the present study would at least record, document and preserve the rich and amazing indigenous skills and knowledge system of these communities which are still untouched.

A Brief Review of the Works Done

In the recent decades, there has been a great spurt in studies related to indigenous knowledge system. Lots of works have been done in relation to indigenous knowledge among various tribes and communities of India. But the North East India, which is the treasure house of indigenous communities, is still left behind.

Anthropological studies have revealed that every known human society has its own concept regarding health and disease and the methods of coping with them. Dube (1977) in his paper "*Cultural factors in rural community development*" emphasized how cultural factors play a critical role in development. Mathur (1977) in his edited book "*Anthropology in the Development Process*" has projected the role of cultural factors. Belshaw (1977) in the paper "*The Contribution of Anthropology to Development*" rightly projected the role of Anthropologists in the developmental process.

Many works have been reported specially from among the rural and tribal communities of India (Chaudhury, 1986, Bhadra and Tirky, 1997, Sharma Thakur (1997). The problems of health and indigenous method of treatment have been reported by Chaudhury (2000), Duarah and Pathak, (1997), Kohli, (1999) and Bhasin, (1997, 1999, 2002, 2003 and 2005).

Chaudhuri (1986, 1990) emphasized the study of health and culture among the Tribal people. Kapoor (1994, 1996) studied the Tribal population of Central Himalayas and Rajasthan and found that still they have more faith in traditional practices. Mahapatra (1994) analyzed the Santal view of health and sickness, disease and death. He also tried to explore the linkage between traditional and modern system of medicine. Mishra and Kapoor (2003) reported the herbal and magico-religious-spiritual means of treatment among the Saharias, a primitive tribe of Rajasthan. It was found that many of the diseases are treated by the traditional healers through herbal medicine. Sachidananda (1994) pointed out that the success of any health programme in the tribal areas largely depends on the understanding of life and culture of the people under study.

The study of Tesfaye and Gautam (2003) in Ethiopia and India reveals the indigenous farmers' technical knowledge and its utilization for pest control.

However, ethno-medicinal studies are relatively less in North East India. Kalita, Dutta and Islam (2005) made a study of the plant and animal based folk medicine used by the people of Dibrugarh District of Assam for treatment of 11 different diseases. Kar (1993, 1997) has reported about cultural dimension of health mainly among the Tea garden communities. Besides using herbal medicine many of the indigenous communities are trying to cure diseases through magico-religious practices as reported by Barua (1990, 2002).

Most of the communities also have their indigenous ways of managing and conserving the natural resources.

Barua (1998, 2000 and 2008) described the indigenous knowledge and belief system among the different communities of North East India. Barua (2004) in her paper "*Maidam: Anthropo-historical Study of Tai Ahom Burial Custom*" reported the indigenous process of construction and preservation among the Tai Ahoms. It was reported that "from the vault of one of the Queens of this country who had been buried 80 years ago, a gold betel basket was taken out within which the betel leaf was still green" (Gait, 1965).

Das and Tag (2006) reported the ethno-medicinal practices among the Khamtis of Arunachal Pradesh.

Devi (2011) in her paper "Plants used by Meitie community of Manipur for the treatment of Diabetes" reported indigenous ways of treatment.

Kala (2005) studied the ethno-medicinal practices among the Apatanis in the Eastern Himalayan region.

Mao and Odyno (2007) in the article, "*Traditional Fermented food of the Naga tribe of Northeastern India* "gives a detail idea about the fermented food of the Nagas.

Nath *et al.* (2011) documented the various medicinal plants used in major diseases by Dimasa tribe of Barak valley.

Pradhan and Badola (2008) highlighted the ethno-medicinal plants used by Lepcha tribe of Dzongu valley of North Sikkim.

Sajem and Gosai (2010) carried out an ethno-botanical investigation among the Lushai tribes in North Cachar Hill district of Assam.

Singh *et al.*, in a paper (2007) "*Cultural Significance and diversities of ethnic foods of Northeast India*" focuses the wide diversities of food preparation and preservation among certain tribes of North East India. The article describes how in each state, the processing method of the food is somewhat different based on culture, variability in materials used in the food, climate and overall knowledge of the processing and preparation.

Singh *et al.* (2008) in the article "*Traditional skill among the Adi tribes of Arunachal Prodesh*" highlights the rich knowledge of Adis in various aspects of their material culture.

Sukla and Haridasan (1995) in the article Ethno-forestry-its relevance in Arunachal Pradesh have dealt with the higher degree of people's dependence on the forest. They also highlighted people's co-existence, in-depth knowledge of forest utilization, management and conservation through their own indigenous ways.

In the field of reproductive health also various beliefs and practices exist among indigenous communities. It was reported by Erikson (1963) where the mother never offers breast milk immediately after the birth of the baby. Veena and Bhat (2008) reported that after the birth of the baby, the child is fed with honey, sugar, water for the first few days. Dave and Tavkar (1985) reported that among the tribes of Panchmahal district of Gujarat the child is fed with the goat's milk for the first three days after the birth followed by breast feeding which usually continues till the next pregnancy.

Such beliefs and practices are pure fallacies which may hinder the development of the child. There are instances where some beliefs exist among the indigenous communities which reflect the idea of family planning and gap between the two issues. Barua (1998) reported such beliefs in many indigenous communities of Assam and the existence of same beliefs in many communities of Punjab. Such beliefs may be utilized for implementation of the family planning programme.

The Institute for Research in Medical Statistics, New Delhi undertook a study to assess the traditional status of children in Bihar and found out the malnutrition among the children depends on both sanitary condition and on dietary intake.

North East India is the easternmost region of India, consisting of the contiguous seven sister states and is popularly known as "Seven Sisters" (*Sat Bhani*). It comprises the States of Assam, Arunachal Pradesh, Manipur, Meghalaya, Mizoram, Nagaland and Tripura. Of late, Sikkim has also been included in North East India for administrative purpose. North East India is the most sensitive and strategically important as it is situated in the International border. The North East is a true frontier region. No other region of India has international borders as extensive as that of North East India. It has over 5,437 km of border with Bangladesh, Myanmar, China, Bhutan and Nepal. It shares about 1880 km with Bangladesh, about 1,643 km with Myanmar, about 1,300 km with China, about 516 km with Bhutan and about 97 km with Nepal. The following table will provide detailed picture about international border.

North East India is one of the most ethnically and linguistically diverse region in India. Culturally, North East region is situated between the two great traditions of the Indic Asia and Mongoloid

Table 1.1: State-wise Length of International Border of NE Region in km

State	Bangladesh	Bhutan	China	Myanmar	Nepal	Total
Arunachal Pradesh	0	217	1080	520	0	1817
Assam	263	267	0	0	0	530
Manipur	0	0	0	398	0	398
Meghalaya	443	0	0	0	0	443
Mizoram	318	0	0	510	0	828
Nagaland	0	0	0	215	0	215
Sikkim	0	32	220.35	0	97.80	350.15
Tripura	856	0	0	0	0	856
Total	1880	516	1300.35	1643	97.8	5437.15

Source: Ministry of Development, NE Region.

Asia. This geographical cultural condition of "in-betweenness" is an important factor for the crisis of identity. The region provides shelter to numerous people of various ethnic affiliation having different social structures, cultural heritages and cultural linkage across the international borders. North East India is the home for more than 166 separates tribes speaking a wide range of languages. Many scholars have considered the North East region as a cultural corridor between India and South East Asia. A great majority of the tribes have migrated from South East Asia long back and still retain their own cultural values and traditions. This has also helped the scholars to identify and trace their original homeland. But slowly with the passage of time, they have started to change their traditional culture and the process of assimilation and acculturation plays its role in developing an ethnic mosaic in this part of North East India. Another significant feature of North East India is that each tribal group can be called an ethnic group since each of them is a social unit, having a common culture, language, common goals and is at the same time self-conscious as a group. The plain areas are inhabited by both tribal as well as the non-tribal populations. It is significant that, one-third of the total number of the listed tribes of the whole of India is found in this region.

The region can be physiographically categorized into the Eastern Himalayas, North East Hills (Patkai-Naga Hills and Lushai Hills) and the Brahmaputra and the Barak valley plains. The North East is a true frontier region. Along with the west coast of India; this region has some of the Indian subcontinent's last remaining rain forests which support diverse flora and fauna and several crop species.

Similarly, reserves of petroleum and natural gas in the region constitute a fifth of India's total potential. The region is covered by the mighty Brahmaputra-Barak river system and their tributaries. Geographically, apart from the Brahmaputra-Barak and Imphal valleys and some flat lands in between the hills of Meghalaya and Tripura, the remaining two-thirds of the area is hilly terrain interspersed with valleys and plains.

Assam is the heartland of North East India. Assam, a land of the blue hills and green valleys is situated in North East India occupies a strategic importance since Independence. It has become a museum

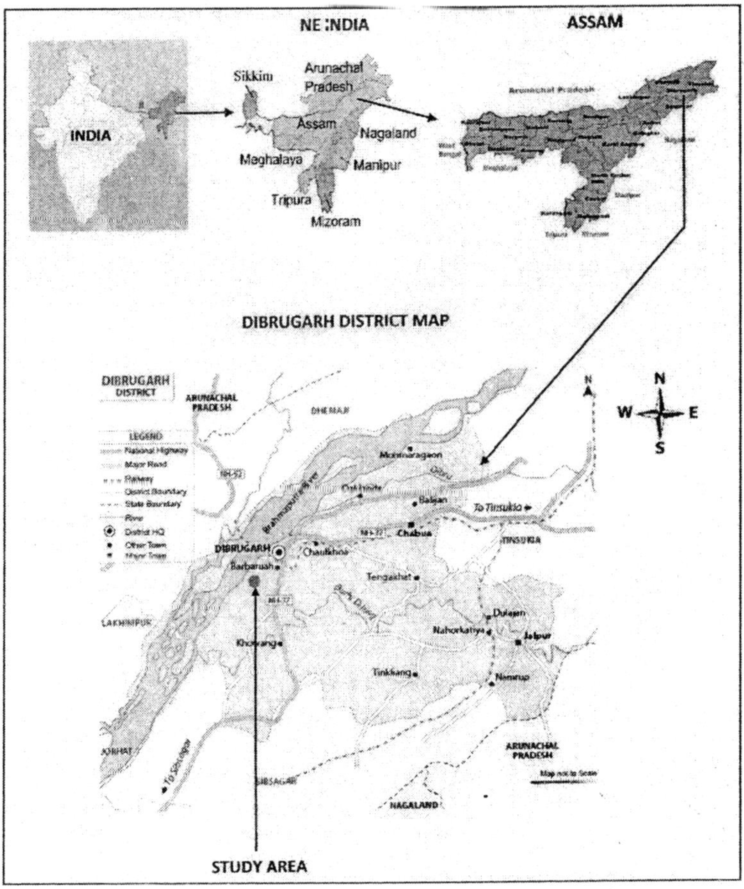

Map 1.1: Location of the Study Area

of races, being situated in one of the great migration routes of mankind. "The various racial elements from India on the one side and from South-East Asia on the other, passing through Assam left their substratum in both hills and plains." (Choudhury, 1959:82). Various races, viz. Austro-Asiatic, Negritos, Dravidians, Alpines, Indo-Mongoloids, Tibeto-Burmese and Aryans entered into Assam at different times through different routes carrying with them distinct cultures and trends of civilization. These different types of people contributed in their own way towards the unique fusion of a new community which came to be known as Assamese. Assam, however, remained predominantly a land of Tibeto-Burmese.

There is no doubt that Mongoloid contributes a major stock of population in Assam. Risley rightly remarks that Assamese are unmistakably Mongoloid. Elwin considers them a rather modified Mongoloid. The Mongoloid strain entered Assam mainly through Patkai ranges of eastern India. The mountain pass across the Patkai ranges has a historical significance for the country; it can easily be described as the Khyber of the east. Like the Pataki range, the Namkin range, though less known constitutes a natural boundary between India on the one hand and Burma and China on the other.

The State of Assam spread over an approximately 78,523 sq. km. The topography of the state is mainly composed of plains and river valleys. Geographically, the state can be divided into three major regions, i.e. the Brahmaputra valley and the Borak valley, named after the two great rivers, and the Cachar hills which divide both the valleys. But the Brahmaputra valley occupies major part of the state, running from north to south.

The state is on the foothills of the eastern Himalayas. On the north lies the country of Bhutan, while in the east, the state is covered by the state of Arunachal, Nagaland and Manipur. To the west of Assam, are Meghalaya and Mizoram and in the west is Tripura and Bangladesh. The state is surrounded by a ring of blue hills. Assam bears its own distinct identity as the homeland of a number of tribal and non-tribal communities with heterogeneous language and culture. The tribal population includes both hills and the plain dwellers. Some of the important tribes are the Bodos, Kacharis, Karbis, Mishings, Rabhas, and Tiwas and among the Tai speaking communities there are Ahoms and the Tai Buddhist communities.

As per 2011 Census (Provisional), the total population of Assam is 31,169,272, out of which 15,954,927 are males and 15,214,345 are females. The sex ratio of females per 1000 males is 954. The population density per sq. km is 397. The percentage of decadal growth rate is 16.93. The literacy rate is 73.18 per cent (Male - 78.81%, Female - 67.27%). The percentage of female literacy rate is low as compared to male. The number of child population within the age of 0-6 years is 45,11,307 (Male - 23,05,088, Female - 22,06,219). The percentage is 73.18. The percentage of child population above 7 years is 67.27. When we look the population strength of the North-eastern states in the total population of India (1,210,193,422) according to 2011 Census (Provisional), it is found that in Assam it forms the 2.58 percentage of the total population of India. While each of the remaining states has below 1.00 per cent of the total population of India. It also indicates that among the North-eastern states significant majority, i.e. 68.37 are found in Assam. It forms the 2.58 per cent of total population of India. Growth of population in Assam has experienced a very high trajectory since the mid-decades of 20th century. Population grew steadily from 3.29 million in 1901 to 6.70 million in 1941, while it has increased unprecedently to 14.63 million in 1971 and 22.41 in million in 1991 to reach the present level. The Scheduled Tribe population forms a significant section in the North-eastern states forming 12.41 per cent of the total Scheduled Tribe population of India. In case of Assam as per 2001 Census the total Scheduled Tribe population is 3,308,570 forming again 12.4 per cent of the total population of Assam (26,655,528). The Scheduled Tribe population of Assam have secured highest number (31.61%) in the total Scheduled Tribe population of North East India (2001 Census). The state has registered 15.1 per cent decadal growth of Scheduled Tribe Population 1991-2001. There are total twenty three (23) notified Scheduled Tribes in the state. Among the Scheduled Tribe Population Boro (40.9%) represent half of the total population of the state. The other Scheduled Tribe population of Assam are Mishings, Karbis, Rabhas, Sonowal Kacharis, Tiwas, Dimasa, Deoris, etc.

The present study deals with two major Scheduled Tribes of Dibrugarh district of Assam.

Dibrugarh District

It is situated in the extreme north-eastern corner of Assam on the southern bank and upper reaches of the river Brahmaputra. Dibrugarh became a separate district when it was split from the earlier Lakhimpur district in 1976. On first October 1989, Tinsukia district was split from Dibrugarh. Presently Dibrugarh district has an area of 3,381 sq. km. It comprises the southern part of the undivided Lakhimpur district and is bounded on the north by the river Brahmaputra and Lohit, on the east by a part of Lohit of Arunachal Pradesh; on the south by Tirap district of Arunachal Pradesh. The south-western boundary of the district runs along the eastern boundary of Sibsagar district. The district headquarters is Dibrugarh. It consists of a fairly high plain. A vast area along the foot of the hills is covered with dense evergreen forest. Tea gardens cover a vast area of the District. The population of the district is composed of members of various ethnic, linguistic, social and religious affiliations and mainly dominated by Mongoloid and Caucasoid element and an admixture of these two. The large labour force working in tea-garden belongs to various castes and tribes. According to the 2011 Census, Dibrugarh District has a population of 1,327,748. This gives it a ranking of 367th in India (out of total of 640). The district has a population density of 398 inhabitants per sq. km. Its population growth rate over the decade 2001-2011 was 12.04 per cent, and the male female ratio is 1000:952; the literacy rate being 76.22 per cent.

2
The Setting

In this chapter, the data have been arranged systematically under two broad settings, viz. **Section A** and **Section B**, that deals with the main population considered in the study. These sections have been further divided into **A.1**. and **A.2** Sub-Sections. In Sub-Section **A.1** emphasis has been made to highlight the origin, history, socio-cultural life and the present distribution of the population as a whole in Assam. In Sub-Section **A.2**, an effort has been made to give a detailed description of the micro field wherefrom the field data have been collected and incorporated.

A. Population: The Sonowal Kacharis

A.1: Historical Background

Sonowal Kacharis are one of the most ancient Scheduled (Plain) Tribe living within the geographical perimeter of Assam. They are a sub-group of the great Kachari tribe of Assam belonging to the Asiatic Mongoloid race of Sino-Tibetan stock.

Endle (1990) describes the Kacharis as the earliest known inhabitants of the Brahmaputra valley. All the scholars who studied this tribe from various angles were of the opinion that the origin of the Kachari race is still very largely a matter of conjecture and inference, in the absence of anything entitled to be regarded as authentic history. Endle remarked that in feature and general appearance they approximate very closely to the Mongolian type; and this would seem to point to Tibet and China as the original home of the race (Endle, 1990: 3).

Chatterjee has speculated that these Mongoloid groups might have migrated to the alluvial plains of the Brahmaputra valley, from the northern plateau, along the sub-Himalayan water channels like the Brahmaputra, during 200 BC for the purpose of extending their trade and commerce and these were the people who are also mentioned as the "*Simantubasi*" or the frontier dwellers or "*Kiratas*" in the Hindu mythologies like the *Mahabharata*. The most important of these stocks is a group called the Bodos (Boro) who form the major bulk of the non-Aryan population of Assam, including the Koch, the Kachari, the Lalung, the Chutiya, the Garo, the Moran and so on. Of these, Bodo groups, a certain group had migrated further southwards, to reach the low lands of the present Cachar district. The Sanskrit word for the term "Low land" is the "*Kuskhyata*" and it is from this very word, the term Cachar (Kachar) and subsequently the 'Kachari' is supposed to have been evolved.

Endle (1990:4) was of the opinion that there were at least two great immigrations from the north and north-east into the rich valley of the Brahmaputra, i.e. one entering through North-east Bengal and Western Assam through the valley of the Tista, Dharla, Sankosh and founding there what was formerly the powerful Kingdom of Kamrupa; and the other making its way through the Subansiri, Dibong and Dihong valleys in eastern Assam where a branch of the underspread Kachari race, known as Chutiyas, undoubtedly held sway for a lengthened period. The capital city was at or near the modern Sadiya. It is emphasized by all scholars that in earlier days the Kacharis, who also referred themselves as *Badas*, (*Bara)* were in earlier days the dominant race in Assam. Their existence no doubt was reflected in many of the nomenclature of Assam. The Kachari word for water (*di; doi*) apparently forms the first syllable of the names of many of the chief rivers of the province, such as *Diputa*, *Dihong*, *Dibong, Dibru, Dihing*, *Dimu, Disang, Diku* (ef. *Khu, Tista*) and to these may be added *Dikrang, Diphu, Digaru*, all near Sadiya, the earliest known centre of Chutiya (Kachari) power and civilization. But the Kachari race is a much more widely distributed even outside the limits of modern (Political) Assam, i.e. in North East Bengal, Koch-Behar and also in Hill Tippera (Endle, 1990:4).

Endle (1981) also opined that the word Mech was coined by the non-tribal people outside Assam to denote the Kacharis of those places. For him, the Bodo or '*Bodofisa*' of Brahamaputra valley and the Dimasa or *'Dimafisa'* of North Cachar hills are the Kacharis. But he expressed his inability to trace the origin of the term Kachari. Endle (1926) also refers to the popular opinion concerning the origin of the term 'Kachari' or 'Kacharis' from the country known as Kachar. But he strongly opposes the idea that the Kacharis got their name from Khacher or Kachar as popularly believed. He emphasized the point that the people living in other parts of the state situated far away from Cachar were also known as 'Kacharis'. No doubt, a section of the Kacharis dominated Cachar, but they were already known as the Kacharis before their settlement there.

So far as the historical records of the past heritages of the Kacharis are concerned, we can satisfactorily trace up to the beginning of the 13th century only. During this period, the Kacharis were known to have a well organized social and political set-up, which covered the entire valley of the Brahmaputra. It was also evident that the eastern branch of the race showed up under the name of Chutiyas. They had established a powerful kingdom in the eastern corner of the province, the seat of Government being at or near the modern Sadiya. How long this kingdom existed, it is now impossible to say, but what is known with some degree of certainty is that they were engaged in a prolonged struggle with the Ahoms, a section of the great Shan (*Tai*) race, who crossed the Patkai Hills from the South and East about AD 1228 and invaded the valley and at once subdued the Morans, Borahis and other Kachari tribes living near the northern slope of these hills. For the Chutiyas, the strife would seem to have been a long and bitter one, lasting for some 150 to 200 years. But the Kacharis could not resist the mighty power of the Ahoms, who drove their opponents and compelled them to take refuge in or about Dimapur on the Dhansiri at the foot of the Naga Hills. It seems that they lived there in comparative peace and security, which is still reflected in their civilization in the ruins of material remains. However, about the middle of the sixteenth century, the Ahoms succeeded in capturing and sacking Dimapur itself. The *Kachari Raja* then had no other option than to move to Maibong (much paddy). There the dynasty would seem to have maintained itself for some two centuries. Finally, however, under pressure of an attack by the Jaintia Raja, the Kachari sovereign withdrew from Maibong to Khaspur in Kachar (circa 1750 AD). There they seem to have come more under Hindu influence. It would seem that the movement was only a very limited and restricted one, confined indeed very largely to the Raja and the members of his court. The great majority of his people remained in the hilly areas, where they retain their language, religion, and custom, to the great extent, intact to this day. It was assumed that the Kacharis who remained in the rich valley of Assam came to terms with their conquerors (the Tai Ahoms) and gradually became amalgamated with them. Endle remarked their amalgamation with that of the Saxons, Danes, Normans, who slowly but surely became fused into one nationality in the centuries following the battle of Hastings (Endle, 1990:7). Though amalgamation has changed their ethnic identity to a certain extent, yet the Kacharis as a distinct tribe still exist. But it is also a fact that as a result of the fatal invasion of 1706, the main Kachari stream became disintegrated into several minor sub-groups which diffused in the surroundings localities under various groups, titled like the Dimasa, the Lalung, the Rabha, the Tengal, the Sonowal and so on. The remnant of the original stock the Barmans, representing the Royal dynasty clan is inhabited in certain places of the present Cachar district (Sonowal, 2001).

Waddle (1901, 1975) says that the title Kachari is usually interpreted as being the Indian term denoting an inhabitant of the Katch or submountainous marshy tract. He rejects the opinion that the term Kachari is derived from Cachar. Again he suggested that the Sonowal or the Sadiola were mostly the legendary gold washers in Lakhimpur district of Upper Assam.

Rajguru (1988) makes a survey of the distribution of the Kacharis in the state. His data are based on chronology and he also states that there were two main branches of the Kacharis, namely Sadial Kachari and the Hidambial Kachari. But Barua (1985) contradicted the statement of Rajguru about the presence of Sadiyal Kacharis; she indicates that at the time of the appearance of the Tai Ahoms in the Brahmaputra valley, the Chutiyas were ruling the Sadiya. Her opinion was that the Chutiyas drove away the Kacharis from Sadiya before the advent of the Tai Ahoms.

Though Kachari is the earliest inhabitants of Assam, yet they have no written history about their administration. From the administration of Ahoms, i.e. only from the history of Tai Ahoms of 13th century, we have come to know something about them. From the Ahom history it is known that when the Ahoms entered in the Brahmaputra valley at the earliest part of the 13th century, the southern part from Dikhow to Kolong was under the Kachari Kingdom. North Cachar hills and Dhansiri valley were also within their Kingdom. Dimapur was the capital of this Kachari Kingdom.

The Sonowal Kachari does not have any authentic history and written record about their migration and settlement. But there exists various oral tradition based on folk beliefs and customs. There is one view that the Kacharis entered through the northern bank of river Brahmaputra during 830 AD and settled in Darrang, Tezpur, and Lakhimpur. After crossing the Subansiri River, they started to settle permanently in Sadiya. They established 'Halali' Kingdom at Dimlong and Kaudilaya during 830 AD and this fact is historically established. The etymological meaning of Halali is (*Ha*—soil, *Lali*—bright and prosperous, i.e. a prosperous kingdom). According to folk tradition, the descendents of this bright soil are the Sonowal Kachari (Sonowal, 2001:195). Dimasa have close affinity with the Sonowal Kachari and in Dimasa language also *Sonowal* means prosperous. After ruling nearly 500 years successfully, they had to face the mighty power of the first Tai Ahom King Sukapha. They could not resist the invasion and the entry of Tais into Assam not only changed the entire history of ancient Assam but totally disintegrated the Kacharis who had to migrate to the plains of upper Assam and distributed in various places.

The Kacharis were in opinion that earlier they occupied a hilly territory called 'Mahang'. The Sonowal Kacharis, during their settlement in Halali Kingdom, had to collect salt from a hill named Mahong. As this place was far away from Ahom Kingdom, and under the subjugation of Halali Kingdom, it was not easy for the Ahoms to collect salt from that area. Probably because of it, there exists a term in Assamese language, i.e. 'Mehenga' which literally means rare/precious. While singing Bihu song, a village damsel addresses her paramount as "*my dearest, do not go to Mahong, we will survive without salt of Mahong; on the way to Mahong the enemy might kill you and who will weep for you*". The love song indicates that Mahong was a place under the dominion of the Kacharis, but it was surrounded by enemies, possibly by the Nagas. Thus, it may be presumed that their folk tradition clearly indicates the existence of Kachari Kingdom at Halali and they emphasized that it was their homeland which was lost to the Nagas.

The Genesis of Sonowal

With regard to the genesis of the term Sonowal, no definite information could be collected. Whatever is available so far is purely on the basis of certain legends and cannot, therefore, be accepted at the final verdict. The following legends, however, may indicate certain possible genesis of the term:

(i) The Ahom Kings engaged different tribes and communities in various professions. One section was engaged in sieving gold from the sand (gold panning) and the Ahom Kings allotted them the river bank for their settlement. It was from the very nature of the profession that they have been called the Sonowal (*Son*—gold, *Wal*—profession).

(ii) Another view suggests that the term Sonowal has got a semi-historical fact in which the King 'Arimatta', the Chutiya King who killed his father with his own hand, because of some political conflicts, was later on subjected to a tremendous strain of mental agony and restlessness. He arranged a ritual performance so has to neutralize his guilt. Huge treasure of gold was offered to the Brahmins in that ritual, but none of them accepted the presents. When the King found no other way, he threw the treasure in the river Sowanshire. The river is also known to have refused it and the discarded treasure of the gold was thrown out to the sand. This particular group of the Kacharis came to know about the gold being thrown into the sands and engaged themselves in its recovery and subsequently got involved in the gold discovery profession. Hence, they came to be known as Sonowals.

(iii) Another view suggests that the title has got a religious background. It is said that once a highly spiritualistic head of the Vaisnava religion known as Keshardeva established his monastic abode during the time of Ahom King Gadadhar Singha in the eastern sector of the valley of Brahmaputra. His spiritualistic power impressed the local people and many of them converted into *Vaishnava* religion. A section of the Kacharis who were without any *Guru* (priest), wanted to know the reason behind of so much conversion. So, they threw a burning bamboo pipe with a gold coin inside it along with a betel nut and leaf in the river and said that if the *Guru* had real power, the pipe would stop at his *Ghat* (bank) by floating against the current of the river, but if he had no such qualities, it would float in the direction of the current. Surprisingly, the pipe stopped at the *Guru*'s *Ghat* and those who were already aware of the incident came out and accepted the pipe with the gold. From that day they accepted him as their '*Guru*' and called themselves as Sonowal, as their conversion was linked to the offering of a gold coin. Whatever might be their origin, at present the Sonowal Kacharis are mainly concentrated in several villages in the district of Dibrugarh, Sibsagar, Lakhimpur and Tinsukia.

(iv) The Sonowal Kacharis do not have their own language. Majority of them speak Assamese. In their day-to-day life, they are using a language which is slightly different from Assamese language, having a different tune. This colloquial language might have developed due to their interaction with other tribes and communities. Some of the words from the original Kachari dialect which are still in use are:

Thunderbolt — "*Chang patang*"
This way that way — "*Giding – gadang*"
Go and sleep in the outer edge of mud flood house – Go and sleep in "*Kaitali*"
Near — *Hadang*
Tomato — *Jamuna*
Thick — *Doka*
Branch tree — *Kepong*
Gate — *Dhoina*
To catch cold — *Ghaga loga*
An implement for catching fish — *Hooping*
Relaxation — *Hiriong Hiring*
Sweet fragrance — *Mdham Madham*
Weak — *Lelong Palong*
Sharp tongued lady — *Chatai*
Baby — *Kukai*
Place — *Khol*
Heat — *Una*
Plinth — *Kaitali*
A little amount — *Usuman*

Similarly, in Assamese, it is said *ki karu, ki nakaru lagise ei*, i.e. what to do and what not to do. The Sonowal Kacharis would say "*ki karang ki nakarang lagsi ei*". The tune and pronunciation make it different from the Assamese speakers.

Endle (1911) describes the Sonowal Kacharis as the earliest known inhabitants of Brahmaputra valley. According to 2001 census their total population in Assam is 235,881.

The Sonowal Kacharis are medium stature people. Their skin colour is yellowish black and straight hair, broad and flat face and mesorrhine nose (Das, 2006). They display the high incidence of HbE gene (above 50%) (Das *et al.*, 1975), The mean menarcheal age among the Kacharis is 12.77 ± 0.12 (Deka, 1975).

The Sonowal Kacharis as an ethnic group has been living in Assam from time immemorial. Though, they have lost many valuable customs and traditions, yet their distinct identity is reflected in their customs and traditions. This is an important criterion to be considered by the Constitution of India to declare any community to be tribe in India and providing Autonomous Council. At present, along with the ethnic consciousness, they are trying to revive many of their traditional customs and practices. The ethnic consciousness among the Sonowal Kachari is a very recent phenomenon in the history of Assam.

As the Sonowal Kacharis fulfilled most of the criterion of having Autonomous Council, the Government of Assam has declared the Sonowal Kacharis Autonomous Council in May 2005. The main objective of setting up the Administrative Authority is to provide maximum Autonomy within the framework of the Constitution of India for the social, economic, educational, ethnic and cultural advancement of the Sonowal Kachari people in the state. But it is felt that the declaration of Autonomous Council could not put an end to the anxiety of the community. As a result besides the Autonomous Council, various organizations like the All Assam Sonowal Kachari Student's Union, Sonowal Kachari Jatiya Parishad and All Assam Sonowal Kachari Women's Association were formed and from time to time they are putting their demand to the Government. It is to be noted that unlike all other ethnic groups of Assam, their identity movement is by and large peaceful in nature.

The main demand of these associations includes the socio-economic development of Sonowal Kachari society. They have identified various demands, e.g. providing land *patta*, educational facilities, employment opportunity and appointment of Sonowal Kachari youth under Assam Scheduled Caste and Scheduled Tribe Reservation of Vacancies in Services and Posts Act, 1978. They have also given stress on transforming the Forest villages to Revenue villages, to identify the Tribal belt and blocks and steps to be taken for preservation of Sonowal Kachari culture and customs. Now-a-days, each and every member of the community tries to focus the customs and traditions in a conscious way. As a part of revival process, they have started to observe some of their traditional festival, dance (*Bahua* dance) in a greater community level. Through such customs and tradition, they are trying to identify their individual ethnic identity in the midst of greater ethnic communities.

A.2: The Areas of Study

The present study has been carried on intensively in two forest villages, namely Paroliguri and Nahoroni. The villages are exclusively inhabited by the Sonowal Kacharis. The two villages are situated adjacent to each other and are nearly 28 km away from Dibrugarh town. Socio-demographic data has also been collected from one of the oldest Sonowal Kachari village, namely Duliagaon which falls under the jurisdiction of the Barbaruah sub-division of Dibrugarh district of Assam having its headquarters at Dibrugarh town. It is located eastwards at a distance of 15 km from Dibrugarh town. Relevant data were also collected from other Sonowal Kachari villages situated within a radius of 20 km from Dibrugarh town.

In the present study, two forest villages were selected keeping in mind that the indigenous knowledge,, beliefs and customs may distinctly be traced in these villages, because, there exists a symbiotic relationship between the tribal population and forests. Forest provides them the means of sustenance, like food, fruits, timbers, wild animals for hunting, fuel wood, etc. The word forest is derived from Latin word "foris" meaning outside, the reference being to a village boundary or fence, and it must have included all uncultivated and cultivated land (Sagreiya, 2000). Technically forest has been defined as,

(i) In general: An area set aside for the production of timber and other produce, or maintained under woody vegetation for certain indirect benefits which it provides, e.g. climatic or protective;
(ii) In Ecology: A plant community predominantly of trees and other woody vegetation, usually with a closed canopy; and
(iii) In Law: An area of land proclaimed to be a forest under a forest law.

The creation of forest villages was a part of forest management in the early part of the last century. The first National Policy on Forest was formulated in 1894. Thereafter, the state began to manage the affairs of the forest. At the same time, the commercial exploitation of forest also began. The British government had to meet the supply of raw materials first for ship building process and secondly, for the expanding of railway tracks. But the need for exploitation of forest resources required maintaining a regular supply of labour. In the early phase of forest exploitation, this need was met through the introduction of '*Taungya*' system as was earlier practiced in Burma and Malaysia.

The general conditions governing the forest villages are:

> The forest department and its contractors have the first claim to its labour of the forest village on payment of wages at the market rate. The villagers may not accept other employment without the prior sanction of the forest department and they are expected to comply with the orders of the Divisional Forest Officers. Besides, they can be summarily evicted for non-compliance of the term and condition.
> Assam is the heartland of North East India. The area is characterized by rich bio-diversity and is ideally suited to produce a whole range of plantation crops, spices, fruits and vegetables, flowers and herbs. The area of reserved forest in Assam was 33,550 sq. km during 1951-52. But, it has been reduced to 17,317 sq. km in 1981-82. To maintain the bio-diversity and ecological balance, 33 per cent of the total geographical area should be reserved as forest area by the state. In the initial stage, most of the forest areas were devoid of population except for a few dispersed pockets of indigenous tribal population. Habitation was difficult in those areas as people were suffering from Malaria and Kalazar. Due to unfertile environment and lack of communication, even the fringe areas were not suitable for proper habitation.

The reservation of forest land in Assam is no doubt the result of colonial phenomena in Assam. After the formulation of reservation of forests, considerable importance was given to the scientific and systematic management of forest. Initially, the authority had to face certain problems in respect of man-power as in those days density of population in and near the forest areas was remarkably low. Assam in those days, particularly before independence, was famous for dreaded disease like malaria, kalazar, and wild animals, flood and contagious magic were creating problems. Habitation and communication facilities were not congenial. It was difficult task to mobilize labour force for harvesting and silvicultural operations. The forest authorities had a trying time to mobilize labour force and sometime scheduled works had to be suspended. Against this backdrop the necessity for the creation of regular labour force was urgently felt and the concept of forest village gained currency. Forest villages were set up within the limits of reserved forest in the nineties of the last century, 1901-05 to be precise. At the outset 35 numbers of forest village covering three erstwhile districts of Assam were established. Forest areas in Assam fall mainly under three broad categories.

Reserved Forest

The forest is managed by the trained staff of Forest Department and provisions of scientific silvicultural working plan are implemented under the guidance of experts who are the government employees.

Unclassed State Forest

These forests are theoretically under the control of the Forest Department of state, but they are governed by the customary law prevalent in an unregulated State of Assam. In fact, these forests came under heavy *jhuming.*

Protected Forests

Protected forests are very limited and can be granted to limited tribal population. Even the forest officials have restricted authority to operate among them.

Forest villages are established mostly in reserved forest areas. But the structure and functioning of forest villages in Assam are a bit different from other states of India. Most of the forest villages were established to rehabilitate the flood affected communities in the initial stage. Later on, many of the areas specified for the forest land was occupied by the illegal migrants. There is also evidence especially from Madhya Pradesh and Gujarat (Prasad and Jahagirdas, 1993) that some revenue villages were transferred to forest department to form forest villages. These types of villages are known as Revenue

Forest Village. The typical forest villages on the other hand are the ones where the labour camps have been transformed into semi-permanent or permanent settlements (Sonowal, 2007:48).

To get the benefits of the labour force, decision was also taken to establish forest villages in land suitable for wet rice cultivation within the reserved forest. In the process, by the year 1902-03 as many as 15 forest villages came up and the number increased up to 145 in 1913-14 (cited from Sonowal, 2007: 49). The population of forest villages comprised Tribal communities, Scheduled Caste and other communities including caste Assamese, Nepalese and Muslims. As per the record of forest department till 31st March, 1984 there were total 450 forest villages. In the state of Assam, only 47 per cent villags are inhabited by tribal communities. While nearly 13 per cent of the forest villagers were occupied by Scheduled Caste communities and other communities represent the remaining 40 per cent of the forest population. Thus, the common perception is that the forest villages are basically inhabited by the tribal communities contradict the present scenario. The tribal communities showed a marginally numerically dominated group in forest villages of Assam till 1984. The tribal population growth is gradually showing a negative trend and the trend of population increase in forest villages once inhabited only by the tribal people is even more distressing.

Table 2.1: Name and Extent of Reserved Forests in Dibrugarh District

Sl. No.	*Area (sq. km)*	*Name of reserve forest*
1.	47.27	Dihingmukh
2.	18.47	Jokai
3.	84.61	Joypur
4.	18.57	Namdang
5.	13.31	Telpani

Dihingmukh Reserved – 7 forest villages (all established in 1951)
Source: Forest Range Office, Dibrugarh.

There are five reserved forests in Dibrugarh district, viz. Dihingmukh Reserved forest, Jokai Reserved forest, Namdang Reserved forest, Telpani Reserved forest, and Joypur Reserved forest. Almost in all cases the forest villages were established under the rehabilitation programme for the flood affected people by the devastating earthquake in Assam in 1950.

According to the records of Forest Department, the villages under Dihingmukh reserved forest were established around 1951. There were 7 forest villages in the reserved forest. Records showed that each of the adult member registered with the forest department was given 10 *bighas* of land by the forest department. Like all the other forest villages, the people of these villages also had to render free physical labour to the forest used, to keep the record of the amount of due free labour. The record showed that there were certain households, whose due free labour was nearing thousand man-days by now.

As per rule, every forest villager was allotted up to 5 *bighas* of land including homestead land. Besides each working member living in that household was entitled to get 10 *bighas* of land, but the ceiling, however, was fixed at 35 *bighas* per household on payment of nominal land revenue. The people of these two forest villages were allotted land as per rule of forest department. According to the record of forest beat office in the village Paroliguri, initially, i.e. in the year 1951 only 26 families were allotted land. Out of these 26 families, there were 20 families who were getting land up to 35 *bighas*. The number of families who were allotted land up to 25 *bighas* of land was only 2. There were only 4 numbers of families who were allotted 12 *bighas* of land. While in the village Nahoroni, in the initial stage, only 6 families were allotted forest land. Out of these 6 families, only 4 numbers of families were allotted 4 *bighas* of land. There were only 2 families who were allotted 15 and 12 *bighas* of land, respectively.

This information was recorded during 1950-51. No official record was available after that. In the household survey of the present study in the year 2011, it is revealed that there are 61 families in the village Paloriguri and 30 families in Nahoroni. Of late, the population is increasing rapidly. The families are multiplying with separate establishment and the number of households is increasing. Thus, in most cases the figures of households in the official records do not tally with the actual households in the field. The same trend may also be reflected in the village level and this may be due to two reasons. Firstly, new families might have migrated to this area after the original settlement. Secondly, the breaking up of joint families might have given rise to nuclear families. In both cases, it was not reported to the forest department and the original record remained as it is. Moreover, most of the families have cleared the marginal forest area for cultivation, and in many cases have utilized the peripheral land for seasonal cultivation. But under no circumstances were they allowed to enter or damage the core area/wooded area of the forest. Though the forest officials were aware about such encroachment for cultivation, yet they did not take any rigid step. The villagers do not have the right to transfer or sell the land. They were given only right of use and occupancy over the land. On enquiry, the forest officials informed that the villagers were repeatedly asked to update the official record by enrolling the names, in case of division of joint families or new settlement. But the villagers did not pay any attention to that till today and the forest department is getting nominal land revenue of Rs.12.00 from these families whose names were formally recorded in the official record. In lieu of the allotment of forest land, the forest villagers were required to render 5–20 days free labour to the forest department by cleaning, planting new trees, constructing/repairing bamboo fencing or any emergency works where their services were required by the forest department. In the course of discussion, it was found that at present no regular services are forced upon the villagers, but each family has to supply one bamboo either for repairing the fence or for other purposes. It seems that this act signifies the official responsibility towards the forest department. But in situations like flood or danger from wild elephant, their services are immediately recruited and the villagers are prompt to extend their services as it becomes a question of security of the entire villages. During our stay in the village, it was reported both by the villagers and the forest officials that the herd of wild elephants has already started to damage the rice fields. The forest officials were to go for patrolling at night and asked the villagers to join in this mission. In each village, there is a committee of joint forest management with 9 members and the information is communicated through the committee. Such type of services is known as *Tangia* and this is an additional labour force to help the forest department.

Forest villages were established within Reserve Forest and these were governed by the rules for establishment of forest villages and overall provision of the Assam Forest Regulation, 1891 (Vol.1). The responsibility for providing the basic amenities rest on forest department. In the initial stage the forest department has supplied tube well and ring well to the villagers. For electrification also the forest department has taken initiative and introduced *desi* fire system for producing electricity. As the wood required for running the system has to be supplied by the villagers, it did not continue for long. At present some of the families are getting connection from electricity board.

As the forest villages are outside the purview of the *Panchayat Act*, they were not in a position to get the benefit from DRDA and banks as their land could not be mortgaged. On enquiry, it was reported that some of the villagers have mortgaged their land by showing the original land record which was given at the time of allotment. Such incident indicates that they may be allowed to mortgage the land for getting loans and the rule is not much rigid. Most of the villagers were of opinion that they are deprived from various benefits due to not getting status of revenue village.

The Micro Field: Paroliguri and Nahoroni (Forest Villages)

As noted earlier, the present study has been carried out intensively in two forest villages of Dihingmukh Reserved Forest, i.e. Paroliguri and Nahoroni in Dibrugarh district of upper Assam. The villages are entirely inhabited by the Sonowal Kacharis. A brief introduction of the micro field is being presented under the following headings.

Location

The villages fall under the jurisdiction of Dihingmukh Reserve Forest. It is located westward at a distance of 28 km from Dibrugarh town and 11 km from NH 37 at Medeluwa Tiniali. The villages are within jurisdiction of Barbaruah Police Station. The road transports are available at the *Tiniali,* i.e. the road from NH 37 up to the drain is *Pucca* and the village road is *Katcha.* All village paths become muddy and inaccessible during rainy season.

The village is bounded in the north by Brahmaputra River, which is nearly 3 km away from the village. During summer the river water badly affected the village. There is Nahoroni village in the west, Tinsukia in the north and Gorudhoria in the south.

The village path runs almost straight from south to north. The road is *Katcha* and various lanes bifurcate from this path towards the eastern direction and the houses are constructed sometimes on both sides of the lane and sometimes houses are there only on one side. Reserved forest is on the north-western side.

The village primary school is situated on the eastern side of the path. There is a big pond on the northern side of the village. The village *Namghar* (Prayer hall) is situated on the western side of the village path, surrounding an open area. Youth club is there near the *Namghar*. Paddy fields are situated on the sides of by-lanes and on western side of the village. Bamboo grooves are seen by the side of individual families.

Boundary and Settlement Pattern

With regards to Nahoroni village, it is found that Tinsukia and Deori villages are situated on the western side. The Paroliguri is on the northern side and in the east Garndharia village is situated. The part of the Dihing reserved forest is on the southern side.

The households are situated on the eastern side of village path. Bamboo groves are seen by the side of settlement. On the west, a few households are there. Youth club and *Namghar* are found just near the entrance of village. The school is situated on the western side in the midst of paddy field. There is a village shop which caters to the needs of the people.

As both the villages are situated adjacent to each other, the other features would be described considering the two villages together.

Transport and Communication

The communication system of these villages may be considered suitable. The auto-rickshaws and "*bikram*" ply up to the drain. Both the public and private transport plies on the NH 37 throughout the day. One can avail the facility of shared auto rickshaws which regularly run from Dibrugarh auto stand. From there, one has to walk up to the villages during rainy season. But during winter one may take the vehicle up to the village. The common villagers have bi-cycle and scooter for communication. The telephone facility and mobile network is also available. There is no post office in the villages. For postal purposes, they are to go either to Barbaruah or Dibrugarh town.

The villagers have to come to the health centre for medical purpose. It is situated near the forest beat office and nearly 9 km away from the village.

Origin of the Name Paroliguri

Regarding the origin of the name of the village, it was reported by the villagers that originally, they were residing in the Dikhowmukh area of Sibsagar district. In the year 1950, their original settlement

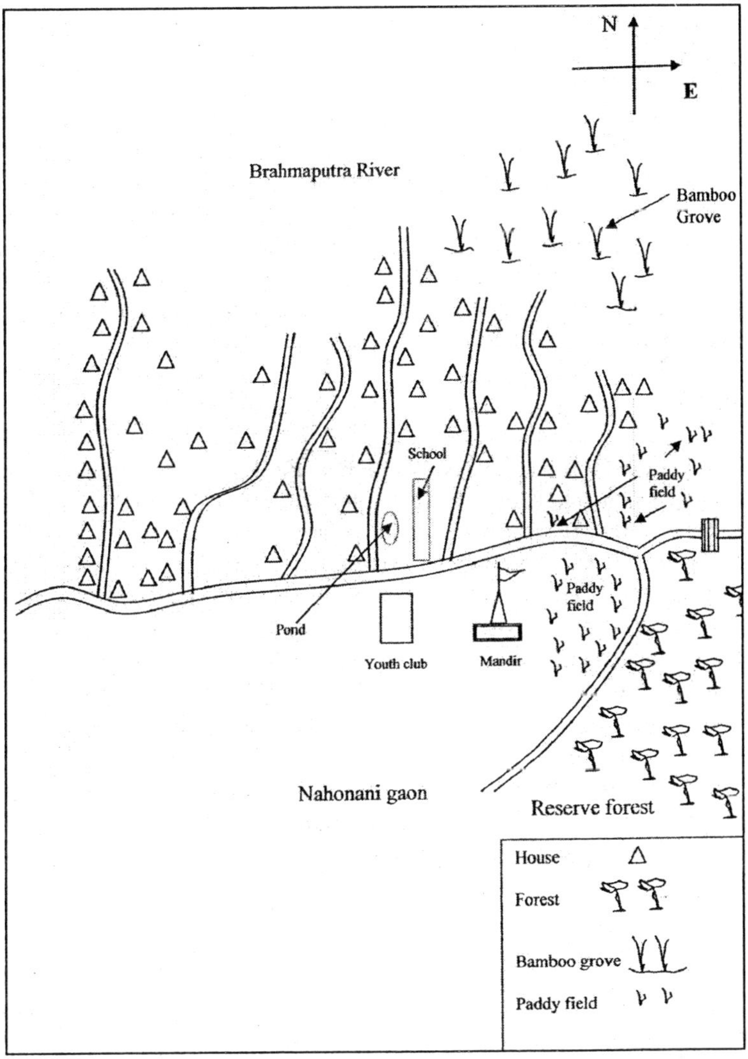

Map 2.1: Notional Map of Paroliguri

was badly affected by the flood and they lost their entire cultivable and residential plot. In that crisis situation, they were rehabilitated in this area with the permission of the then Forest Minister. When they first came to this area, the entire area was covered with *Paroli* tree. As it was dense forest area, various valuable plants were also available in the forest which was useful for different purposes.

The Scientific name of *Paroli* is "*Stereospermum chelonoides DC and Stereospermum tetragonum DC*" and the Family name is "*Bignoniaceac*".

Paroli is a large deciduous tree and is moderately hard and durable, fine grained. Used for railway sleepers, house building, canoes, tea boxes, furniture, fire wood, etc. Decoction of leaves, roots and barks is used to reduce fever. Their flower mixed with honey is good for hiccough. The tree is fairly common in Assam and Nagaland (*Source*, Dutta, 1985: 206-207). Because of the large scale availability of *Paroli* tree, the original settlers decided to name their new settlement as Paroliguri.

Nahoroni Village

The people of this village were the inhabitants of Nahoroni village of Sibsagar district. The lush green environment with abundant *Nahor* (*Mesuaferrea Linn*) tree created an enjoyable environment. But due to frequent flood and in search of more land, initially 6 families shifted to this area. They observed that their new forested area was also surrounded by *Nahor* tree. So, they decided to retain the name of their original settlement. Slowly more families started migrating from the flood affected area. Thus, the village came into existence. *Nahor* (*Mesuaferrea Linn*) tree is a valuable plant and available in most of the areas of Assam.

Both the villages are situated adjacent to each other and exclusively inhabited by the Sonowal Kacharis, therefore it is decided to present the socio-demographic analysis of these two villages together.

Population Analysis

The distribution of population by age and sex in the forest villages Paroliguri and Nahoroni has been presented in Table 2.2.

Table 2.2: Distribution of Population by age and sex in Paroliguri and Nahoroni

Age Group	*Male*	*Percentage*	*Female*	*Percentage*	*Total*	*Percentage*
0 – 5	20	3.88	20	3.88	40	7.76
6 – 10	24	4.66	17	3.30	41	7.96
11 – 15	28	5.43	21	4.07	49	9.50
16 – 20	25	4.85	29	5.63	54	10.48
21 – 25	28	5.43	20	3.88	48	9.31
26 – 30	27	5.24	23	4.46	50	9.70
31 – 35	33	6.40	32	6.21	65	12.61
36 – 40	25	4.85	25	4.85	50	9.70
41 – 45	11	2.13	10	1.94	21	4.07
46 – 50	15	2.91	10	1.94	25	4.85
51 – 55	10	1.94	13	2.52	23	4.46
56 – 60	7	1.35	11	2.13	18	3.48
61 – 65	6	1.16	6	1.16	12	2.32
66 – 70	8	1.55	3	0.5	11	2.05
71 – 75	3	0.58	1	0.19	4	0.77
76 – 80	2	0.38	2	0.3	4	0.68
Total	272	52.81	243	47.18	515	99.70

The total population of the village is 515 distributed in 91 households. Out of total 515 individuals, 272 (52.81%) are male and 243 (47.18%) are female. The entire population has been divided into 16 age group categories ranging from 0-5 to 75-80. It has been observed that 16-20 age group category has the highest number of individuals, i.e. 54 (10.48%) out of which 25 (4.85%) are male and 29 (5.63%) are female.

Again the lowest number of individuals which is 4 with a percentage of 0.77 is found in the 71-75 and 75-80 age group categories. It has also been found that 31-35 categories has the highest number of males with 33 (6.40%) individual, while the highest number of females, i.e. 32 (6.21%) are also found in the 31-35 age group category. The lowest numbers of males are found in the 75-80 categories with only 2 (0.38%) individuals and the lowest numbers of females are found in the 71-75 categories with only 1 (0.91%) individual.

The children (0-5 years) constitute approximately 7.76 per cent of the population, whereas the figure in the next higher group (6-10 years) stands at 8 per cent, approximately. This may reflect a reducing trend in the birth rate during the last five years.

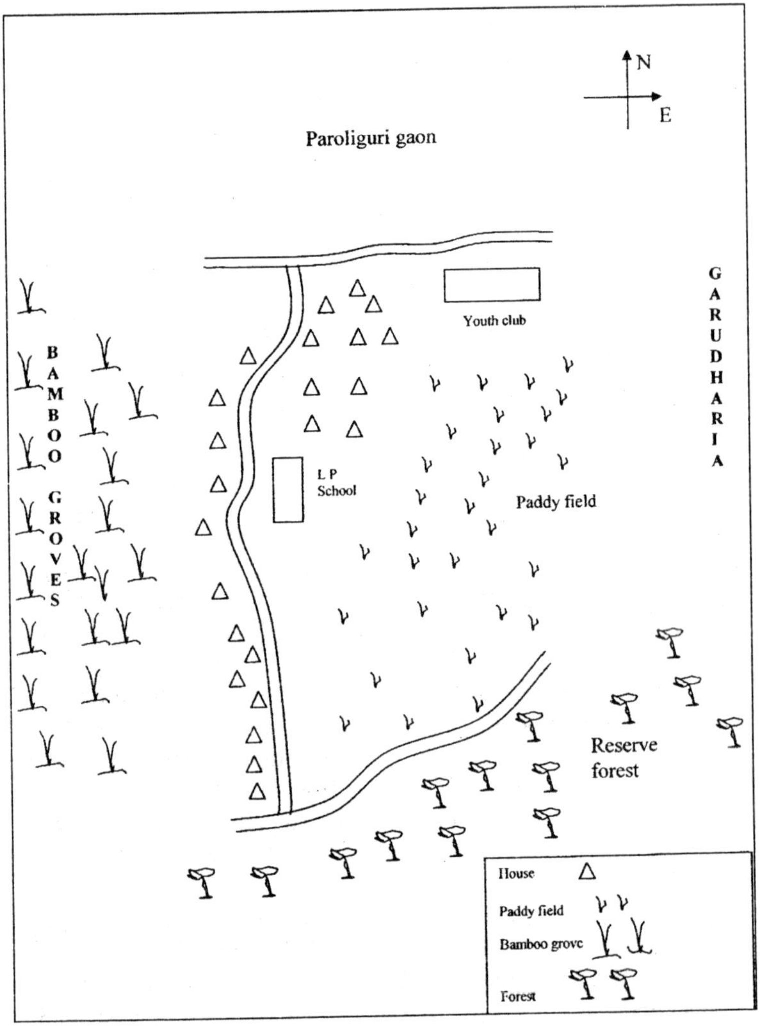

Map 2.2: Notional Map of Nahoroni

The table further reveals that the active labour force (16-55 years) is composed of 336 (65.24%) of the population that is supposed to look after the 34.75 per cent dependents, i.e. children and adolescent.

An effort has also been made to reveal the educational status in the villages Paroliguri and Nahoroni. Table 2.3 reveals that literacy rate is moderately high. The highest number of individuals who read up to ME level is quite high. There are 140 (27.18%) individuals, out of which 73 (14.17%) are male and 67 (13.1%) are females. The number of individuals who read up to LP level is 92 (17.86%). There are 78 (15.14%) who read up to ME level, but could not clear the matriculation 43 individuals (8.35%) are matriculate, out of which 24 (4.7%) are males and 19 (3.68%) are females.

The number of graduates recorded in the present study are 11 (2.13%) out of which 6 (1.16%) are males and 5 (0.97%) are females. 1 male (0.19%) who have obtained the engineering degree and another male individual (0.19%) who took degree in ITI. The number of illiteracy is 80 (15.53%). There are 31 (6.1%) children who are too young to study during the period of field survey.

Table 2.3: Educational status in Paroliguri and Nahoroni

Type	*Male*	*Percentage*	*Female*	*Percentage*	*Total*	*Percentage*
Too Young to Study	17	3.30	14	2.7	31	6.1
Illiterate	37	7.18	43	8.34	80	15.53
Up to LP (I-IV)	48	9.32	44	8.54	92	17.86
Up to ME (V-VII)	73	14.17	67	13.1	140	27.18
Up to HSLC	40	7.76	38	7.37	78	15.14
HSLC Passed	24	4.7	19	3.68	43	8.35
HS Passed	25	4.85	13	2.52	38	7.38
Graduate	6	1.16	5	0.97	11	2.13
Engineering	1	0.19	—	—	1	0.19
Others (ITI)	1	0.19	—	—	1	0.19
Total	272	52.81	243	47.18	515	100

Though the educational status in the two forest villages and the revenue village is more or less the same, yet the numbers of highly educated persons are significant in the forest villages. In each village, there is lower primary school and for higher education they have to go to Barbaruah and Dibrugarh town.

The Micro Field: Dulia Gaon (Revenue Village)

The villagers could not definitely tell the year of the establishment of the village. Some of the elderly persons of the village were of the opinion that during the reign of Ahom Kings, the villagers were entrusted with a particular function, i.e. to carry the *Dulla* (palanquin).

They referred to themselves as *Dullavari*, who carry the palanquin of king and high officials. That is why the village is known as Duliagaon.

Location

Duliagaon falls under the jurisdiction of the Barbaruah sub-division of Dibrugarh district of Assam having its headquarters at Dibrugarh town. It is located eastwards at a distance of 15 km from Dibrugarh town and about 5 km from Barbaruah Tiniali and is connected with NH 37 at Barbaruah. The village is within the jurisdiction of Barbaruah Police Station and is included under Dulia Kakoti Panchayat. The road transport is available at Barbaruah Tiniali. The main road adjacent to the village is *Pucca* and the village road is *Katcha* and more or less zigzag. All the village paths became muddy and inaccessible during rainy season.

Boundary and Settlement Pattern

The village is bounded on the east by cultivable land and the west by the gas cracker project. On the north, the village Dainijan is situated and on the south, there is Kakati village. The neighbouring villages are mostly inhabited by the Sonowal Kacharis and the Ahoms.

The village is by and large situated on a plain terrain. Soil is alluvial, brown in colour and fertile summing up to make good agricultural land especially for paddy cultivation. There are no natural water sources within the village. Almost all the households have tube wells within their compound. For agricultural purposes, they are dependent mostly on rain water and sometimes use water from the pond. There are both *Katcha* and RCC houses found in the village. The number of RCC houses is less in comparison to *Katcha* houses. The *Katcha* houses are built on bamboo, thatch, wooden posts, etc. Raw materials are easily available for constructing these types of houses. Their houses can be grouped into two categories: (i) l-patterned and (ii) L-patterned. The houses are constructed mainly on both sides of the village path. Sometimes they keep large open space in the front. Every household has a granary. Cowshed is normally seen in the front.

Almost each house has electricity connections. Compared to other rural areas of Assam, the electricity supply is good because there are two transformers within the village.

Sanitation system of the village is good. Most of the houses have sanitary latrine. For bathing purposes, they have separate bathroom. In certain cases, they are to make pit latrine and a separate enclosure is made with bamboo stripes. Most of the people take bath regularly, but sometimes children are irregular. There are four shops in the village, which cater the needs of their day-to-day necessity.

As the people are *Vaishavas* by religion, there are two *Namghars* (local centre of worship for Assamese *Vaishnavite*). There is also a *'Bathou Mandir'* at the extreme boundary of the village.

There is only one lower primary school in the village. For higher studies, they have to go to Barbaruah or Dibrugarh.

Transport and Communication

The communication system is good, because the village is located in the eastern side of NH 37. Both public and private transport plies on this National Highway throughout the day. To come to this juncture, the villagers mostly use bi-cycle. One can avail the facility of auto rickshaw and the villagers may intimate the auto rickshaw owner by the mobile phone. Tele-communication facility is well developed and a good number of families have telephone in their house. Moreover, mobile network is also available. Most of the families have TV and Radio set in their home. The villagers have the habit of reading newspaper regularly. They are getting postal facility from the Barbaruah town which is within their easy reach.

Health Care

There is no health sub-centre within the village. But they are getting all the facilities at Barbaruah town. "Asha Karmis" have been regularly monitoring the womenfolk of the village. Thus, for medical and health care facilities, people either go to Barbaruah or direct to Assam Medical College hospital in Dibrugarh.

The village seems to be rich in having a wide range of bio-diversity. Both wild as well as household plants are observed in the area. The village has a common forest, wherefrom they are allowed to take away their day-to-day necessary herbs, shrubs and firewood. Wild animals are occasionally seen in the village.

The village is homogeneously inhabited by the Sonowal Kacharis. For the present study 110 families were considered for intensive socio-demographic study. Systematic classification of the investigated population according to age and sex has been presented in Table 2.4.

Out of the total population of 534, it has been found that 270 (50.56%) are male and 264 (49.44%) are female. It can be observed from the Table that the entire population has been divided into 20 age group categories ranging from 0-5 to 96-100. It has also been revealed that 21-25 age group categories has the highest number of individuals, i.e. 62 (11.61%) out of which 17 (3.18%) are male and 45 (8.43%) are female.

Table 2.4: Distribution of Population by age and sex in Duliagaon

Age group	*Male*	*Percentage*	*Female*	*Percentage*	*Total*	*Percentage*
0 – 5	24	4.49	24	4.49	48	8.98
6 – 10	31	5.80	19	3.56	50	9.36
11 – 15	26	4.87	22	4.12	48	8.99
16 – 20	21	3.93	26	4.87	47	8.80
21 – 25	17	3.18	45	8.43	62	11.61
26 – 30	25	4.68	25	4.68	50	9.37
31 – 35	23	4.31	19	3.56	42	7.88
36 – 40	24	4.49	25	4.68	49	9.17
41 – 45	17	3.18	20	3.75	37	6.93
46 – 50	18	3.37	14	2.62	31	5.81
51 – 55	7	1.32	10	1.87	17	3.19
56 – 60	15	2.80	8	1.50	23	4.30
61 – 65	10	1.87	7	1.32	17	3.18
66 – 70	6	1.12	6	1.12	12	2.24
71 – 75	1	0.18	1	0.19	2	0.37
76 – 80	2	0.37	—	—	2	0.37
81 – 85	3	0.56	—	—	3	0.56
86 – 90	1	0.18	—	—	1	0.18
91 – 95	—	—	—	—	—	—
96 – 100	—	—	2	0.37	2	0.37
Total	270	50.56	264	49.44	534	100

Again the lowest number of individuals which is 1 (0.18%) is found in the 86-90 age group categories, comprising a single male member. It has also been observed that highest number of males, i.e. 31 (5.81%) are found in the age group of 6-10 years, while the highest number of females is 45 (11.61%) are found in the age group of 21-25 years category. The single number of male is found in 71-76 years of age group category.

The children (0-5 years) constitute, approximately 8.9 per cent of the total population, whereas figure is the next higher age group

(6-10 years) stands at 10 per cent, approximately. This may reflect the reducing trend in the birth rate during the last 5 years.

Table further reveals that the active labour force (16-55 years) is composed of 62.73 per cent of the population, that is supposed to look after the 37.26 per cent dependents, i.e. the children and adolescent.

An attempt has also been made to describe the educational status of the population in the village Duliagaon. There is only one LP School in the village. But the children can avail the educational facilities of Barbaruah and Dibrugarh town which are 5 and 15 km away, respectively.

Table 2.5 reveals that the percentage of illiterate population is negligible. There are 12 males (2.25%) and 15 females (2.81%) illiterates. The percentage of illiteracy is only 5.06 per cent. In the village there are 39 individuals (7.30%) who are too young to go to school.

Table 2.5: Educational Status in Duliagaon

Division	*Male*	*Percentage*	*Female*	*Percentage*	*Total*	*Percentage*
Too Young to Study	23	4.31	16	2.99	39	7.30
Illiterate	12	2.25	15	2.81	27	5.06
Up to LP	37	6.23	46	8.61	83	15.54
Up to ME	45	8.43	42	7.86	87	16.29
Up to HSLC	78	14.61	73	13.61	151	28.28
HSLC Passed	28	5.24	31	5.81	59	11.05
HS passed	37	6.93	34	6.37	71	13.30
Graduates	10	1.87	7	1.31	17	3.18
Total	270	50.56	264	49.43	534	100

The number of individuals who studied up to HSLC but could not clear the matriculation examination is 151 (28.28%) out of which 14.61 per cent are males and 13.67 per cent are females. The highest level of educational degree obtained by the individual is graduate level. There are 17 individuals (3.18%) who have got the degree, out of which 10 (1.87%) are males and 7 (1.31%) are females.

Socio-Cultural Life

The Sonowal Kacharis are peace loving people enjoying the mixture of both the traditional and modern system of living. They are agriculturist and in recent years major sections have opted for diverse occupation.

The Sonowal Kachari villages represent the overall picture of rural Assam. Houses are arranged mostly on both sides of the village path. Some by-lanes are bifurcated from the village path and the by-lanes are invariably *Katcha* and remain muddy during the rainy season. Each house with its granary and other outbuilding is surrounded by fence, made of split bamboo. As the forest villages, Paroliguri and Nahoroni are rehabilitated villages; their environment seems to be slightly different from revenue villages', i.e. Duliagaon. The socio-economic condition is reflected from their surrounding areas. It has already been mentioned that they have expanded their agricultural land after clearing the marginal forest land. They do not have the right to transfer the land but only given occupancy right.

In the villages, most of the houses are *Katcha* and they raise the plinth of the land for prevention of flood. But majority of the families use CI Sheets for roofing. There are only a few *Pucca* houses, noticed in the villages. Whereas in the village Duliagaon, the number of *Pucca* houses are significant.

Most of the houses are erected facing to the east. They generally follow the old saying of Assamese folk culture:

Pube Bharal, Pachime Goral, Uttare Charu, Dakhine Garu.

This means, the granary (*Bharal*) is in the east of house, the poultry (*Goral*) to the west, the kitchen to the north and cowshed must be towards southern direction of the houses with bamboo, thatch and wood. They select *Nahar (Mesuaferree Linn), Hallokh* (valuable wood, etc. for their good qualities. They generally collect it from the nearby reserved forest and sometimes purchase it from the market. They try to select as far as possible such types of wood which protect/prevent the houses from lightning. The houses vary in length according to the economic status and size of the family. Before construction of the houses, they erect one post in the eastern side that is the main post of the house known as *Bor-Khuta* or *Ghai Khuta*. After erecting the main post, they erect the other posts and walls.

Normally, there are two houses in a household. The main house is called *Bor-ghar* which is oriented north-south. The *Mar-ghar* is made according to necessity. The kitchen and dinning space is found in the *Bor-ghar*. There is a fire place in the dining area, known as *Jui-ghar* or *juhal*. At the floor of the kitchen, they make a fire place with the earth for cooking. There is a bamboo tray above the fire which is used for drying fish or meat and keeping domestic utensils and fishing implement and firewood. The materials kept in the tray vary from family to family. They built their granary 3 to 4 feet above the floor with bamboo, wood thatch and cane.

Family System

The social system of the Sonowal Kacharis is very unique. There are many families or *Hanch* among the Sonowal Kacharis. Several *Hanch* constitute the *Bangsha*. Each family or *Hanch* perform their rituals in their own way, which may be different from other family or *Hanch*. However, certain rituals are performed uniformly by the Sonowal Kacharis irrespective of *Hanch* or family background.

A Sonowal Kachari family comprises father, mother, children and grandchildren. It is also seen that in a family there are members belonging to several generations.

Size of the Family

The total population under investigation is 515 (male – 272, Female – 243) who are distributed among 91 families. Thus, the average size of the family stands at 5.65.

To have a better understanding of this aspect, the families have conveniently been distributed in the following size categories.

Single member family	1 member
Small members	2 – 3
Medium members	4 – 6
Big members	7 – 9
Very big members and above	10

Distribution of the families according to size in two forest villages is presented in Table 2.6. A cursory glance of the table makes it apparent that the medium-sized family occurs in the highest frequency, i.e. 40 (43.95%).

Table 2.6: Distribution of the Families according to size in Paroliguri and Nahoroni

Family Size	*No. of Individuals*	*No. of Families*	*Percentage*
Single	1	—	
Small	2 - 4	32	35.16
Medium	3 - 6	40	43.95
Large	7 - 8	5	5.49
Very Large	9 - above	14	15.38
Total		91	99.98

It is followed by small family, the number of which is 32 (35.16%). It is followed by the very big family, the number of which is 14 (15.38%). The number of big family is 5 (5.49%). During the present investigation, not a single individual has been found in the category of single member.

Distribution of the families according to size in the Duliagaon has been presented in Table 2.7. A cursory glance reveals that small size family occurs in the highest frequency (49.1%). It is followed by medium family, the numbers of which are 36 (32.73%). The strength of large family is 11 (10.0%) and very big one is 7 (6.36%). There are 2 families (1.81%) with single individual.

Table 2.7: Distribution of families in Duliagaon

Family Size	*No. of Individuals*	*No. of Families*	*Percentage*
Single	1	2	1.81
Small	2 - 4	54	49.10
Medium	3 - 6	36	32.73
Large	7 - 8	11	10.00
Very Large	9 - above	7	6.36
Total		100	100

A study of family in two forest villages and one revenue village reveals that in the forest village the number of medium family is found to be highest (49.1%). However, in the revenue village, the small size family is found in the highest frequency (49.1%). In the forest village not a single family with one member is recorded, but in the revenue village, there are two families (1.81%) with single individual. The very large family is found to be significant in forest villages (15.38%), whereas in Duliagaon 6.3 per cent of very big families are recorded. The differences may be due to their location and set-up.

Type and Composition

An analysis of the type and composition of families under investigation in two forest villages is presented in Table 2.8. It is evident from the table that the most frequently observed type of family among the Sonowal Kacharis is the nuclear 45 (49.5%). It is followed by the joint/extended type 20 (21.97%) and broken type is also 20 (21.97%). There are 6 families (6.54%) that fall under the miscellaneous type.

Table 2.8: Distribution of the families according to the type and composition in Paroliguri and Nahoroni

Type	*Composition*	*No. of Families*	*Percentage*
Nuclear	Husband, Wife and Unmarried children	45	49.45
Joint	Husband, Wife with married and unmarried children	5	5.49
	Husband, Wife and married children and grandchildren	15	16.48
Broken	Widow with unmarried children	5	5.49
	Widow with married and grandchildren	15	16.59
Miscellaneous		6	6.59
Total		91	100

The distribution of family according to type and composition in the village Duliagaon reveals that the highest number, i.e. 52 families are nuclear type and the percentage is 47.27. The largest number of a family is found in the extended category which has only 2 families, the percentage being 1.8. Besides 36 families (32.73%) fall in the joint family and 19 (17.28%) fall under the broken family.

A study on type and composition in two forest villages and one revenue village reveals that nuclear family predominates in both the villages. The percentage is slightly higher in forest village (49.45%) than the revenue village (47.27%). The number of joint family is comparatively higher in revenue village, i.e. 36 (32.72%) than the forest village, i.e. 20 (21.98%). It is also revealed that the number of broken families are slightly lower in forest villages, i.e. 20 (21.98%) in comparison to revenue village, where there are 22 (20%) broken families. The percentage of extended family is not significant in both the villages.

Among the Sonowal Kacharis, the father is the central figure of the family. All the authority is vested into him and lineage and descent are traced through the father line. In the Sonowal Kachari family, the relationship between different members of the family is based on marriage and descent. This relationship is threefold in nature, that between husband and wife, between parents and children, that between children's. Position and status of the males are a bit higher.

Both the husband and wife contribute to the maintenance of the families. Among the Sonowal Kacharis the succession of authority is on the male line. Their division of labour is based on sex and age. The husband goes for cultivation and fishing, wife collects firewood and edible herbs and shrubs from nearby forest areas or jungle. Throughout the day women remain busy in various household

Table 2.9: Distribution of families according to type and composition in Duliagaon

Type	*Composition*	*No. of Families*	*Percentage*
Nuclear	Husband, wife and their unmarried children	52	47.27
Joint	Husband, wife with married and unmarried children	20	18.18
	Husband, wife, married children and grandchildren	16	14.55
Broken	Widow with married children and grandchildren	8	7.27
	Widow with married and unmarried children with grandchildren	3	2.72
	Widow with married and unmarried children with grandchildren	3	2.72
	Unmarried brothers	2	1.82
	Widower with married children and grandchildren and unmarried sisters	6	5.45
Extended	Husband, wife with married and unmarried children and grandchildren and married and unmarried brothers and sisters	1	0.91
	Husband, wife, married children, husbands brother and his wife and children	1	0.91
Total		110	99.08

activities. Co-operation in a Kachari family is a noteworthy feature. Most of the families depend on agriculture. They also earn cash amount by selling the excess paddy or in emergency to meet the need of the family members. Nowadays many of them have opted for services and this may be one of the main reasons for the emerging of nuclear family.

Marriage

Sonowal Kacharis consider marriage as indispensable for the adult boys and girls. Monogamy is the most common form of marriage though polygamy is permissible. But in the present investigations not a single polygamous marriage is noticeable. The practice of widow remarriage and divorces in the Sonowal Kacharis society is very rare. Marriage among the Sonowal Kacharis is marked by clan exogamy. It is believed that members of the same clan are brothers and sister and it is sin to marry within one's clan or lineage. There is no hard and fast rule about the age at which a boy and a girl may enter into conjugal life. In general, they consider the marriageable age for girl is 18-20 years, while the marriageable age for boy is 22-25 years.

Widow marriage is prohibited, though society recognizes those who became widow at tender age. In such cases, the widow shares her second husbands house without performing any marriage rituals. Sometimes the village elders are invited to bless the couple. Bride price and dowry are not found among them. Although there is no social custom for divorce, yet quarrel between the couple may lead to separation. But in the present study, not a single case of divorce is found in both the forest villages and revenue village.

The Sonowal Kacharis perform the marriage ceremony in four different ways, i.e. (i) *Noa Dhoa* or *bor-biya*, (ii) *Hom diya biya*, (iii) *Gandharba biya* and (iv) *Churchurria or Rabha Sarakai biya.*

The *Noa Dhoa Biya* is performed by the Sonowal Kacharis by observing certain formalities. This type of marriage is normally performed by the wealthy section and marriage is arranged by the parents. As huge expenditure is involved very few families are able to perform it. Generally, non-tribal influence is visible in such type of marriage.

Hom Diya Biya is a type of marriage and rarely visible among the Sonowal Kacharis. Brahmin priest conduct this type of marriage.

Gandharba Biya or love marriage is the common form and traditionally Sonowal Kacharis marriages were performed by this type of marriage. The main reason to support such type of marriage is to avoid vast expenditure which is required in formal marriages. A nominal bride price is charged in this type of marriage and normally they are to offer symbolically Rs. 300.00 because of violation of existing formal social rule.

The *Churchuria* or *Rabha Sarakai Diya Biya* is the fourth category of marriage noticeable among the Sonowal Kacharis. This type of marriage is observed when the people cannot afford the expenditure for celebration of *Bor-biya*. This is popular type of marriage; where the runaway couple is formally recognized as married couple. In such type a few elderly persons are invited to bless the couple who recognize them as husband and wife.

An analysis of marital status in two forest villages has revealed that out of total 515, persons, 125 (24.27%) males and 96 (18.64%) females are unmarried. On the other hand in the category of married, there are 136 (26.40%) males and 135 (26.21%) females. There is not a single case of divorce recorded in the village during the field-work.

Table 2.10: Distribution of marital alliances according to spatial distance in Paroliguri and Nahoroni

Spatial Distance (in km)	*Number of marriages*	*Percentage*
0 – 1	55	34.60
1 – 10	4	2.52
11 – 20	14	8.81
21 – 30	32	20.12
31 – 40	8	5.03
41 – 50	26	16.35
51 – 60	2	1.25
61 – 70	3	1.88
71 – 80	10	6.28
81 – 90	2	1.25
91 – 100	—	—
100 km and above	3	1.88
Total	159	99.97

Among the Sonowal Kacharis, both intra and inter-village, marriages are found. From Table 2.10, it is revealed that village endogamy is very common. 55 marriages (34.60%) have been performed within the village. There are 32 marriages (20.12%) which have been performed within a spatial distance of 21-30 km. Next higher percentage, i.e. 26 marriages (16.35%) occur within the range of 41-50 km. It has been found that 14 marriages (8.81%) are performed within the spatial distance of 11-20 km. There are only 3 marriages (1.88%) which took place beyond 100 km.

Mating Pattern

The Sonowal Kacharis are endogamous; having a number of exogamous clans. Clan exogamy is most important consideration that the tribe most strictly adheres to. They no doubt prefer to confine their marriage within the same tribe, but in exceptional circumstances, they may marry from other tribes/castes.

Table 2.11 indicates that maximum number of marriages, i.e. 128 (80.50%) took place within the same tribe and it is good example of tribal endogamy. Significant number of marriages, i.e. 16 (10.06%) occurred with other backward communities, i.e. the Ahoms, Chutias, etc. There are 8 cases (5.03%), where marriage took place with other Scheduled Tribes and Scheduled Caste Communities.

The Sonowal Kacharis are living side-by-side with Deoris and they have a congenial relationship from the past. There are 7 cases (4.40%) where marriage took place with Deoris. The Sonowal Kacharis are using surname like Hazarika, Saikia, Bora, etc. in the process of assimilation with other cognate communities like the Ahoms, Chutias, etc. which started during the Ahom administration in Assam.

Table 2.11: Mating Pattern in Paroligori and Nahoroni

Type	*No. of Marriage*	*Percentage*
Sonowal with Sonowal	128	80.50
Sonowal with OBC, e.g. Ahoms, Chutias, etc.	16	10.06
Sonowal with Deoris	7	4.40
Other SC and ST	8	5.03
Total	159	100

The distribution of population by age, sex and marital status of the people of Duliagaon revealed that out of the total population of

534, there are 121 (22.15%) males and 91 (17.03% females are unmarried. In the category of married population, there are 142 (26.91%) males and 170 (31.83%) females. There are 7 (1.31%) widowers and 3 (0.56%) widows recorded in the village. Not a single case of divorce is recorded in the village.

An analysis of marital status of the population in Duliagaon also represents that they mostly confine their marriage in the same village. Table 2.12 reveals that the villagers prefer to confine their marriages within the same village. There are 92 (60.14%) marriages which have been performed within a spatial distance of 0-1 km, i.e. within the same village. Next higher percentage is noticed within the range of 21–30 kms where 15 (9.81%) marriages took place. There are 10 marriages (6.54%) which occurred within the range of 1–10 km. Similarly, 10 marriages (6.54%) took place within a spatial distance of 71–80 km, 5 numbers of marriages took place each within the range of 91–100 km and 101–110 km, respectively. There are only 3 numbers of marriages (1.96%) which took place beyond 111 km.

Table 2.12: Distribution of Marital alliance according to spatial distance in Duliagaon

Spatial Distance (in km)	*Number of marriages*	*Percentage*
0 – 1	92	60.14
1 – 10	10	6.54
11 – 20	—	—
21 – 30	15	9.80
31 – 40	—	—
41 – 50	8	5.23
51 – 60	—	—
61 – 70	5	3.27
71 – 80	10	6.54
81 – 90	—	—
91 – 100	5	3.27
101 – 110	5	3.27
111 km and above	3	1.96
Total	153	100

A study in two forest villages and one revenue village reflect more or less the same picture. Child marriage is absent in all the villages. In the forest villages there are only 3 females (0.58%) who are married within the age group of 16–20 years. In the revenue village, there are 6 males (1.12%) and 10 females (1.87%), who are married in the age group of 16–20 years. Thus, among the Sonowal Kacharis, marriage starts from the age group of 16–20 years. Not a single case of divorce is recorded among the Sonowal Kacharis.

B. Population: The Deoris

B.1: Historical Background

The Deoris are a major tribe of Assam inhabiting Lakhimpur, Dhemaji, Sibsagar, Jorhat, Dibrugarh, Tinsukia and Sonitpur districts. The Deoris constitute one of the distinct Scheduled Tribe of Assam. Linguistically they are affiliated to the great Tibeto-Burman group and racially, they belong to the Mongoloid stock. Mongolian characteristics are still visible among them.

There are several interpretations about the word 'Deori' which differ from scholar to scholar. According to some, the word 'Deori' comes from the word '*Deu*', meaning great, wise and O and R denoting male and female, respectively. Deori thus refers to a great or wise male/female human being (Borah, 2007:13) (*Assam Tribune*). According to U.N., Goswami's "Deori Chutia", the term Deori, refers to a person who is well versed in worshipping God. Hemkosh (1900) refers to Deoris as one of the disobedient tribes who live in the plains of Assam. Chandrakanta Abhidhan (1933) refers that they were originally hill people, now living in plains of Assam as priestly class of the Chutiyas. According to Gait (1963), the Deoris were considered as the priestly section of the Chutiya king of Sadiya who worshipped the Goddess Tameswari or Kechaikhati and Baliababa. Dr. B.K. Kakati wrote, "…they (Deoris) are a new Indo-Aryan formation connected with *Devagrhika*".

According to Brown, "the Deoris are known as a branch of the Chutiyas which belong to the Great Bodo race. They speak the Chutiya language which also belongs to the Bodo group. The Chutiyas were the ruling race in Upper Assam (Chutiya Rajya) before the Tai Ahom invasion in 12th century AD. Kacharis, Mech, etc. at one time extended their rule throughout the Assam valley that continued to Eastern Bengal, where the Maharaja of Koch Bihar is still the representative of one branch of the family. The contention is proved beyond any shade of doubt by their Mongoloid features which are as prominent as those of the Bodo-Kacharis (cited in Gogoi, 1990). The historians claimed them as one of the four divisions of the Chutiyas who reigned over eastern Assam prior to the advent of the Ahoms. It is historically proved that the Ahom kings after their arrival in the soil of Assam extended their territories by conquering the various ruling tribes of Assam. It is also commonly referred that the Deoris were the priest of the Chutiyas though at present the Chutiyas and its four divisions have acquired self-identifying features. Differences of opinion still exist among the scholars with regard to the existence of Deori as a division of Chutiya.

The Deoris proudly introduced themselves as *Jimo-Chanya*, meaning they are the children of the sun and the moon (Borah, 2007:13). In fact, Deoris were respected among the tribal communities as priests or worshippers, even after the annexation of the Chutiya Kingdom by the Ahom King Suhungmung in 1523 AD. Chutiya families were dispatched into various places by the Ahom King as a state policy, but the Deoris continued their positions in the shrines of Sadiya and nearby areas with Royal Ahom patronage.

History is, however, silent about the Deoris except a handful of scholars. Due to lack of scientific study about the indigenous tribes of the state, one cannot find a general acceptable term on the Deoris. It was also mentioned in the history that the Deoris faced a serious crisis from 1794 AD for which the Moamoria rebellion widely spread up to Sadiya and the Ahom monarchy gradually declined. Then the Khamtis who were Buddhists, occupied Sadiya from the Ahoms, and as a consequence, the Deoris were stopped from making human sacrifice in the Tameswari temple and celebrating certain traditional rituals. Because of the crisis situation in the state, the Deoris lost their support from the Ahom kings and felt insecure as the Khamtis killed the chief priest Kendukalai Bordeori in the temple itself. Without royal patronage, they had no resources to repair the Tameswari and other temples of the region that were damaged in natural calamities. So in 1800 AD when the Ahoms re-occupied Sadiya, the Deoris had already left Sadiya for the Choukhowa area.

The Deoris are believed to have come to Sadiya before the first century AD. Up to the 4th century AD was the "pre-history period" of Assam history and our sources for that period are the relics like caves, pots, megaliths and legends and tradition as found in the ancient literatures like the epics and the Puranas. In the *Bhagavata* there is a reference about the legends of a king named 'Bhismak' who ruled over a kingdom called 'Vidarbha' with its capital at Kundima. This kingdom was in the north-eastern corner of Assam near Sadiya. The

Deoris were the royal priests of the kingdom. It was specifically mentioned that the Deoris were the royal priest of king 'Bhismak' and the gods and goddesses which were propitiated by the Deoris were patronized by the king. It is a fact that the Deoris were the ancient indigenous tribes of Sadiya. In 1901 census report, reference has been made about their habitation and it was clearly mentioned that Deoris as a tribe lived on the bank of the river Kundil, i.e. east of Sadiya (Deori, 1948). In 1837, Brown in the book 'Deori-Chutiya' mentioned that the original abode of the Deoris were on the other side of Sadiya. Slowly they moved to their present habitation and many of them still frequently visit their ancient abode for religious purpose.

The historical record reveals that when the Ahoms (the great branch of Tais) entered Assam and established their kingdom in the south-eastern corner of Assam or south bank of the river Brahmaputra, and, in between the rivers Buri Dihing and Disang in the 13th century, one of their immediate neighbours were the Chutiyas, who ruled the land east of the river Subansiri and Disang. During that time both were independent powers and faced no problems from each other. Both came into contact in the middle of the 14th century AD. In course of time hostilities broke out between the Ahoms and the Chutiyas and in the 16th century, the Chutiya Kingdom was annexed to the Ahom Kingdom.

Dalton (1972) writes about the Deoris as "An isolated colony on the river Dikrang in Lakhimpur calling themselves as Deori Chutia who had a peculiar language which they called Chutiya and they were styled as Deoris" (Dalton, 1872:5). Thus, it has been established that the original abode of the Deoris was on the bank of Kundil River of Sadiya. But due to constant feuds with the neighbouring hill tribes', i.e. Mishimis, Adis and other powerful tribes, they had to move westward and spread in the riverside areas. According to Sadiya Frontier Tract Gazetteer, the Deoris are the oldest priestly community and the attendants and worshipper of god. According to Goswami (1994) the meaning of the word 'Deori' is the people who can worship god. During the early Ahom period, the king held the Deoris in high esteem. They were exempted from services and provided with guards and slaves. When the four Deori chiefs paid their annual visit to the Ahom court, the Raja rose and stood to receive their salutation.

According to 1951 census, the number of Deori population was about 11,000 (Deori, 1964:8). As per 2001 Census, their total population was 41,161. In the year 2005, the Deoris got their Autonomous Council to fulfil their longstanding demand according to the felt need of the people as grassroots level. As per the report of the Deori Autonomous Council, Narayanpur, district-wise concentration of the Deori population in Assam is presented in Table 2.13. The total population according to it is 1,27,086.

Table 2.13: Districtwise Deori population

District	*Population*
Jorhat	11,500
Sibsagar	16,369
Dibrugarh	5,411
Tinsukia	13,585
Dhemaji	15,106
Sonitpur	6,000
Guwahati	1,331
Lakhimpur	57,784

There are four great territorial groups or *Khels* among the Deoris, namely, (i) Dibongia or Dibongiya, (ii) Tengaponia or Tengaponiya, (iii) Borgaia or Borgonya, and (iv) Patorgoia or Patorgoiya. Each one derived its name either from a particular place or river. The Dibongiyas were believed to reside on the bank of Dibang River, whilst Tengaponiyas on the bank of river Tengapani and Borgoiya *Khel* settled on the bank of the river Borpani or Borgang. The people who lived in Pat-Sadiya were named as Patorgoiya. Because of their settlement on the bank of different rivers, they were known accordingly. The last group reportedly became extinct. According to some elderly villagers, the Deoris had to migrate from Sadiya to avoid the frequent troubles created by the neighbouring hill tribes. They left the place in a country made boat (*Mar-nao*). Unfortunately, one such *Mar-nao* carrying the Patorgoiya group became traceless in the middle of the Brahmaputra. Brown also mentioned this story while narrating the migration history of the Deoris. According to some, this group might have amalgamated with the Dibongiya, while other's claim that the group merged with the Chutiyas and lost their identity. Whatever the fact is, now three distinct groups exist among the Deoris.

Each of this division is composed of a number of exogamous clans called *Bangshas* (*Jakus*). There are slight differences of opinion among the scholars regarding the number of *Bangshas* of each group. Each *Bangsha* is entitled to perform certain ritual obligations. The Dibongiya is the only division, who speaks of Deori language or dialect. Their main deities are *Gira-Girasi* or *Burha-Burhi*. *Gira* refers to Lord 'Mahadeva' and *Girasi* refers to goddess 'Parvati'. Their place of worship is *Than* and is found in every village. Sharma Thakur (1987:27) mentioned about 8 *bangshas* among the Dibongiya. Whereas Deori (1964:15) refers that there are 12 *bangshas* among the Dibongiya, i.e. *Sundariya* (*Bordeori*), *Patriya* (*Sandeori*), *Airio* (*Bharali*), *Sariyo* (*Bora*), *Chitigaya* (*Bhog Randhoni*), *Kamtayo*, *Sukrayo*, *Dhupiya*, *Murangyo*, *Kumaroi*, *Lakachukoyo* and *Kalichakoya*.

The Tengaponiya speak Assamese language and maintain close relation with other Deori divisions. They worship *Pisa-Dema*; commonly referred to as *Bolia baba*, who according to them is the son of 'Lord Mahadeva' and 'Parvati' or Gira-Girasi. Their place of worship is also *Than*. There are seven clans in this *Bangsha*. Both Sharma Thakur and Deori were of the same opinion. The *Bangshas* are *Machiatika* (*Bordeori*), *Bikramiyatika* (*Sarudeori*), *Khutiyotika* (*Bharali*), *Sakuchaintika*, *Pagimegeratika*, *Phapariyotika* and *Chenabariyatika*, etc.

The Borgoiya are the worshipper of *Pisasi* or *Tameswari* or *Kesaikhati*, who according to them is the daughter of Lord 'Mahadeva' and 'Parvati'. Their place of worship is also *Than*. They speak Assamese in their daily life and have 6 clans, e.g. *Ikucharu* (*Bordeuri*), *Chimucharu* (*Sarudeori*), *Hizaru* (*Borbharali*), *Busharu* (*Balikata*), *Lufaru* (*Bora*), *Gosaru*. Only six clans have been identified (Deori, 1964: 16). The last clan no longer may be traced.

Each *Bangsha* is entitled to perform certain ritual obligations. The function of certain *Bangsha* may be identified and in general discourse, the people refer to it as *Khel or* group. But clan (*Bangsha*) distinction within a group plays major role, particularly in marriage. The members of the same *Bangshas* are considered as brothers. There is social prohibition to marry within the clan. At the time of birth and death, members of the same clan are to observe ritual purity and prohibition.

At present, the Deoris are found in North Lakhimpur, Dhemaji, Tinsukia, Dibrugarh, Sibsagar, Jorhat and Sonitpur districts in the State of Assam. While in Arunachal Pradesh, the Deoris are found in Mahadevpur, Tezu, Namsai, Sumpoi and Udampur areas.

Since the last quarter of the 19th century, the Deoris started mobilizing their resources to revitalize their traditional culture and language in order to establish their group identity and heritage in the multi-ethnic setting of different tribes/caste in Assam. To fulfil their objective, various associations and organizations have been established, e.g.

(i) Sodou Asom Deori Chatrahanta,
(ii) Deori Sahitya Sabha,
(iii) Deori Pujari Sanmilan,
(iv) Sodou Deori Mohila Samiti,
(v) All India Deori Student Association
(vi) Deori Janojati Mancha
(vii) Deori Sayatya Hakhita Dabi Samiti (Deori Autonomous Demand Committee)

Out of these associations, Deori Sahitya Sabha (1965), literary association is playing the most important role in Deori identity formation. In this regard, the association is trying to preserve the existing culture and make effort to revitalize their old vanishing culture. In the year 2005, the Deoris got their Autonomous Council. Though they have got Autonomous Council for their development, yet like most of the other tribes having Autonomous Council, they too are not satisfied with it. They feel that the common people are not benefited from it and 9 members of the council may not represent the entire Deori community.

B.2: Areas of Study

In the present study, the Deori villages were selected in the same ecological condition as of the Sonowal Kacharis. The forest village is situated adjacent to the villages inhabited by the Sonowal Kacharis. One of the oldest revenue villages was also considered for the present study, situated about 10 km away from the forest village.

Micro Field: Modhupur Deori Village (Forest Village)

Data on Deoris have been collected from Modhupur Deori village, situated 28 km away from Dibrugarh town. The village falls under the jurisdiction of Dihingmukh Reserved Forest. Initially there were 55 families with 275 *bighas* of homestead land and 803 *bighas* of cultivable land. The total land areas of Modhupur were 1078 sq. km.

The two villages, inhabited by the Sonowal Kacharis are also situated adjacent to the Deori village. Thus, it is found that all the three villages occupied by the Sonowal Kacharis and the Deoris are situated in the same environmental situation having same kind of facilities.

The village is bounded in the north by the river Brahmaputra, which is nearly 2.5 km away from the village. The Nahoroni and Paroliguri, the two Sonowal Kachari villages incorporated in the present study are situated in the eastern direction. In the South, there is Gorudharia village inhabited mainly by the Sonowal Kacharis. The village path runs straight from south to north. The road is gravelled and various lanes bifurcate from this village path towards the eastern direction. The houses are constructed sometimes on both sides of the bylane and sometimes only on one side. On the western side adjacent to the village road, the school is situated. The community hall is also on the western side. There is a small shop near the village path on the western side. Most of the north-eastern sides are covered by the reserved forest. Near the forest *Baliababa Than,* i.e. the religious institution is situated.

Regarding the origin of the village, the village elders were of the opinion that the entire area was a part of the Reserved Forest. Various types of trees, big and small were found in the area and it was suitable for resting the Hong Bees nest. When the flood affected people were rehabilitated in the area, they observed the unique scene and named the place as Modhupur. *Modhus* means honey and *Pur* means full. Most of the villages agreed about the origin of the name in this way.

Population Analysis

The distribution of population by Age and Sex in Deori village has been presented in Table 2.14.

The total population of the village is 406 distributed in 62 households, giving the average size of the family as 6.5. Out of the total population of 406 individuals, 196 (48.27%) are Males and 210 (51.72%) are Females. It indicates that the number of females is slightly higher than the males. It has been observed that 26-30 age group category has the highest number of individuals, i.e. 48 (11.82%) out of which 23 (5.66%) are males and 25 (6.15%) are females.

Again the lowest number of individuals which is 1 with a percentage of 0.24 per cent found in 86-90, 91-95 and 96-100 age group categories, respectively. While the highest number of females,

Table 2.14: Distribution of Population by Age and Sex in Deori village

Age Group	Male	Percentage	Female	Percentage	Total	Percentage
0-5	18	4.43	23	5.66	41	10.09
6-10	20	4.92	15	3.69	35	8.62
11-15	12	2.95	17	4.18	29	7.43
16-20	13	3.20	16	3.94	29	7.43
21-25	16	3.94	20	4.92	36	8.86
26-30	23	5.66	25	6.15	48	11.82
31-35	23	5.66	23	5.66	46	11.33
36-40	17	4.18	15	3.69	32	7.88
41-45	11	2.70	11	2.70	22	5.41
46-50	7	1.72	11	1.72	18	4.43
51-55	7	1.72	7	1.72	14	3.44
56-60	8	1.97	7	1.72	15	3.69
61-65	3	0.73	6	1.47	9	2.21
66-70	5	1.23	5	1.23	10	2.46
71-75	5	1.23	3	0.73	8	1.97
76-80	4	0.98	4	0.98	8	1.97
81-85	2	0.49	1	0.24	3	0.73
86-90	1	0.24	—	—	1	0.24
91-95	—	—	1	0.24	1	0.24
96-100	1	0.24	—	—	1	0.24
Total	196	48.27	210	51.72	406	98.57

i.e. 25 (6.15%) are found in 26-30 age group category. The highest number of males, i.e. 23 (5.66%) are found in the age group of 26-30 and 31-35 age group category. The children (0-5 years) constitute approximately 10.09 per cent of the population, whereas the figure in the next higher group (6-10 years) stands as 8.62 per cent, approximately

The table also reveals that the active labour force (16-55 years) is composed of 245 (60.34%) of the population that is supposed to look after 39.6 per cent dependents, i.c. children and adolescent.

Socio-Cultural Life

The Deoris are peace loving and hard working people, enjoying the mixture of both the traditional and modern system of living.

Family and Household

A family is the basic social and cultural unit of a society because the seeds of culture originate in the family. Among the Deoris, family

Table 2.15: Distribution of Families according to size in Deori village

Family Type	*No. of Individual*	*Total no. of Family*	*Percentage*
Single	1	—	—
Small	2-4	14	22.59
Medium	5-6	28	45.16
Large	7-8	9	14.50
Very Large	9 +above	11	17.74
Total		62	100

plays an important role of uniting the members. Distribution of the families according to size in forest village is presented in the Table 2.15.

An analysis of the families according to size in Table 2.15 reveals that the medium sized family occurs in the highest frequency, i.e. 28 (45.16%). It is followed by small family, the number of which is 14 (22.59%). Very big family is also reported from the village and the number of which is 11 (14.5 %.). During the present investigation, there is not a single family with one member. They are patriarchal people and traced their descent through male line. The Deoris generally observe a harmonious family life.

An analysis of the type and composition of families in Table 2.16 reveals that in the village both joint and nuclear families are found. Earlier joint family was preferred which was the distinguished characteristics of Deori society. The eldest male member is considered as the head of the family. But the situation is changing due to various

Table 2.16: Distribution of Families according to type and composition in Deori village

Type	*Composition*	*No. of Family*	*Percentage*
Nuclear	Husband, Wife with un-married children	27	43.54
Joint	Husband, Wife with married, un-married and general children	17	27.42
Broken	Widow with un-married children or widow with married and grandchildren.	13	20.96
Extended		5	8.06
Total		62	99.98

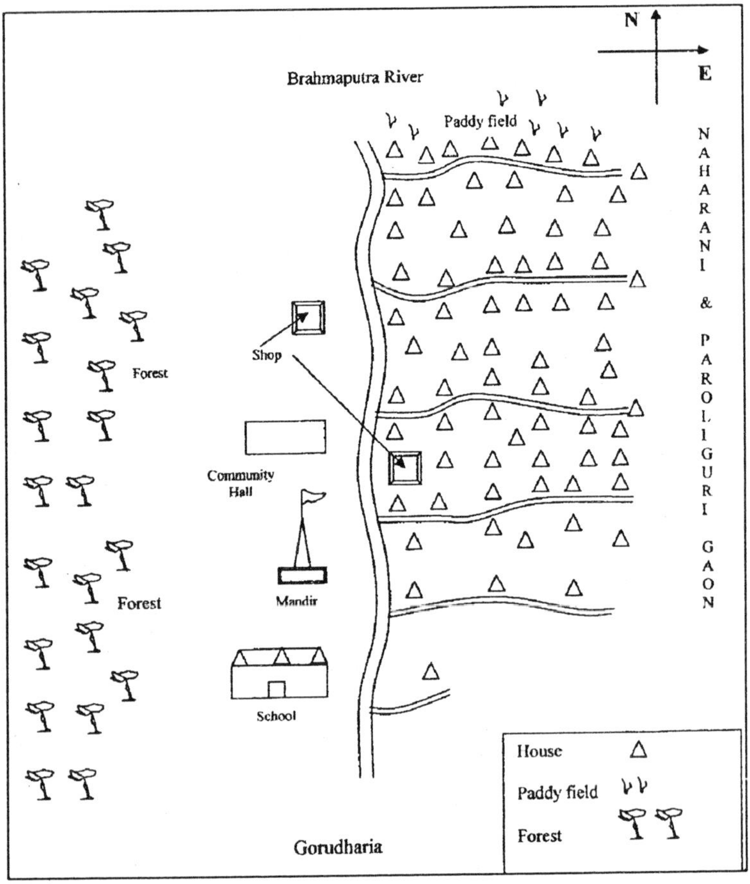

Map 2.3: Notional Map of Modhupur Deorigaon

socio-cultural factors. The present analysis reveals that the number of nuclear family is found in highest frequency, i.e. 27 (43.54%). There are 17 (27.42%) joint families found in the village. The number of broken family is also significant and 13 (20.96%) families fall in this category. The number of extended family is 5 (8.06%).

The Deoris follow a specific tradition in constructing their houses, and are guided by tradition. Though, Sonowal Kacharis and Deoris are living in the same environmental situation, frequently effected by flood water, yet not a single platform type of house is visible among the Sonowal Kacharis. Of course, they raise the plinth of their houses slightly higher to prevent the flood water. Whereas among the Deoris all the households are of platform type, normally referred as *Chang-ghar*. This indicates that material culture more or less reflects their tradition.

The *Chang-ghar* is generally built in 'L' or 'I' shape. The villagers were of the opinion that the Deoris prefer to settle on the river side and consider themselves as a riverine people. So, to protect themselves from flood and wild animals, they prefer to live on platform type house. As many of their customs and traditions are associated with livelihood pattern, the *Chang-ghar* became their traditional pattern of household. In the forest village, all the houses are of platform type. The roof of the house is made up of thatch whereas sidewalls are made up of *Ikora* (reeds) and sometimes bamboo splits are used. The side walls are plastered by a mixture of mud and cow-dung. There is no ventilation in this type of house. The floor is generally made of bamboo splits or by wooden planks. The posts are either wooden or concrete. The *Chang-ghar* contains two verandahs or *mishang*, one at the front side and another at the back side of the house. Their houses are mostly facing towards the east. As an alternative south facing households are also preferred. A home generally possesses one main post named *Subachani* post. Every household possesses two ladders (one in the front and the other at the back), which are generally made up of wood. The steps of the ladder are usually odd in number, i.e. 7/9/11. Most of the tribes of Assam, who are living in *Chang-ghar,* keep odd numbers in the ladder. The real reason behind it cannot be explained by common people.

Like the peasant communities of Assam, the Deoris also store paddy in the granary. The granaries are also of platform type. They normally construct granary in the front of the house in sunny and airy spot. Following the tradition, the Deoris do not use nail in constructing the granary. The roof of the granary is made up of thatch or CI sheets. The side walls are plastered from the inner side with a mixture of mud and cowdung. They use a narrow movable ladder which is made up of single tree trunk or bamboo. There is an extension in front of the granary which is normally used for keeping paddy or to store hey stack. The space beneath the granary is used for keeping their domesticated animals, i.e. cows, buffalos, etc.

A traditional Deori kitchen possesses a *Tipa*i (*Thi-Pai*) or *Juhal*. The hearth in each household plays a significant role in the life of the members. Besides cooking it is also utilized for preservation and drying. Two hearths are found in each household, one is used for cooking purposes and the other is used for sitting or entertaining the guest and family members over a cup of tea. Hearths are made of a square platform raised with mud or cowdung. In the middle they make the actual fire place or sometimes iron rod is used for making the fire place. The platform is polished with thick mud so that fire of the hearth cannot burn up the wooden platform. Just above the hearth there are small square shaped *Chang* (platform), made of bamboo. They use it to keep their daily use utensils and other cooking materials, e.g., salt, chili, turmeric, pepper, etc. so that they get it easily while cooking. Occasionally, fishes, bamboo shoots, chilies are kept for drying/smoking. Above the first *Chang*, there is another big platform which is referred as *Lueng*. They normally keep the utensils which are used for preparing rice-beer. Different kind of bamboo containers, e.g., *Dola, Chaloni, Pasi* are kept here. They also keep the raw materials like cane, bamboos which are used for making baskets of various kinds. It is believed that if these are kept in that way, these are protected from insects. Moreover, the fire cannot reach the roof easily and the process prevents the house from catching fire.

Marriage

The Deoris practice different types of marriages, e.g. (i) Monogamy and (ii) Polygamy but in the present study not a single case of polygamous marriage was reported. They perform marriage in 3 different ways, e.g. (a) Elopement, (b) Negotiation and (c) *Bar-biya*. It is reported that third type of marriage is rarely practiced as it is an elaborate ceremony where huge amount of money and materials like rice, meat is required in large quantity. Most of villagers are not aware about the know-how of the entire procedure of *Bor-Biya*.

Thus, elopement is the common type of marriage prevalent among the Deoris. In this type of marriage, the boy after elopement seeks the permission of the parents to take the girl home. The girl is welcomed by the boy's family after observing a simple rite. Next day or after 2-3 days, the boy's family arranges a feast for the villagers. They inform the community members about the incident and seek formal permission. Before arranging the feast, it is the responsibility of the boy's side to inform the girl's parents about it through a middleman. In the feast, fowls, ducks, pigs, etc. are arranged and pig is a must in the feast. The host family is to invite selected novices and the bride is to prepare and distribute meal for the novices, by herself. While for the invitees as a whole, the cooking may be done by professional cook. Before serving the meal, the couple first offer the meal in the *Than*. After it, they bow before the gatherings, who bless them for a happy married life.

Negotiated marriage is performed with the formal permission of both the families. Proposal for marriage is first initiated from the boy's side. When it is agreed, the groom family visits the prospective bride's house carrying with them the *Bhuja*. It is a traditional system of offering goods to the bride's family. The *Bhuja* is a kind of bamboo basket, where they take rice-beer, fowl, mustard-oil, salt, rice, etc. Normally, the boy's elder brother and father perform this formality and the date of marriage is fixed on that day.

Bridal dress and ornaments are also ceremoniously presented from the groom's side and it is referred as *juran* like other rural communities of Assam. On the day of marriage party also they are to carry *Bhuja* and it contains fowl, fish, *Shukati*, rice, *dal* and rice-beer that are needed for arranging a feast. These are all under the charge of *Pathoria* (middle-man). The *Pathoria* plays an important role in Deori marriage. Both the families appoint *Pathoria*. On the marriage day, he is to wear a special dress and he must be a person who is conversant with the folk songs/folk lore and other marriage formalities.

The system of bride price was prevalent among the Deoris (Bordoloi *et al.*, 1987:29). But no rigid system exit at present period. A token amount of bride price is to be offered by the groom's side and the amount increases in case of elopement marriage. An elaborate feast is arranged in the bride's house, though in practice it depends on the economic condition of the family. A portion of food which is prepared for the *Bhakats* is kept separately for the bride's mother, which is traditionally known as *Pat purani-bhat*. The bride's mother is to take this meal on the next day.

The field study in the village Modhupur reveals that they prefer to confine their marriage within the village. Table 2.17 reveals that out of 103 marriages, 19 (18.44%) marriages were held within the village. But the same percentage is also found where marriage took place within the spatial distance of 91-100 km. A significant number of marriages, i.e. 16 (15.53%), took place beyond a distance of 100 km.

Table 2.17: Distribution of marital alliances according to spatial distance in Deori village

Spatial distance in km	*Number of marriage*	*Percentage*
0–1	19	18.45
1–10	3	2.91
11–20	1	0.97
21–30	7	6.80
31–40	4	3.88
41–50	11	10.68
51–60	5	4.85
61–70	6	5.82
71–80	9	8.74
81–90	3	2.91
91–100	19	18.45
100–+ above	16	15.53
Total	103	100

Mating Pattern

The Deoris are endogamous, having a number of exogamous clan/ *Bansha*. In no cases, they are to marry within the same clan. In general, there is a tendency to confine their marriage within the same tribe, but the marriage may take place with other tribes and communities according to the demand of the situation.

Table 2.18: Mating Pattern among the Deories

Type	*No. of Marriages*	*Percentage*
Deori with Deori	80	77.6
Deoris with Ahoms	5	4.85
Deoris with Kacharis	12	11.65
With others (S.C., Mishing, Rabha, Khamyangs)	6	5.82
Total	103	100

It is revealed from Table 2.18 that maximum number of marriages, i.e. 80 (77.66%) took place within the same tribe. This is no doubt a clear indication of maintaining tribal endogamy. Significant number of marriages, i.e. 12 (11.65%) occurred with the Kacharis. There are only 5 (4.85%) cases where marriage took place with the Ahoms, a dominant community of upper Assam. On the other hand, marriages took place with ST and SC communities, i.e. Mishings, Rabha and Khamyags. The percentage of such marriage is 5.82.

Economy

Economy of a group cannot be considered as independent unit, because it is closely linked with the total socio-cultural life. Economic activities are essential for a group not only for their survival, but also to retain/reflect their cultural identity. Thus, communities living in the same ecological conditions have different ways of technology/ belief system.

The Deoris are agriculturist and agriculture is the primary means of livelihood. They cultivate different types of paddy like *Sali*, *Ahu*, and *Bao,* etc. As they live in the flood prone areas, their lands are not suitable for *Sali* paddy cultivation. *Ahu* and *Bao* are widely grown by the Deoris and they relish on *Ahu* rice. In the Modhupur Deori village, their cultivable lands are on one end of the village in the northern side and lands are very low. They produce paddy mainly for home consumption and only in rare occasion are they able to sell it. But in emergency, they invariably sell paddy to meet their immediate need.

For cultivation, the Deoris use plough drawn by bullocks. Sometimes to plough their low land, they hire buffaloes from nearby villages. As they entirely depend on plough cultivation, the implements used for cultivation is religiously taken care off: "If the yoke is broken, they keep fast on that day" (Deori, 1964:363). It has also been mentioned that they never use any part of the plough as fire wood. It is believed that if they do it, the weather becomes averse for cultivation. All the members of the household extend their helping hand towards different economic activities. The community life is still strong among the Deoris. But the strong bond and co-operation, which characterized Deori society no longer, exist. The system of '*Haria*' was widely prevalent among the Deoris. On the basis of type of work, there are 'male *Haria*' and 'female *Haria*'. The host specified the type of work and invites one member from each family. The next day, the members jointly complete the work and the host is to arrange a feast when they go for *Haria*.

There was another type of exchange of work known as *'Hedari'* or '*Haldari*' (Deori, 1964:365). It is one type of learning process. If someone wishes to learn something from another, one may go for it, e.g. if a person does not have his own plough he may extend his service to a person according to the necessity of that person for a period of 7 days. In return, the person helps him by providing the plough. Moreover, to learn a particular skill, whether weaving/embroidery one may extend her service to another who knows the art. Because of her service, she gets the opportunity to learn the skill from that girl. This no doubt develops their unity and fellow feeling. But unfortunately, such system of reciprocal help is gradually vanishing from the society.

Besides paddy, they cultivate various types of seasonal vegetables in large scale, if one possesses sufficient land. They cultivate cabbage, different types of gourd, chilies, brinjal, potatoes, mustard, etc. From this point of view they may be considered as self sufficient and their economy may be considered as slightly above the subsistence level. The kitchen garden provides the herbs and shrubs which are automatically grown in their soil.

The present study also reveals that though they are agriculturist, yet significant number of persons has gone for other occupation. As the village is not far from Dibrugarh town, most of the villagers are able to utilize the educational facilities in the town. This on the other hand helps in increasing literacy rate. The present study reveals that the percentage of literacy is roughly 75 per cent. There are four persons; two males and two females who have received medical degrees. Three persons have achieved engineering degree and another two have qualified for ITI.

Religion

The Deoris are Hindu and followers of *Sakta cult*. They believe in spirits and sacrifice different animals in every religious ritual. There is no definite worshipping room or alter in their home, except the *Subachani* post, where they believe the household deity resides (Barua & Bharali, 2001:89). The main religious institution of the Deoris is *Thanghar* or *Goshani Sal* and all religions rituals and festivals (community level) are performed in the *Thanghar*. In almost every religious ritual, they sacrifice animals like pig, goat, duck, fowl, etc. whether performed at the *Thanghar* or in the family. There are nine office bearers who manage all the religious activities of the *Thanghar*. They have been assigned specific duties in relation to *Thanghar*. Certain restrictions are to be observed by the priests, particularly in relation to food habits and daily activities. They observe elaborate family/community level rituals (Barua & Bharali, 2001:90).

3

Indigenous Health Care System

In this chapter, an effort has been made to highlight the indigenous health care system. Beliefs and practices associated with the system have also been described citing suitable examples.

Indigenous Health Care System

From time immemorial, the people of India have depended on their natural environment for various necessity of their daily life. In the initial stage, human society had to develop various measures for their survival, e.g. protection from enemies, supply of food for their existence, etc. Besides food and shelter, people are to develop measures for health and well-being. Since ancient times, it has been the endeavours of the society to seek ways and means for eradicating illness and sufferings.

The history of diseases in human society is as old as man himself. Since, human being is living in cultural environment; every known human society has developed a pharmacopoeia and therapy, be it is magico-religious, secular and scientific. Thus, medicine and diseases have an undeniable effect on the history and culture of mankind. Every culture, irrespective of its simplicity and complexity has its own notion regarding health and health seeking behaviour and this is often referred to as "health culture". It is an integral component of the overall culture of the community. Culture is unique in human society. The "established pattern of living" is a very composite term; this could be referred as culture. One recent Encyclopaedia of social and cultural Anthropology even explains, "Culture is plural and realistic". This clearly indicates that gradually the concept and boundary of culture studies expanded.

Health is a common theme in most cultures. In fact, all communities have their concept of health, as part of their culture. The most prevalent and oldest definition is the "absence of diseases", which may be referred as "bio-medical concept". Development in medical and social sciences led to the conclusion that the bio medical concept of health was inadequate. Medical professionals tend to consider illness and diseases as a bio-medical phenomenon and thus they treat illness with only bio-medical approach, while social scientists perceive illness and diseases as an outcome of macro-interactions of the bio-socio and environmental factors.

In every culture, a substantial and integral set of beliefs, knowledge, techniques and practices are related to the major life experiences of health and disease. Researches indicate that health condition of an individual is not always due to physiological condition, but depends on various cultural and social factors. Man is a cultural animal and it is not possible to discuss any human problem without social and cultural factors. The social dimension of health includes the levels of social skills one possesses, social functioning and the ability to see oneself as a member of a larger society. Health is multi-factorial.

Various factors internal as well as external create health problem; conceptually the health of individuals and whole communities may be considered to be the result of many interaction, e.g. heredity, environment, life style, socio-economic conditions, health and family welfare services and other emerging factors.

Health care can never be adequately protected by health services without the active understanding and involvement of communities. The individual and community responsibility are complementary, not antithetical. This implies a more active involvement of families and communities in health matters, viz. planning, implementation, utilization, operation and evaluation of health services. In other words, the emphasis has shifted from health care for the people to health care by the people. From the view of the anthropologists and of the holistic understanding of the behaviour of human beings, the point is precisely stated that, "we cannot explain acts solely in terms of the biological properties of the people concerned, that any comprehensive study person must involve not his biological properties", but also that of the past and present experience of human being that we call culture, "Since culture is prior to the person and indeed the organism becomes a person principally as a direct effect of cultural stimulation and organization which has inherited potentialities and his acquired behaviour undergo it becomes of the first importance to understand the nature of culture or cultures in which the person was culturalized if one is to understand the person" (Montagu, 1963:151).

Health Care Practices

The nature and extent of acceptance of a particular type of Medicare system before a cultural group, especially by a simpler society generally depends on a number of factors.

The prevailing healthcare system among the people can be categorized as:

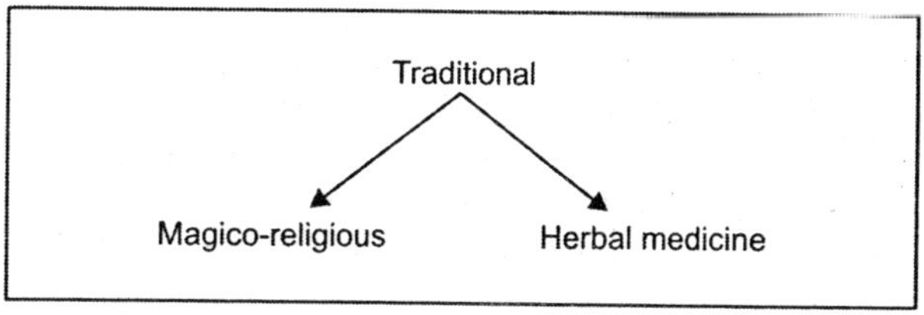

In traditional healthcare, the people resort to both super natural (Magico religious) as well as natural (Herbal) means. Magic occupies a very important role in primitive society and it is considered to be the aggregates of superstition.

Though there is no direct relation between religion and health, yet the role of religion in the sphere of health and diseases cannot be ignored. River's, pioneering theoretical classic, "Medicine, magic and religion" defined medicine as a cultural system. He perceived medicine, magic and religion as "three sets of social process...so closely interrelated that the disentanglement of each from the rest are difficult or impossible" (Rivers, 1927: 1).

Explanation of illness and its preventive, curative measures reflect the knowledge, cultural values and traditions of a society. Social and cultural elements as a whole do influence the health of a community both positively and negatively. The belief that illness is a punishment for wrong doing is widespread in human society. It is commonly believed that if man offends supernatural forces, their mystical powers would punish the individual or the family by causing sickness, death or other natural calamities. "The attribution of illness to misconduct may have been a very early form of social control in the development of human society" (Hallowell, 1963). Various scholars also express the same view. When the advantages of modern medicine are not convincingly apparent, traditional medical beliefs provide a ready frame of reference. These beliefs are linked to other ideas and patterns of behaviour (Firth, 1959). They are particularly interwoven with magic, religion and traditional social values and they serve cognitive functions (Hughes, 1963). Thus, to a tribal mind, the real enemies of human health and prosperity are the gods and the malevolent spirits of the dead. In traditional societies, people believed that evil spirits, black magic, breach of taboo, sorcery, etc. might lead a person to illness. Explanation of illness and its preventive, curative measures reflect the knowledge, cultural values and traditions of a society. The people are so emotionally attached to these beliefs that even after the availability of modern medical system they could not abandon their belief and practices. As a result, it is still possible to trace such belief and practices in the socio-religious life of many indigenous population. It is a natural tendency among human being to seek good health; they take certain precautions with regard to food and hygienic conditions. Equally, in the folk conception of diseases, health, etc. is prerequisite to know the overall view of the villagers. Most of the plain tribes are superstitious and they firmly believe that most of the diseases or natural calamities are caused by the wrath or displeasure of deity or ancestral spirit. Therefore, every effort is made to appease these supernatural agencies, which are believed to be responsible for particular diseases.

In the same way tribal communities all over the world are very rich in ethno-medicine. Ancient Indian and world literature on medicine suggest that indigenous and tribal people use several kinds of medicinal plants for the treatment of diseases. This knowledge of medicinal herbs has been handed down through generations and some of these have been survived through time among various tribal communities of India. It has been estimated that there are around 3 lakh village-based herbal healers in India, who with their knowledge, cure various ailments and diseases (Darshan, 1998, cited from Maiti, 2005). According to Government of India (GoI, 1994) report, out of 7500 wild species used by the tribes in India for medicinal purposes, about 950 are found to be new claims and worthy of scientific investigations (Cited from Maiti, 2005:137).

Etymologically, ethno-medicines mean medicines which are traditionally associated with specific ethnic group. This can also be conceived as "folk medicine" or "traditional medicine" or even indigenous medicine. In a simple way, it may be conceived as rural wisdom.

There should not be any doubt that ethno-medicine, an inherit component of traditional wisdom of rural communities or people's knowledge have been acquired over generation of environmental adaptation. David Alle, an economist, who has studied African indigenous knowledge system, explains, "It is an unwritten body of knowledge. There is no systematic record to describe what it is, what it does, how it does it." However, such knowledge is not getting due importance and it is undervalued, ignored, despised, rejected and treated by the so-called modern trends.

In course of development, ethno-medicine emerged as an important branch of medical anthropology. Hughes (1968) defines ethno-medicine as a term that has been used to refer to those beliefs and practices relating to diseases that are products of indigenous cultural conceptions and are not explicitly derived from the conceptual framework of modern medicine. Ethno medical approach is to study how a particular group of people perceive and deals with its health and illness.

Since the beginning of evolution, human-kind has always been able to find some medicines in the nature that surround them. Early therapeutic treatments were derived from the surrounding environment of human beings, who were forest dwellers. They made use of plants, animals and other substances naturally available to them for treatment. The knowledge of many medicinal herbs is derived from the direct observation of animals that consume herbs when ill. Complex health care system of simple societies was evolved, based on deep observation of the nature and environment.

The health-sickness process is a tangible veracity for all people all over the world. Man has always been concerned about his ailments and he has complex conceptions of life, death, sickness and its treatment. All cultures have shared ideas of what makes people sick, what cures them of these ailment and how they can maintain good health through time. This cognitive development is part of the cultural heritage of each population and from it, empirical medicine system has been formed, based on the use of natural resources. The indigenous medicines have developed out of cumulative human experiences and depict the folk wisdom. And the folk world is a blend of rational, experimental and supernatural. The common members and health professionals on the basis of their experience tend to combine their society's models of beliefs, which are reflected in their ethno-medicine, socio-religious life and superstitious beliefs.

The analyses of data have been arranged separately and systematically on the basis of community. **1.A** deals with Sonowal Kacharis and **1.B** incorporated data on the Deoris.

1.A. The Sonowal Kacharis

Ethno-Medicine

In the present study, the data have been incorporated under three broad categories:

(i) The medicines which are found in two forest villages, i.e. Paroliguri and Nahoroni are analyzed.
(ii) Secondly, data collected from one of the oldest revenue village inhabited by Sonowal Kacharis, i.e. Duliagaon are analyzed. Some more data were collected from two other villages. Only relevant portion are included here.
(iii) The selected published data have also been incorporated.

The tribal people mainly depend on their forest environment from where they collect the medicinal herbs, plants, roots, tubers, fruits, flowers, etc. to treat the ailment. In the present study, a brief ethno-botanical study was conducted in two forest villages, i.e. Paroliguri and Nahoroni, which are exclusively inhabited by the Sonowal Kacharis. They use various herbal medicines to treat the patients and the diseases and ways of treatment are described below. Sustainable exploration of the rich medicinal flora from the neighbouring reserved forest has resulted in establishing a close link between man and environment. In the forest villages 17 different types of illness were recorded which are treated by their indigenous method of herbal treatment. A part of the data was published in paper form in the journal *Ne BIO*, Vol. 11, 4.2011 (Barùa & Sonowal, 2011). The paper documented 34 species of medicinal plants distributed across 32 genera and 24 families used in the treatment of various diseases.

The entire finding has been compiled under the following disease heads alphabetically. The folk ways of treatment have also been described. The medicinal plants are described with botanical names, local names (Assamese), part/s used along with method of remedy preparation.

Micro Field: Paroliguri and Nahoroni (Forest Village)

1. Blood Pressure

If somebody is suffering from high blood pressure, he is advised to eat tamarind.

2. Bleeding During or 2/3 Months of Pregnancy

Leaf buds of *Bholuka bah* (*Bambusa balcooa*) – 5 numbers and 250 gm of semi-rotten flesh of *Kumura* (*Benincasa hispida*) are crushed and mixed with about 700 gm of jaggery (from old stock at least 1 year old). This preparation was very effective in giving relief.

3. Diabetes

Kola jamuk (*Syzgium jambolanun)* are crushed and kept dipped in water overnight. The filtered water is taken in empty stomach.

4. Dog Bite

Roots of *Korobi* (*Thevetia peruviana*) – about 2.5 inches and 2-3 numbers of *Jaluk* (*Piper nigrum*) are grinded to extract the juice. The patient is given one dose of the remedy immediately after the bite.

5. Gastritis

(i) *Bilokhoni* (*Cassia tora*) roots — 5 numbers, 1 *Leta guti* (*Caesalpinia crista*) are grinded with little amount of water and kept dipped in water for some time. The colour becomes as tea. The filtered juice is taken early morning in empty stomach for three days.

(ii) Leaf buds of *Modhuri* (*Psidium guajava*) — 7 numbers; bark and roots of *Kothona phool goss* (*Caffea bengalensis*); *Jomlakhuti* (*Dracaena angustifolia*) roots—about 3 inches and 7 numbers of *jaluk* are properly crushed and boiled in water. The filtered water is taken for relief.

6. Indigestion

Leaf buds of *Medelwa goss* (*Cassia occidentalis*)—9 numbers are roasted and taken. Also, small tablets are prepared by crushing the leaf buds and taken.

7. Jaundice

(i) Tender shoots of *Tubuki lota* (*Stephania hernandifolia)*—9 numbers; *Kopalphoota tree* (*physalis peruviana*) and *Damdewka goss* (*Impatiens roylei*) are properly grinded and mixed with 100 gm of jaggery. The mixture is administered raw in empty stomach.

(ii) In severe infection, a patient is also given a filtered juice prepared from the roots of *Tora plant* (*Alpinia nigra*), *Patidoi plant* (*Clinogyne dichotoma*) and *Jomlakhuti plant* (*Dracaena angustifolia*) mixed with milk.

8. Pet Phula (in Small Children)

Roots of *Bilokhoni* (*Cassia tora*) and *Hati bhekuri* (*Solanun torvum*) treated with appropriate magico-religious *mantras* are packed with a small piece of black cloth as an amulet and tied with a black string around the neck.

9. Piles

(i) *Bonjalook goss* (*Oldenlandia corymbosa*)—3 numbers and 9 numbers of *Kolajamuk* (*Syzygium jambolanum*) are grounded and kept in water. The filtered juice is taken in empty stomach till it provide's relief.

(ii) In severe infection, leaf buds of *Tangloti* (*Aleurite cordata*)—1 number, *Modhuri* (*Psidium guajava*)—3 numbers, *Maduri lota* (*Croton caudatus*)—3 numbers and leaf axil of *Bhim kol* (*Musa sapientum*)—3 numbers are grounded with 3 numbers of black pepper. The mixture is boiled in water and the juice is taken in empty stomach till relief.

10. Pneumonia

Leaf buds of *Paspotia goss* (*Dioscorea pentaphylla*)—5 numbers,

Som goss (*Machilus bombycina*)—3 numbers and *Titakuchi* (*Solanum spirale*)—5 numbers are grinded properly with 9 numbers of *Laung* (*Syzygium aromaticum*). The paste is eaten early morning in empty stomach.

11. Sinus

A paste is prepared by grinding leaves of *Durun bon* (*Leucas linifolia*) —7 numbers along with 21 numbers of *Amloi porua* (*Oecophyla smaragdina*) and very little amount of cow dung. Three small tablets are made from the paste and are held one after the other over the nose to inhale the strong smell. 3 to 4 drops of the juice extract from the paste is also taken in the nose.

12. Stomach Pain

Tender leaves of *Bilokhoni goss* (*Cassia tora*)—7 in numbers, roots of *Bhim kol* (*Musa sapientum*)—2 to 3 pieces and *Leta guti* (*Caesalpinia crista*) are grinded to make a paste and given to eat during pain.

13. Tonsillitis

(i) Roots of *Nora bogari* (*Prunus persica*), *Dighloti* (*Litsea salicifolia*) and *Hukloti* (*Pogostemon benghalense*); and tendrils of *Akashi lota* (*Cuscuta reflexa*)—about 3 cm in size; 9 numbers are properly grinded with 21 numbers of pepper. The mixture is put in a bamboo tube and boiled in water. Patients are given the filtered solution to gargle.

(ii) In case of severe infection, the above medicine is followed by another one. Here, 2 numbers of *Jaiphal* (*Myristica fragrans*), 7 numbers of *Leta guti* (*Caesalpinia crista*), and 15 numbers of *Hilikha* (*Terminalia chebula*) and *Laung*; and 21 numbers of *Latummoni* (*Abrus precatorius*) are grinded properly. The thick paste is stored in bottle and eaten two times, i.e. one in the morning in empty stomach and the other after meal before bed.

14. Urinary Trouble

Roots of *Bhat kerela* (*Momordica dioica*) and *Kolajira* (*Nigella sativa*) are grinded and mixed with one egg yolk and the remedy is taken in empty stomach till relief.

The villagers also use different types of herbs and shrubs as a curative and also as a preventive measure.

15. Headache (Pain on Head)

If somebody is suffering from acute headache, the medicine man takes some cotton in his hand and chant's *mantras* with *Bilokhoni* (*Cassia tora*). Then this chanted cotton is tied on the right arm in case of male and left arm in case of female.

16. Fever

In case of fever, occasionally the decoction of leaves, roots and barks of *Paroli* tree (*Stereospermum chelonoides* D.C. and *Steroespermum tetragonum* D.C.) is used to reduce fever. Flowers of *Paroli* tree is also mixed with honey in case of hiccough.

17. For Healing Wound or Any Internal Damage

If somebody is suffering from ulcer/cancer, they use the roots and leaves of *Sengmara Alu* [*Lasia spinosa (L) Thw*] in a variety of ways. The villagers, in their day-to-day life, use leaves of *Sengmora* either by preparing curry or using it in *dal.* But when they are aware about ulcer/cancer, they use the roots. They cut small pieces of the root and dry it in sun. They put one or two dry pieces in the curry or *dal* and it is believed that it acts as a strong remedy for ulcer.

The Sonowal Kacharis also believe in chanting hymns (*mantras*) in curing various diseases.

Ram Mantra or Mar Mantra

It is a set of hymns (*mantras*) effective for a number of diseases like headaches, stomach pain, gas formation, fever and body pain. The patient is treated by chanting the *mantras* with 7 numbers of *Bilokhoni* (*Cassia tora*) leaves. The medicine men states that the *Bilokhoni* leaves must be of female gender. They can identify it by looking at the tender leaves as female plants have soft leaves and male plants have hard and coarse leaves. Moreover, the space between two male leaf formations is greater in comparison to the female leaves (This can be termed as a typical example of indigenous knowledge of ethno-botany).

Deo Loga

As they are living in forested area, now and then evil spirit affect's any person. In such cases, the medicine man only needs *Panikait* (a thorny creeper found in water) and garlic. It is grinded and then the paste is applied on the Navel (*nai*) of the affected person.

Pani Bhut

It is believed that the cause of certain diseases is due to the spirits living in water. The villagers could identify it by observing certain symptoms, e.g. if the affected person touches water; he feels pain and sensation in hand. Then the family members come to know about it. To get relief from the spirit, the members go to the bank of river or pond to appease the spirit by offering a *sarai* with betel-nut and rice powder (*pithaguri*). By chanting the names of affected person the relatives pray to the spirit for the welfare of the person.

The wrath of the evil spirits is evident from the incidence like bad dreaming, unusual behaviour, various types of diseases, etc. When the persons are affected by evil spirits, they reflect such unusual behaviour. In most cases, the medicine man first offers a *sarai* before the patient. Then taking some mustard seed and white garlic, he chant's some *mantras* and asked the evil spirit to leave the body of the affected person.

Mukh Loga

It is common to the child and beautiful girls. There is a belief that some persons possess evil powers and if he/she looks at someone or passes comments with evil motives then the other party is affected. Here the medicine man chant's *mantras* on water. The patient is to drink half of the water and rest is applied on the body from head to toe.

Dulia Gaon (Revenue Village)

Survey was made in the village Duliagaon in the year 2010-11 to have an idea about their healthcare practices. The information was collected particularly to understand the nature of diseases that affected the villagers, the concept of disease and therapeutic practices – both traditional and modern. 53 individuals were personally interviewed to find out the nature of ailment that affected the individual during the last 5 years. All total 30 different ailments were reported from the villagers. It is found that the nature of treatment is not uniform. As the common villagers also have the knowledge of know how of the treatment, they immediately prescribe the medicine with the available herbs in the vicinity. The analysis reveals that during the last 5 years, maximum number of 7 persons suffered from jaundice.

1. Anaemia

(i) In most cases, they started to take *Kajus* and *Atlas* (*Anona reticulate Linn*).
(ii) Tomatoes are also considered effective.

It is believed that normal, rich diet would improve their condition.

2. Boil and Itches

(i) Leaves of *Kerela* (*Momordica charatia Linn*), leaves of *Neem* (*Azadirachta officinarum*) are pasted and mixture is applied on the effected area.
(ii) *Chitronola* oil or few drops of *Chitronola* (*Cymbopogon winterianus Jowitt*) is put in water and applied on affected area or advised to take bath with it.
(iii) Root of *Tita bhekuri* (*Solanum indicum Linn*) is pasted and applied.
(iv) *Neem* (*Azadirachta officinarum*) and leaves of *Tulsi* (*Ocimum sanctum*) are prepared as a mixture.

3. Cough/Pneumonia

(i) Honey is used extensively.
(ii) A mixture is prepared with ginger (*Zingiber perpureum*), *Kala haldhi* (*Curcuma caesia Roxb*) and *Tulsi* leaves (*Ocimum sanctum*) and is considered effective.
(iii) In case of dry cough leaf of *Kerela* (*Solanum indicum Linn*),

Tulsi (*Ocimum sanctum*) and root of *Patidoi* (*Clinogyne dichotoma*) are mixed and the patient is advised to gargle for a few days.

4. Constipation/Indigestion

(i) *Moran Ada* (*Zingiber perpureum*), *Duron ban* (*Lecas aspera*), *Bel (Aegle marmelos*) are prescribed.
(ii) *Duronban* (*Lecas aspera*) and lemon juice are also used.
(iii) Lemon juice (*Citrus aurantifolia*) and a kind of turmeric, *Kala haldhi*, (*Curcuma-caesia Roxb*) in the form of paste are taken.
(iv) Papaya (*Carica papaya*) and *Triphala* arc also prescribed.

5. Diarrhoea

A significant number of people were suffering from diarrhoea.

(i) Bark of *Hilikha (Terminalia chebula*) and the bark of mango (*Mangifera indica*) are mixed to make a juice.
(ii) In certain cases, tender leaves of Mango (*Mangifera indica*) is also prescribed.
(iii) Papaya (*Carica papaya*), *Manimuni (Centila asiatica*) and *Khutura* (*Amaranthus viridis Linn)* are also considered effective.
(iv) Tender leaves of *Madhuri* (*Psidium guajava*) mixed with water is taken by some. Ripe *Madhuri* (*Psidium guajava*) is also considered effective.
(v) *Manimuni* (*Centila asiatica*), *Khutura (Amaranthus viridis Linn*) and lemon (*Citrus aurantifolia)* mixed with salted water is taken by some patients.
(vi) Curry prepared with leaves of *Narasingha* (*Murrya koenigil*) and bud of banana (*Musa paradistaca*) is also prescribed in certain cases

6. Dhatu Rog

(i) Bark of *Amora* (*Sponlias mangifera*) mixed with jaggery is fully boiled. It is believed that normal, rich diet would improve their condition.

7. Dog Bite

(i) *Nahorlota* (*Mesuaferrea Linn*), *Boga phutuka* (*Melastoma malabarthricum Linn*) mixed with *Garia alu* (*Dioscorea spinosa Roxb*). These roots are mixed with water and are to drink in the morning in empty stomach.

(ii) *Malbhog* banana (*Musa sapientum Linn*) and *Haldhi* flower mixture is also prescribed.

Patient is not allowed to eat *Jatilao* (Longurd), *Jika* (Ribgourd) *Urahi* (*Vicia sativa Linn*) and Duck's meat while taking this medicine.

8. Gastritis

The number of persons who were suffering from gastritis is also significant.

(i) Papaya (*Carica papaya*), *Manimuni* (*Centila asiatica*) and *Vedailata* (*Paederia foetida Linn)* are prescribed edible for the patient. In certain cases, these are grounded together to prepare a mixture.

(ii) In certain cases papaya (*Carica papaya*), gum (*Colatroptis*) and Black *Haldhi* (*Curcuma caesia Roxb*) are prescribed.

(iii) Sometimes, patient is treated with *Papaya* (*Carica* papaya), *Manimuni* (*Centila* asiatica) and *Khutura* (*Amaranthus viridis Linn*).

(iv) Juice of *Vedailata* (*Paederia foetida Linn*) and water is used by some patient.

(v) In certain cases it was reported that cool water mixed with sugar is also taken.

(vi) Some patients take water mixed with *Manimuni* (*Centila asiatica*).

9. Gall Bladder/Appendix

Water melon mixed with water is prescribed. In most cases operated later on.

10. High Blood Pressure

(i) Immediate remedy is to start taking garlic and mixture *of Nefafu* (*Clerodendrum Colebrookianum Walp*) and *Harpagandha* (*Hemidesmus indicus R.Br*).
(ii) Garlic and bitacord are considered appropiate by most of them.
(iii) Garlic and *Manimuni* (*Centila asiatica*) controls the pressure.
(iv) Leaves/barks of *Arjun* tree (*Terminalia Arjuna wight and Arn*) are kept in water and juice is considered as an effective medicine.

11. Heart Problem

(i) Bark of *Arjun* tree (*Terminalia arjuna wight and Arn*) and *Nefafu* (*Clerodendrum colebrookianum Walp*). These are kept in water and juice is prepared.

12. Headache

(i) Apply externally a paste prepared from the bud of Banana (*Musa paradisitacal*) and young shoots of bottle gourd (*Lagenaria vulgaris sering*) on the forehead in order to get rid of acute headache.
(ii) Sometimes a paste of the spongy portion of the ash gourd (*Lagenaria vulgaris sering*) is used externally for the purpose.
(iii) Onion, garlic and pepper is taken to get relief.

13. Inadequate Supply of Milk

A lactating mother who does not have sufficient milk is provided with a medicinal food. The food is prepared from *Papaya* (*Carica papaya*), *Jaifal* (*Myristica*), turmeric and salt.

14. Jaundice

Different types of herbal medicines are used for treating jaundice.

(i) In most cases, the patients are advised to drink the juice of sugarcane (*Saccharum officinarum*) and juice of *Kardoi* (*Averrhoa carambola*) for immediate relief.

(ii) Some treat with *Jetuka* leaves (*Landsonia Innermis*), bark of *Jam Lakhuti* (*Dracaena angustifolia*) which is then mixed with goat's milk.

(iii) In certain cases, leaves of *Dupartenga* (*Bryophyllum pinnatum kuntz*), leaves of *Jetuka* (*Landsonia Innermis*) are mixed with milk.

(iv) Leaves of *Dupar tenga* (*Bryophyllum pinnatum kuntz*) along with juice of sugarcane (*Saccharrum officinarum*) and *kardoi* (*Averrhoa carambola*) are also prescribed.

(v) *Mohaneem* (*Azadrachta indica*) as juice is also prescribed or as edible item.

15. Joint Pain

(i) Root of *Birina* [*Vetiveria zizanioides (L) Nash*], *Nefafu* (*Clerodendrum colebrookianum Walp*), *Tagmuri* (a kind of medicinal herb), *Vageoti* (i*mpatiens balsamin*a) mixed with garlic and boil it. Mixture preferably of half a glass is taken twice.

(ii) Fowl curry prepared with ginger, black pepper, onion, garlic and salt are prescribed.

(iii) Juice of *Okyothera* (a kind of medicinal herb) is mixed with ground mustard seeds to prepare a paste. To be smeared as the joints and is to message it.

16. Kidney Problems

(i) Immediate relief is to take the juice of tender leaves of *Dupar tenga* (*Bryophyllum pinnatum kuntz*).

(ii) Leaves of *Dupar tenga* (*Bryophyllum pinnatum kuntz*) is also mixed with cucumber juice.

17. Liver Enlargement

The number of persons suffering from liver problem is significant.

(i) In most cases *Papaya* (*Carica Papaya*) is taken immediately as these are available in most of the households.

(ii) *Manimuni* (*Centila asiatica*), *Veddailata* (*Paederia foetida Linn*) and *Mosandari* (*Houttuynia cordata Thunb*) mixture is taken by some.

(iii) *Kardoi* (*Averrhoa carambola*), thorny *Khutura* (*Amaranthus vividis Linn*) and *Garakhiya tiyoh* (a kind of cucumber) is also effective.

In some cases juice mixture is taken and sometimes these are considered as edible item.

(iv) *Kardoi* (*Averrhoa carambola*), *Kasu-thuri* (*Colocasia esculenta* (*L*) *Schotl*) and *Ul-kasu* (*Amorphophalus colebrookianum Roxb*) mixture is prescribed, 2 teaspoon to be taken once daily.

(v) A kind of thorny climber, i.e. *Kaitia lota* mixed with water is also taken by some.

18. Measles

(i) Leaves of *Mahaneem* (*Azadirachta officinarum*) are used on skin.

(ii) Leaves of *Mahaneem* (*Azadirachta officinarum*) and *Ou-tenga* (*Dillenis Indica*) are kept under the bed.

19. Menstruation Problem

Mixture from *Dubarigrass* (Family – *Gramineae*) is used in one case.

20. Nerve Problem

(i) *Brahmi sak* (*Herpestis monnieria*) and *Manimuni (Centila asiatica*) are taken to get relief.

(ii) In some cases *Brahmi sak (Herpistis monnieria*), *Vedailata* (*Paederia foetida Linn*) and *Manimuni (Centila asiatica*) are taken together.

21. Nari Utha

In rare occasions, such cases are found:

(i) Roots of *Hukloti* (*Pogostemon benghalense*), root of round lemon [*Citrus lemon* (L) *Burm*, f.] and root of *Bilokhoni* (*Cassia tora*) are mixed with pepper and water.

(ii) Roots of *Bilokhoni* (*Cassia tora*), *Hukloti* (*Pogostemon benghalense*), *Vageoti* (*Impatients balsamina*, and *Tongloti* (*Aleurite cordata steud*) are mixed with water. Everything is mixed with the same proportion and is taken in empty stomach.

A medicine man was asked how this ailment was identified. He replied that when the patient's navel cord is enlarged and eyes become unusual it can be identified.

22. Pain in the Ear

Juice of onion is put in the ear to heal earache.

23. Pregnancy Related Case

Mixture is made from *Tulsi* (*Ocimum sanctum*), *Bel*, (*Aegle marmelos), Duran ban* (*Lecas aspera*) and *Dubari* grass (Family – *Gramineae)* are prescribed and used.

24. Piles

(i) Common treatment is to collect *Kesumata* (mud extracted from earthworm) which is heated and mixed with water.

(ii) There is a medicine woman. She collects red lotus and dries it over fire. Then the dried substance is given to the patient to apply in the anus through which bleeding takes out.

25. Stomach Pain

Stomach pain is common in the village.

(i) Commonly *Cirota* (*Swertia Chirata)* mixed with salted lemon are taken to get immediate relief.

(ii) Bark of *Kadam* tree (*Anthocephalus cadamba Miq*), root of *Matar* tree mixed with water. Patient is to take 2 tea spoonfuls, once daily.

(iii) *Duran ban* (*Lecas aspera*) and lemon juice (*Citrus aurantifolia*) are also taken by some.

(iv) *Bar manimuni* (*Centella asiatica*) with jaggery is also prescribed.

26. Toothache

(i) Paste of *Tajmui* (a kind of medicinal plant), *Akan* (a kind of medicinal plant). Gum (*Colatroptis*) is applied on the affected area.
(ii) Paste is prepared with the bark of *Bakul* tree (*Mimusops* *'elengi Linn*).

27. Urinary Problem

(i) Leaves of *Patagoja* tree [*Kalanchoe pinnat* (*Lamk*) *Pers*], *Leta guti* (*Caesalpinia crista*) are taken by some patient.
(ii) Leaves of *Purnonoba* tree (*Boerhavvia diffusa Linn*) mixed with juice of sugarcane (*Saccharum officinarum*) and water are also taken by some.
(iii) Leaves of *Dupar-tenga* (*Bryophyllum pinnatum kuntz*) and cucumber (*Cucumis sativus Linn*) are mixed with water.

28. Viral Fever

(i) Tender leaves of *Salkowari* (*Aloe Vera*) is pasted and applied on the forehead of the patient.
(ii) Hot water and boiled food is prescribed.

29. Worms

(i) Leaves of *Mahaneem* (*Azadirachta indica A. Juss*), *Chirata leaves* (*Swertia chirata*), and *Tita kerela* (*Momordica and charantia Linn*) soaked in water and make a juice.
(ii) Leaves of *Chirata* (*Swertia chirata*) only soaked in water.

30. White Spot on Tongue

(i) The patient is to collect *Agoni pan* (*Pachyrhigus angalatas*) which is then put with other leaves and is put on the white spot.
(ii) Sometimes a mixture is prepared with it and the patient is to take it in the morning and night.

(iii) *Jetuli Poka guti* (*Rubus moluccanus Linn*) is also suitable for curing this disease.

A study was also conducted in two villages, namely Rowmari and Gazai village of Dibrugarh district, Upper Assam. 13 different ailments were recorded from the village medicine-man whose treatments is believed to be very effective. Some elderly persons of the community also have a good knowledge about indigenous herbal medicine that is acquired from their elders. The data has been published in the journal *Studies on Ethno-medicine,* Vol. 2, No. 1 2008 (Das, Barua & D. Dutta Das, 2008: 33-37).

The study reveals that Sonowal Kacharis rely heavily on Ethno medicine in case of disease and illness. The patient is treated with available herbs, flora and minerals. Some of these are home remedies and some are specially prescribed by herbalist or folk medicine man available in the community.

An effort was made to collect some data from S.S. (76 yrs. old), an experienced and renowned herbal medicine man. He learnt this expertise from his grandmother.

1. Jaundice

While treating jaundice, he needs the leaves of *Jam-Lakhuti* (*Dracaena angusti folia*), black pepper, clove, cinnamon, black cumin (*kal-zeera*) a little amount of salt and mustard oil. At first he boils the leaves of this plant along with black pepper, clove, cinnamon, black cumin with salt and then gives it to the suffering one. He prescribes his patient to drink two tablespoon of juice twice/thrice a day in an empty stomach depending on the intensity of the disease.

He also chants hymns (*mantras)* on the mustard oil and give it to the patient to apply on the body. The oil is believed to absorb the germs of the disease which become yellow in colour. The patient is not allowed to eat meat, fish, egg, mustard oil and other spicy food for some months.

2. Piles

In case of piles, he needs *Hag-fish* (*Kuchia*) and also collects the bark of the plant (The name of the plant could not be made available, because medicine-man himself does not know the name but he can identify it), and then boil it in water with a little amount of salt. It is then given to the patient to drink in empty stomach. He prescribes three doses on alternative days. He charges Rs. 50.00 per dose.

3. Unusual Behaviour of Child

He also treats the children who are behaving unnaturally, like crying continuously. For this, he needs the root of the *Bosh plant* (*Acorus calamus Linn*). Then with the help of this root, he prepares amulet, (*Tabij*) and after chanting hymns, he gives it to the suffering child to wear for about one/two month depending on the intensity of the disease.

4. Rheumatic Pain

For this he needs mainly, the *Paspotia goss* (*Dioscorea pentaphylla*) along with some other plants (name of the plant could not be traced). With the help of this plant, he prepares a paste and gives it to eat or apply on the body for about 10 days to two months depending on the intensity of the disease.

In another case, it was found that to treat the paralytic ailment, the medicine man takes two pieces of bamboo splits in his right hand, gently beats the same on the infected part of the body and simultaneously chants hymns (*mantras*). This ailment is believed to be inflicted by some spirit and locally known as *Jara-phuka*.

Religion and Health

During the present investigation, it has been observed that the Sonowal Kacharis believe in both natural and supernatural causation of disease. Some disease is believed to be caused by the malevolent spirits whereas some other is ascribed to natural causes. It is also believed that annoyance of the deities or the benevolent spirits may also ultimately result in the occurrence of any type of ailment or disease.

The indigenous system of medicine to treat various ailments among Indian tribes depends upon their forest environment. Different Indian tribes have distinctive ethno-medicinal practice which persists even though modern Medicare is available to them. Among the Sonowal Kacharis, there are folks medicinemen, commonly referred to as *Bez* (Barua & Phukan, 1998: 354). Of course, folk medicine man is commonly known by this in rural Assam. The folk medicine man treats patients with herbal or indigenous medicines. They collect the required herbs and shrubs from the nearby forest. Certain herbs, their roots or shoots or flowers and barks and leaves are prescribed. Besides the treatment of herbal medicine, they also suggest measures for protection from the effect of some deities, ghosts and devils. When astrological calculation indicates that the cause of diseases is an evil eye, appropriate remedies are suggested. They also prescribe wearing some enchanted articles like a rupee or *tabij* (amulet), etc. Besides, the specialists, the elderly persons or women of each village have the knowledge of treating the patients with herbal medicine. In most cases, the immediate treatment is provided by the elderly persons with the available herbs and shrubs.

In every society the belief that illness is a punishment for wrong doing is widespread and it has developed on the basis of their life experiences. The Sonowal Kacharis are also superstitious and they firmly believe that most of the diseases or natural calamities are caused by the wrath or displeasure of deity and ancestral spirit.

Sorcery or Black Magic (Ban Mora)

It is believed that some ailments identical to that of a naturally caused disease (viz. fever, indigestion, vomiting, chest pain, paralysis, epilepsy, etc.) may be caused by magical powers. The people believe that there are some sorcerer or black magicians among the people who may cause illness to some one by his/her magical powers. It is locally known as *ban*, here, a magical object (viz a piece of cloth, nail, hair, etc.) is hidden in the roof of the house or in the ground under the raised floor of the household or sometimes under the bed of the person intended to be affected. The magical object causes some incurable ailment to the intended person. It is believed that in such cases, patients cannot be cured with the natural treatment or medicines. Only the counter-magical activities performed by some magico-religious practitioner may cure the ailing person, otherwise it may prove fatal.

A study was made among the Sonowal Kacharis of Lepetkata Kachari village, to discuss the socio-religious aspect in relation to health and well-being of the Sonowal Kacharis of Assam. Though there is no direct relation between religion and health, yet the role of religion in the sphere of health and disease cannot ignored. A portion of data have already been published in the journal *The Eastern Anthropologist* (Barua & Phukan, 1998: 51: 4). The relevant portion has been incorporated in the present study.

Beliefs

In every society there exist certain beliefs which are followed by the people to ensure overall well-being. Such beliefs and superstitions may develop from practical experiences and it is believed that any violation affect's the health and happiness of the people. The Sonowal Kacharis also have certain beliefs, which are closely related to their religious system and become apparent in their day-to-day life. Certain common beliefs are enumerated below:

1. They never spit on cow-dung, because it is believed that if they do so, the person would suffer from neck pain. As a remedy, they are to offer one pair of betel-nut and leaf and a few coins as an *Arihana* (offering) in the name of god of cow-shed (*gohali*).
2. They never eat rice in front of a gathering. If they do so, it may affect the stomach. In such cases, they are to approach the *Bez* (folk medicine man) and drink enchanted water.
3. During mid-day and night, they never go into jungle. It is believed that the gods of the jungle take rest during this period. If they are disturbed, its effect may be seen on human health.
4. If a sick person cannot be cured, even after providing all medical treatment then it is believed that the disease is due to evil spirits, *Deo,* etc. To appease these unknown powers or free oneself from their effect, they wear *tabij* (amulet), use *juru* oil (enchanted oil) and holy thread obtained from the folk medicine men.
5. Pregnant woman should be cautious in her movement. She is not allowed to walk by the side of a burial ground or burning *ghat* and not allowed to touch any cooked food sent by a family where death had occurred recently. It is believed that such acts may cause spontaneous abortion.
6. A pregnant woman should not move during mid-night or noon. It is believed that evil spirits are more powerful during this period and may harm her.

7. They carefully keep the navel cord of a baby delivered prematurely. If the baby is drowned in water, then the cord is dipped into a cup of water. It is believed that the child may regain life if he drinks that water.
8. They keep the navel cord of each child in a specially made cocoon. It is believed that the water extracted from the cord is useful when a child suffers from diseases like dysentery, fever, etc.
9. It is believed that birth of twins is related to eating 'joint fruits'. Therefore, they avoid eating joint or double fruits.
10. They have a belief that ancestral spirits are benevolent spirits and protect the family. If a person fails to offer that particular cock or hen, which he committed to offer in *Mritakak puja* (ancestor worship), the ancestral spirit may be displeased. As a result misfortune may befall on the family.
11. During illness or fever, if a medicine man prescribes *tabij* or enchanted oil, then the the parents of the sick person are not allowed to touch it as in such cases it may lose its magical power.
12. When big crow cries loudly, it is believed that there will be rain with thunder or some misfortune may occur. If a small crow cries on the roof of the house, then it is believed that guest may visit the house.
13. If some articles fall from the hand of the senior most lady of the house, then it is believed that unexpected guest may arrive.
14. If an owl or a dove cries on the roof of the *Borghar* (main room) then it is believed that there might be something wrong in the observances of family customs and tradition.

Restrictions

The Sonowal Kacharis also follow certain restrictions for well-being and keeping good health:

1. They never take an amulet or enchanted oil from the astrologers on Thursday.
2. They never cut bamboo on Tuesday and Saturday, as these days are considered as bad days.
3. They do not perform any ritual or ceremony in the month of

Sawan (August-September). They believe the month to be a male month.

4. They do not eat red cock at home because red cock is offered in *Deopuja* and *Mritakak puja* (ancestral worship).
5. There is also prohibition on eating red duck at home as it is offered in *Jalkhai puja.*
6. They never eat white duck as it is offered in *Ai puja.*

These are some of the common restrictions observed by the villagers. Thus, all such beliefs are linked with health and welfare of the villagers. The people believe that everything that happens has a cause. The cause may be natural or human event or an environmental condition. The cause-effect relationship, which early man observed in the environment might have helped in the development of such belief and practices. It is believed that if these restrictions are not observed, either the individual violating the rules are affected or the whole family may face the wrath of misfortune. Similar beliefs and restrictions are also found to exist among the rural Assamese community.

The aim of the present study is to give an idea about the religious aspects of health and disease. Religion as a whole, serves the spiritual and moral need of the people. The Sonowal Kacharis also perform various religious rites and rituals with that aim in view. At the same time, they firmly believe that most of the diseases are caused due to the wrath or displeasure of a deity or ancestral spirit. They may even identify specific gods responsible for their health and disease, natural calamities etc. Because, common people generally are not aware of the physiological aspects of a disease, they have the belief that ancestral spirits are benevolent spirits and are worshipped at the family level to bring health and happiness. Certain protective deities and spirits safeguard the village and are worshipped jointly at the village level. The nature of religion may differ from society to society. "Most societies attach enormous importance to their beliefs in the supernatural, which tend to pervade every phase of their culture" (Lowie, 1961:76). Different gods and goddesses are propitiated or worshipped for fulfilment of ambitions and happiness of the people.

The Sonowal Kachari starts the family level rituals from the beginning of Assamese New Year, i.e. from the month of *Bohag-Jeth* (April-May). They never perform any ritual in the month of *Sawan*

(August-September) because this month is considered as a male month. It is believed that if they perform any ritual in that month the very purpose of the ritual will be defeated. The religious authorities of *Namghar* (the congregational prayer hall) also play a role in the welfare of the villagers.

Some of the important rituals performed annually in the family may now be discussed.

Thinbhanga

On the day of Assamese New Year, three *Bhakats* (devotees) from *Namghar* visit each and every household. As soon as they arrive in a particular household, a woman member, after washing their feet, welcomes them to the *Bharghar* (main building). The *Bhakats* take their seats arranged in a circle. The host offers three *Bhujanis*, which contains rice, one pair of betel-nut and leaf and one *Arihana* containing potatoes, *dal*, oil and some rupee as a token of offering. The family members bow before the *Bhakats*, who bless them, wishing a happy life. The host offers light refreshment along with rice-beer. This signifies the role of *Namghar* in their religious life.

Mritakak Diya (Ancestral Worship)

Among the Sonowal Kachari, there are two ways of worshipping the ancestors; one is *Mritakak diya* and the other is *Pi-dia*. They observe these ceremonies regularly thrice a year, i.e. on the day of New Year, after plantation and in the *Magh bihu. Mritakak dia* is performed by offering red cock, rice-beer and other items of feast, e.g. vegetable, *dal*, etc mainly by the *Nakari* lineage. *Pi-dia* is performed occasionally, when someone suffers from serious illness, particularly from dysentery and stomach pain.

Na-purusia Sakam

This ritual is performed twice a year by each family. This is observed to worship the nine ascending generations. It is believed that if the nine generations are propitiated satisfactorily, with all the observances, the family members would not be affected by any disease. For this ritual, they invite nine *Bhakats* from nine lineages of the Sonowal Kachari. The materials required for the feast are one red duck, rice, potatoes and other available vegetables.

Besides, the above mentioned family level rituals, the Sonowal Kachari also performs various religious rites and rituals to satisfy the gods and deities believed to be responsible for particular disease. Table 3.1 describes the various religious rites and rituals which are performed when someone suffers from illness.

Table 3.1: Disease due to wrath of the supernatural agencies

Disease (Rituals)	*Supernatural agencies*	*Pujas*
Dysentry, mental diseases, cancer	Deo	Propitiated by sacrificing two red cocks, one red hen, and one egg, besides other items of feast. Arrangement is made in the forest.
Asthma, mental disease, cancer	Lord of water	Jalkhai puja worshipped by sacrificing one white duck and other items of feast, rice, salt, vegetables, etc.
Accident, sudden illness	Burha dangaria	No sacrifice. Only raw items, e.g. rice, powdered rice, etc. are offered to propitiate Burha dangaria.
Gastritis	Ancestral spirit	Ai Puja, no sacrifice except offering raw articles, powdered rice, gram with betel nut and leaves.
Epidemic	Mother goddess	Community level worship by arranging Bhur utuwa puja. One pair of betel nut and leaf is offered from each family. One red duck is offered on behalf of the villagers. All the offered articles are placed in a boat.
Epidemic and large scale deaths of men and animals.	Mother goddesses of forest	A white duck is a must for the puja, besides other offerings.

Source: Barua and Phukan, 1998:51:4.

Deo Puja

They perform *Deo puja* to propitiate the spirit of *Deo,* who is believed to be responsible for diseases like dysentery, mental disease, cancer, malaria, etc. The materials required for the *puja* are two red cocks, one red hen, one egg, vegetables and other items for feast. The invited *bhakats* carry the materials to the forest. The cock and the hen are sacrificed in the *Deo sal* (sacrificing alter). The cook prepares the items for feast. The food is offered on three leaves, in the name of *Deo*. S.S. performed this *puja*, when her daughter suffered from mental illness.

Habi dangaria puja and jalkhai puja are performed to propitiate the lord of forest and water. The Sonowal Kacharis believe that these gods are responsible for mental disease, pain, cancer and asthma. Normally three *Bhakats* are invited and a white duck is a must for this *Puja*. These items and other articles for feast are taken to the forest. The duck is sacrificed on the altar. D.S. performed the *Puja* when his wife suffered from mental disease.

Ai puja is performed to propitiate the goddess *Ai*, particularly when someone suffers from measles, chicken pox, small pox, malaria, etc. It is performed during day time, inviting nine *Gopinis* (women *bhakats*). Only raw articles like powdered rice, gram, betel nut and leaves, etc. are offered.

Soni puja is performed to propitiate the god *sone*. They believe that this deity is responsible for neurosis and anaemia.

The Sonowal Kacharis also believe that protective deities or spirits safeguard the village. Such deities are worshipped occasionally in the family but mostly at the community level. One such deity is *Burha Dangaria*. It is believed that if *Burha Dangaria* is offeneded even unintentionally, then the person may suffer from sudden illness and accident. During epidemic also, they propitiate *Bura Dangaria* at the community level. *Burha Dangaria* is a benign spirit, almost a demigod to the villagers. He is the presiding spirit of a village. It is believed that he resides either on the *Bakul* tree near the *Namghar* (the congregational prayer hall of the village) or in the big betel-nut tree. *Burha Dangaria* is regarded as the revered sentinel, who wards off the evil spirits of *Haija* (cholera), *Aai* (pox) and other deadly diseases from the boundary of the village. This *Puja* is performed in the forest at noon. No sacrifice is made and the items offered are gram, rice, rice-cake, powdered rice, etc. Villagers hold *Burha Dangaria* in great reverence.

During epidemics like cholera and small pox, the villagers perform *Bhur utuwa puja* at the community level. On the appointed day, all the villagers assemble in the *Namghar* and make necessary arrangement for the *Puja*. The young boys make one boat of banana stem. Each family offers a pair of betel nut and leaf. On behalf of the villagers, one red duck is offered. After lighting incense sticks and earthen lamps, the villagers bow before the boat with a prayer to get relief from the epidemic. The boat is then carried to the river side in a ceremonial way, singing *Ai nam*. It is carried by two young boys, who are dressed in a special way, to be prescribed by the *Namghar* authorities. The boat is finally pushed into the river along with the offered articles.

Moreover, in case of large scale death of men and animals, they perform a *Puja to* propitiate the mother goddesses of forest. Besides the articles of feast, a white goat is a must for this *Puja*. The goat is sacrificed by the *Deodhai* on a specially prepared *Balishal* (sacrificing alter) in the name of mother goddess of the forest. The *Bhakats* bow before it, with a prayer to protect the village from epidemic.

It is a universal human tendency to perform rituals for the overall welfare of the villagers. The Sonowal Kacharis also perform one such ceremony on the last day of *Bohag Bihu* (Mid-April). In the evening, all the villagers assemble near the main entrance road of the village. Before it they ensure that not a single outsider is present within the village. Then they close the main entrance road, making a bamboo barricade. In the middle of the barricade, they erect a post where they fix one sieve (*chaloni*). A cock is sacrificed by a priest and placed near the post as an offering to the spirit. It is performed to ward off the effect of evil spirit. The common belief is that if this is done, no harm will come to the villagers and their animals.

1.B. The Deoris

The present study also incorporated the data collected from the Deoris. Data were collected from two different settings, i.e. (i) Forest village Madhupur and (ii) Kaloluwa Deori village, one of the oldest revenue villages.

Ethno-Medicine

Traditional medicine according to Reddy, (1986:18) "is that whole, which includes holistic knowledge and practices; oral or written and functions in diagnosis, prevention and curative aspects of illness and disease to promote well-being of the community." In almost all communities there are folk or herbal medicine man/ woman that have knowledge of indigenous medicine and prescribe it in time of need.

Micro Field: Modhupur (Forest Village)

In the Modhupur Deori village, there is no professional folk medicine man (*Bez*). The study reveals that for most of the diseases, the people prefer to visit Barbaruah Health Centre or Assam Medical College, Dibrugarh. As such the common people do not have much idea/interest in folk/herbal medicine. However, a few elderly male/female have some knowledge about indigenous medicine and use it whenever necessary.

Some of the common diseases recorded in the village are mentioned below. On the basis of door to door investigation a total of 12 diseases could be recorded which may be treated at home.

1. Blood Dysentery

Tender leaves or small plant of guava (*Psidium guajava*) except the root portion are grounded and mixed with a pinch of salt. The mixture is prepared and the patient is prescribed to take it 2/3 times a day. During this period, the patient is not allowed to take fish, meat or any spicy food.

2. Constipation

(i) Seeds of *Bakul* plant (*Mimusops elengi Linn*) are fried in ghee. When cooled, it is pushed through the anus of the children to treat constipation.

(ii) Ripe fruit or boiled tender fruit of Papaya (*Carica Papaya*) is prescribed to cure constipation.

3. Cough and Whooping Cough

Leaves of *Siju goss* (*Euphorbia nertiifolia Linn*) are crushed together. The mixture is prepared and filtered juice extracted from it is ready to use. It is prescribed to cure cough and whooping cough.

4. Dysentery

(i) If a child suffers from dysentery, juice is prepared from the tender leaves of guava (*Psidium guajava*). Normally a teaspoonful is given at a time. But in serious cases, it is given frequently.

(ii) In case of adult person, curry of *Bhedailata* (*Paederia foetida Linn*) is prescribed to the patient.

The patient is debarred from eating spicy food, meat, chilly, egg, etc. when suffering from dysentery.

5. Gastric Ulcer

(i) Curry is prepared from the tender leaves of *Sookloti* [*Perilla frutescens* (L)]. It is normally taken with the main meal.

(ii) Raw turmeric (*Curcuma domestica Loir*) is crushed completely. The mixture is filtered and the patient is prescribed to take the filtered juice in early morning and evening.

6. Menstrual Problem (When it is not Stopped)

(i) One piece of *Bogadubori* [*Cyndon dactylon* (L)], a few drops of honey and one cup of left over water (which was used for washing rice) are required. These are grinded together. Then it is filtered and the filtered juice is prescribed in empty stomach.

(ii) In case of excessive bleeding during the period, the entire plant, except the root portion of *Helachi* (*Enhydra fluctuans*) is soaked overnight in water. The following day, the juice is extracted from the plant. The patient is prescribed to take it during the day.

(iii) In case of adult women, *Duronban* (*Leucas linifolia spreng*) is collected. A paste is prepared mixing it with salt and water. The patient is prescribed to take it frequently.

(iv) *Misiri* (palm candy) is dissolved in water frequently. *Misiri* may be taken without dissolving in water as well.

7. Pneumonia

(i) Following plant parts are needed to treat the patients; Bark of *Gossmaroli* (*Croton joufra Roxb*), 5 to 7 pieces of leaves of *Goborsuta* (*Cordia myxa Linn*) and bark of leaves of *Titajora* (bitter medicinal herb). These are mixed together adding salt and pepper (*Piper nigram*) for taste. These are grinded and boiled in water and then filtered. After it, only water portion is prescribed for drinking.

(ii) Sometimes the mixture is grinded and the powder is stored in bamboo tube and the mouth is sealed with paddy straw. It may be prepared mixing with water. The patient may take it whenever necessity.

8. Pyoroea

Bark of *Bakul* plant (*Mimusops elengi Linn*) is boiled in water. The lukewarm water is taken in mouth for a few minutes to cure pyoroea.

9. Ringworm

Leaves of papaya (*Carica papaya*) are locally applied on the effected area to cure ringworm.

10. Scabies

Leaves of *Dupartenga* (*Bryophyllum pinnatum kuntz*) are grinded and applied in the affected area.

11. Skin Disease

Leaves of *Siju* tree (*Euphorbia neriifolia Linn*) are grinded and prepare a paste. The paste is applied on the affected part of ringworm or other skin disease.

12. Stomach Pain before Menstruation

One piece of root of *Jamlakhuti* (*Dracaena angustifolia Roxb*), *Bormanimuni* [*Centella asiatica* (L)] and a few pieces of *Dubariban* [*Cynodandactylon* (L)] are required. These are grinded together and mixed with water. The patient is prescribed to take it in empty stomach in the morning.

Kalaluwa (Revenue Village)

Data on indigenous herbal medicine have also been collected from Kalaluwa Deori village. The village is more than 100 years old and has a rich tradition of ethno-medicine. There are two medicine men in the village that have sufficient knowledge about the herbal medicine. Normally, they are referred as *bez.* The information was directly collected from the medicine-men. To give a clear picture some elderly persons who have knowledge of know how of the indigenous treatment have also been interviewed.

1. Asthma (Ha-pani)

To treat it, *Duamali* (*Jasminum sambac Ait*), three pieces leaves of *Duranban* (*Leucas aspera Spreng*) and pepper (*Piper nigrum*) are required. These are grinded and mixed with water. The filtered juice is prescribed to patient.

For children - 1 drop is prescribed.
For adult - 2 teaspoonful (anytime)

2. Bleeding

(i) Medicinal plant *Premlota/Japanilota* (*Mikania micrantha kunth)* is grinded or paste is prepared by rubbing hands. It is then applied on the affected area to get immediate relief.

(ii) Bark or stem of *Kukura thengia* (*Leea Sambusina Willd*) is cut into pieces. A paste is prepared by grinding it. These are then applied on the affected area. It would stop bleeding immediately.

3. Cough (Kah)

(i) Bark of *Bhimkal* (*Musa sapientum Linn*) is dried and burnt. Its ashes are dissolved in water and filtered with cotton cloth. Then the solution is stored in a bottle and the patient is prescribed to take it whenever necessary.

(ii) Three pieces of root of *Kotora* (*Bauhinia veriegata L*) and nine number of pepper (*Piper nigrum*), 50 gm of Ginger (*Zingiber perpureum*) are required. These items are mixed together and boil in water. The prepared boiled water is prescribed as medicine.

4. Cancer

(i) Small piece of *Ulkachu* (*Arum campanulatum*), roots of *Teezmoi* (*Zanthoxylum hamiltonia nụm wall*), *Letaguti* (*caesalpinia crista linn*) and leaves of *Gahorigela* (wild creeper) are required. A few numbers of peppers (*Piper nigrum*) are added to it. These are mixed together and boiled in water. The juice is filtered and is taken once in a day after meal far three days.

(ii) Leaves of *Hengool* (*Carthamus tinctorius Linn*), *Kordoi tenga* (*Averrhoa carambola Linn*) and leaves of *Gorokhia bhendi* (small Lady's finger) are required. These are crushed to make a paste and applied in the affected area extensively.

(iii) Moss (found under the bottom of boats) is collected in large quantity. These are then dried and small tablet is prepared from it. One tablet may be taken thrice in a day.

5. Diabetes (Blood Sugar)

(i) Tender buds of *Bholuka Bah* (*Bambusa balcooa Roxb*) and *Kuzithekera* (*Garcinia kydia Roxb*) are mixed in water. The mixture is prescribed to take before and after meal.

(ii) Tuber at the root of *Simolu* (*Bombax malabaricum D.C.*) is mixed with sugar candy. The patient is prescribed to take one glass as medicine.

(iii) A creeper known as *Amoi lota* [*Tinospora cordifolia* (*Wild*) *Miers*] is cut into pieces. Then these are dried in sunlight. It is prescribed to mix 3 to 4 pieces in a glass of water and the patient is advised to drink it.

6. Dysentery (Grohani)

(i) Round limes (*Citrus aurantifolia*) are rubbed with salt and kept in a bottle or jar for ¾ days. Then the lime is taken out and dried in the sunlight. One-third of the lime may be taken at any time of the day for 3 days.

(ii) 3 to 4 tender leaves of Guava (*Psidium guajava*) are pasted. The patient is prescribed to eat it for 2 to 3 times a day.

7. Dog Bite

Leaves of *Dhatura* (*Datura stramonium Linn*) are mixed with molasses. The person is advised to take it for immediate relief.

8. Dhatu

Young tender shoots of *Bholuka Bah* (*Bambusa balcooa roxb*) and *Kuzithekera* (*Garcinia kydia Roxb)* are mixed together. The mixture is soaked in water for the night. It the next morning the mixture is filtered and the patient is prescribed to take the prepared water.

9. Gastric

Young buds of *Motakuli* (*Flemingia strobilifera R.Br*), young bud of *Tita bahak* (*Adhatoda vasica Nees*) and pepper (*Piper nigrum)* are grinded together. Small tablets are made out of the mixture. The patient is prescribed to take one tablet before each meal.

10. Joint Pain

(i) *Jamlakhuti* (*Dracaena angustifolia Roxb*), and *Sengmora* plant [*Lasia Spinosa* (*L*)] are required in equal proportion. These are then mixed and boiled in water with *Goroi fish* (*Channa punctatus*). The patient is prescribed to take the mixture morning and evening for three days.

(ii) *Sengmora* plant [*Lasia spinosa* (L)] and *Jamlakhuti* (*Dracaena angustifolia Roxb*) are taken in equal quantity. Then it is mixed with *Goroi fish* (*Channa punctatus*). These are then grinded and boiled. Medium round ball/tablet is made out of the mixture. The patient is advised to take it twice daily, i.e. morning and evening.

11. Menstruation Bleeding

(i) Three pieces of tender bud of *Nalgajali* (a kind of acid climbing plant), 3 pieces of *Pani Kalmou* (*Ipomoea acquatica Forsk*) and 3 pieces of *Okara gajali* (bud of climbing plant) are required. These are grinded and mixed in 200 cc of water. The patient is prescribed to drink it for 3 days.

(ii) If a girl menstruates more than once in a month, then leaves of *Tita bahak* (*Adhatoda vasica Nees*) are boiled in water. The water is filtered after cooling and the patient is advised to drink it.

12. Phita Pelu (Worm)

(i) Seeds of *Norabogori* [*Prumus persica* (*L*) *Stokes*] are required. These are grinded and the patient is advised to take it for 4 days.

(ii) Dry coconut measuring 250 gm is grinded and then sugar is added to it. The mixture is then fried in a vessel. The mixture after cooling is administered raw in empty stomach. The patient is advised to drink at least 3 glasses of boiled water after taking it. Each day fresh mixture is prepared, and, it is prescribed to take it for 3 days.

13. Piles

(i) The leaves of *Bakbon* (*Eupatorium cannabinum Linn*) are grinded and small tablet is prepared out of it. The tablet may be attached to the affected area.

(ii) Seeds of *konibih* plant (*Croton tiglium Linn*) are mixed with one portion of earthworm (cut into 3 pieces). A piece of garlic is added to it. These are grinded and small tablet is prepared out of it. It is prescribed to take 3 tablets in a day in empty stomach.

14. Stomach Problem

(i) Leaves of *Narahingha* (*Leucan aspera Spreng*) are grinded. The raw juice is administered at a frequent interval.

(ii) Occasionally curry is also prepared with leaves of *Narahingha* (*Leucan aspera Spre*ng). The patient is advised to take it with rice.

15. Sinus

Leaves of *Duranban* (*Leucas linifolia Spreng*) are grinded to make a paste. It is held over the nose and the strong smell is inhaled.

16. Tuberculosis

Young buds of *Tita bhekuri* (*Solanum indicum Linn*) are mixed with water. Leaves of the bud should be odd in number, i.e. 3 to 5 numbers of pepper (*Piper nigram*) is then mixed with *Titabhekuri* (*Solanum indicum Linn*) and boiled in water. The patient is prescribed to take it.

17. Worms

Leaves of *Tita bahak* (*Adhatoda vasica Nees*) are wrapped in banana leaves. Then the packet is heated over the fire. The patient is prescribed to take it to get relief.

The Deoris use different types of herbs/shrubs as vegetables. The people may not be aware about its medicinal values, but it help in maintaining good health.

Religion and Health

The present study reveals that the Deoris also believe in supernatural forces for disease causation and seek remedies through magico-religious practices. They firmly believe that most of the diseases are caused due to the wrath or displeasure of a deity or ancestral spirits. Therefore, every effort is made to appease these supernatural agencies, which are believed to be responsible for particular disease.

Influence of Evil Spirit (Bhut loga)

The Deoris are of the opinion that evil spirits in many different forms may harm the people. Now and then the evil spirit may affect any person. When they suspect that someone is affected by evil spirits, then they immediately approach the folk medicine man to know about the remedy. There is no medicine man in each and every village, but in a locality covering a large area, there is invariably a person who through magico-religious practices cures the patient. At first, the medicine man through devination, try to identify the spirit responsible for it. Then he prepares a medicine and appropriate remedies are suggested. For preparing the medicine, he needs mustard seeds and a plant known as *Bosh* (*Acorus Calamus Linn*). These two things are grinded together by chanting *mantras.* The patient is advised to take the medicine to get relief from the clutches of evil spirit responsible for the disease.

The Deoris also perform various religious rites and rituals annually both in the family and community level. They have a belief that ancestral spirits are benevolent spirits and are worshipped in the family level to bring health and happiness. They invariably perform a family level ritual known as *Ghar Deo* in the month of *Bohag* (April-May) and *Kati* (October-November). This ritual is performed for the welfare of the household as well as family members. It is also reported that whenever there is a crisis or any unforeseen incident occurs in the family, they perform this ritual. Some of the rituals performed by the Deoris have already been published (Barua & Bharali, 2001:87-94). Only the relevant portions have been incorporated here.

Ghar Deo

The Deoris observe this ritual on Wednesday as it is considered as an auspicious day by them. They invite 3 to 5 *Bhakats* and a *Deodhai* to perform this ritual. Every clan has their own *Deodhai,* whose duty is to perform family level ritual as a priest. *Ghar Deo* is performed to please the deity who is responsible for the welfare of a family. The articles needed for the ritual are: one white hen or duck, *kecha pithaguri* (raw rice powder), banana, betel-nut and leaf, etc. The *Deodhai* chanting the *mantras,* sacrifice the duck with the help of bamboo string and pray for the welfare of the family. No community cook is invited for preparing the meal and any member of the family may do this job. While the preparations are going on, a portion of cooked meal and other items are arranged in a *sarai* (a raised bell-metal dish) in the name of dead ancestor. It is a custom among the Deoris that offering to the ancestor is always done by the *Deodhai* and it is performed in the front side of the household.

While offering to the ancestor, the *Deodhai* chants some *mantras* mentioning the name of dead ancestors. Completing the offering outside, the *Deodhai* returns to the *Subachani room,* where the main ritual is going on. The family members seek the blessings from the *Deodhai* and *Bhakats* for their welfare and offer cooked meal ritually to the *Deodhai* and *Bhakats.* They firmly belief that if they do not get the blessing from their ancestors, they cannot achieve anything and there are possibility of facing unforeseen crisis. Thus, besides regularly performing the ritual; they perform the ritual of *Ghardeo* (*the presiding deity of the household*) in any crisis situation.

Mora-Khuwa

The Deoris observe ancestor worship, i.e. *Mora-Khuwa* regularly in the month of *Bohag* (April-May) and *Kati* (October-November). It is a family level ritual and is performed in the evening. They invite 2 or 4 *Bhakats* and *Deodhai* of a particular clan has to perform this ritual. In exceptional cases, the head of the family can perform this ritual and it is admissible in the society. To perform this ritual, either a pig or a hen is considered essential, and *suje* or rice-beer is a must. The animals are ritually sacrificed by the *Deodhai.* They do not invite professional cook to prepare the meal and any members of the family is permissible to cook the meal. At first, the *Deodhai* offers a portion of cooked food in the name of ancestor and offering is done in front side of the house. While offering, the *Deodhai* chants *mantras* incantation mentioning the name of all the ancestors. After completing the ritual part, the *Deodhai* returns back to the room. The family members offer rice-beer and seek the blessings from *Deodhai* and *Bhakats*. Thereafter meal is served first to the *Deodhai* and *Bhakats*. The family members take their meal after the completion of all activities relating to ritual. Besides performing this ritual regularly in the family level, they also observe it anytime of the year, when someone suffers from prolonged illness or astrological calculation reveals the wrath of ancestor.

During investigation in Kalaluwa Deori village, it was reported that while someone is suffering from Asthma, they observe a magico-religious treatment. It is done by the medicine man and is performed either in Saturday or Tuesday. At first the medicine man cut the neck or throat portion of a duck. A silk cocoon is collected and a small portion is inserted in the cocoon, chanting *mantras* by mentioning the name of the patient. The cocoon is tightly tied by a thread. Then, it is put on the neck of the patient. In case of girl, during the menstruation period, it should be removed for the time being.

In case of Jaundice also, they follow magico-religious treatment. Prior to the day of observance, the medicine man preserves water in a pot in the afternoon. Next morning, the water is purified by chanting *mantras.* Then the patient is asked to take a *Duboriban* [*Cynodon dactylon* (L)] in the hand. The medicine man after taking a little bit of water in his hand sprinkles water in the left hand of the patient starting from arm to finger. During the act, the medicine man chants *mantras* all the time. Sprinkling of water is done for 3 times. The patient is to visit medicine man for 3 to 5 days according to the intensity of the disease. The patient may take only *magu dal* boiled with rice at least for 15 days or till the patient is fully cured.

Besides these rituals, in the community level, the Deoris also observe *Bohag Bihu* or *Bohagiya Bisu* on the *Sangkranti* of *Chat* (i.e. 14th April) while the *Magh Bihu* or *Magiyo Bisu* on the *Sangkranti of Puh* (i.e. 14th January). It may be mentioned that Deoris *Bihus* do not always fall on the *Sangkranti* day; rather these *Bihus* may be deferred to a day or two as they perform the same from Wednesday. The Deoris consider Wednesday as most auspicious and sacred. Like the Deoris, there are many tribal communities who also consider Wednesday as an auspicious day. *Bihu puja*, on the occasion of *Bihus* has much socio-religious significance. The *Deodhani* dance forms the most important and essential part of *Bihu puja.* Through the *Deodhani* dance, the community members try to find out about any misfortune or maladies, etc. that the community may face. It is commonly believed that the term *Deodhani* has been derived from Sanskrit word "*Deva*" meaning god or deity and "*Dhani*" meaning sound, i.e. echo. This popular term literally means the echo or uttering of a deity (Goswami, 1960:46). Among the Deoris, on the second day of the *Bihu,* the *Deodhani* dance starts. In the morning, the priest lights an earthen lamp in each *mandir* at the *Than*. Then the sacrificing of animals begins. In the meantime an individual, who is considered pure from various aspects, is possessed by the spirit. It is mentioned that "on that day, no one is allowed to enter the *Than,* wearing red, black, orange or blue coloured cloth or sporting an umbrella" (Deori, 1964:189). As the *Deodhani* wears such coloured cloth during possession, such restriction is prevalent among the community. The person who is possessed by the deity almost looses his normal sense and starts dancing vigorously. During "possession", he is considered as direct intermediary between this world and supernatural. The *Deo*, is believed to be capable of predicting future, and can even say about the causes of illness, maladies, etc. The devotees came to the *Than* and offer *sarai* and animals to the *Deo*. The *Deo* listens to a devotee and indicates remedial measured to be followed. The priest offers fresh blood of animals to *Deo*, who drinks it while dancing. During *Deodhani* dance "the devotees sing devotional song, welcoming the spirit, but no musical instrument is used" (Deori, 1964:188). Normally, dance starts from evening and reaches its peak at night. The last part of the dance is very emotional and tragic. Being tired and restless, he almost loses his sense and falls in front of the deity. It is an indication that he has been released from the control of deity. Thus, ends the *Deodhani* dance and the person is freed from possession and loses his special divine power. Normally, *Deodhani* dance is performed during *Magh* and *Bohag Bihu*. In case, if any unforeseen incidents occur or during epidemic, flood, the Deoris may invite this power.

Thus, it is revealed that magico-religious practices form one of the significant aspects of Deori's socio-religious life. Beside indigenous/herbal medicine, they depend on spiritual power and perform various rituals to know about the disease or any unforeseen incident. *Deodhani* dance or *Deo utha* forms a part of cultural life of many tribes and communities and it commands respect and fear from all, on account of their power of revelation during the spirit possession that sustains the life and happiness of a household or a village or the community at large. The Dimasa Kacharis and Tiwas perform *Kesaikhati Gosani Puja*, where *Deodhani* dance is a must. Many similarities exist between them and the Deoris. Among the Mishings, only the priest is possessed by the spirit and at the end of the *puja*, only he can predict the future. Among the Kacharis, the person who is possessed, i.e. the *Deodhani*, himself performs all the activities of the priest during *puja*. But the significant point is that "among the Deoris, *Deodhani* never performs any religious activities of the priest" (Deori, 1964:195). It is very difficult to make any scientific analysis behind spirit possession. But it may be considered as one of the earliest beliefs found in human society.

Discussion (Ethno Medicine)

After analyzing the traditional health-care system among the Sonowal Kacharis and the Deoris, an effort has been made to summarise the findings. While summarizing the materials, care has been made to compare the data with the available information from other communities.

Diseases and ailments are common problems in every community and every culture evolves its own method of treatment for health problems faced by its members. In every society there exists a body of beliefs and concept with regard to the nature of disease and its treatment. Indigenous medical treatments are still practiced in many communities in one form or other. The concept of health, disease and treatment is as varied as culture. Health does not mean merely the absence of disease, but complete adjustment of individuals to external environment, both physical and social. Thus, it is a positive state of well-being of the individual having harmonious development of physical and mental capacities. The Health Survey and Development Committee (1947:7) rightly pointed out that: "...the term health implies more than absence of sickness in the individual and indicates a state of harmonious functioning of the body and mind in relation to physical and social environment, so as to enable him to enjoy life to the fullest possible extent and reach his maximum level of productive capacity."

Each group has their own conception of health, disease and well being. But there is no universal definition of health which may be applied to all the communities. However, there is a general opinion that those persons who can continue their day-to-day activities without any stress may be considered as healthy person. Very few persons are aware about the multifaceted aspect of health as defined by WHO "a state of complete physical, mental and social well-being and not merely the absence of disease and infirmity"and the aim of achieving the goal of "Health for all by 2000". The World Health Organization has estimated that 80 per cent of the people in the world rely on traditional medicine for primary healthcare needs. And of the 119 plant based drugs used today by modern medicine; about 74 per cent are from plants traditionally used by herbal cures (Farnsworth, 1990). On the basis of it The World Health Organization in its 29th and 30th Assembly (1976 and 1977) gave formal recognition to traditional medicines and recommended the association of traditional healers with the national health care programme.

The survival of human society depends upon health and well-being of its members. Since ancient time, it has been the endeavour of the society to seek ways and means of eradicating illness and sufferings. The history of disease in human society is as old as man himself. Since the beginning of evolution, human kind has always been able to find some medicine in the nature that surrounds them. Early therapeutic treatments were derived from the surrounding environment of human beings, who were forest dwellers. They made use of plants, animals and other substances naturally available to them for treatment. Since human beings are living in cultural environment, every known society has developed a pharmacopoeia and therapy, be it magico-religious, secular or scientific.

Medical professionals tend to consider illness and disease as a bio-medical phenomenon and thus they treat illness with only bio-medical approach, while social scientists perceive illness and disease as an outcome of macro-interactions of the bio-social and environmental factor.

The present study was confined among two Scheduled Tribes communities of Assam, i.e. the Sonowal Kacharis and the Deoris. It has already been mentioned that data were collected from two different settings, i.e. the forest villages and the revenue villages.

With regard to their concept of disease aetiology (causation) it was reported that ethno medicinal practices has two universal categories of disease etiology: (i) Natural—that naturally stem from natural forces or conditions, e.g. cold, heat and possibly by an imbalance on the basic body elements. The other may be termed as (ii) Unnatural, which may again be divided—(a) supernatural forces, i.e. occult causes which are the result of evil spirits, evil eyes, sorcery or black magic and (b) spiritual, i.e. results of penalties incurred for sins or fault, breaking taboos or caused by God. However, some diseases/ailments are believed to be caused due to both the reasons. Generally, the ailments believed to be caused by supernatural and spiritual agencies are preferred to be treated with the traditional (i.e. magico-religious) system and those believed to be caused naturally are treated either by the herbal (i.e. traditional folk medicine) or the modern ones.

A probing analysis of the data reveal's that both the communities; the Sonowal Kacharis and the Deoris have elaborate knowledge of indigenous treatment—both herbal and magico-religious.

The analysis of data among the Sonowal Kacharis in two forest villages has revealed that there was no professional traditional medicine man in the villages. There are only two elderly persons who could report some of the common diseases and how these may be treated at home. In these villages 19 different ailments were recorded. As there is no professional folk medicine man in the villages, they normally go to the nearby villages for treatment.

A survey was conducted in the revenue village Duliagaon in the year 2010-11 to have an idea about their health care practices. In the study, 53 villagers were personally interviewed to find out the nature of ailment that affects the individuals during the last 5 years. All total 30 different ailments were reported from the individuals. It was found that the nature of treatment is not uniform. As many of the elderly male/female have the knowledge or know- how of the treatment, they immediately prescribe the medicine with the available herbs in the vicinity.

It was also reported that the same disease may be treated with maximum of 5-6 different ways, using single herb or combination of many herbs. As all the prescribed herbs may not be available on the spot, the elderly person immediately treats the individual with the available herbs at that point of time.

Data were also collected from other Sonowal Kachari villages situated within a radius of 30 km around Dibrugarh. A renowned herbal medicine man (S.S. 76 years old) was interviewed. He learnt the expertise from his grandmother, and particularly treats 4 different ailments.

The study reveals that Sonowal Kacharis rely heavily on Ethno-medicine in case of disease and illness. The patient is treated with available herbs, shrubs, creepers, flora and minerals. Some of these are home remedies and some are specially prescribed by herbalist or folk medicine man available in the community.

During the present investigation, it was observed that the Sonowal Kacharis believe in supernatural causation of disease. Some disease is believed to be caused by the malevolent spirits and firmly believe that most of the diseases are caused due to the wrath or displeasure of a deity or ancestral spirit. They may even identify specific gods responsible for health, disease, natural calamities, etc. Because, common people generally are not aware of the physiological aspects of a disease, they have the belief that ancestral spirits are benevolent spirits and are worshipped at the family level to bring health and happiness. Certain protective deities and spirits safeguard the village and are worshipped jointly at the village level.

A study on health-care system among the Deoris also reveals the same trend as those of the Sonowal Kacharis. The Deoris have a rich tradition of indigenous healthcare system which is very much followed by them. Data have been collected from two settings and slight differences are noticed in two settings. In the forest village Madhupur, there is no professinal folk medicine man. It was also reported that in most cases, people prefer to visit either the Borbaruah Health centre or Assam Medical College, Dibrugarh. As such the common people do not have much idea/interest in herbal medicine. There are a few individuals in the village, who had obtained Medical degree and are practicing in the state. However, there are only a few elderly male/female that have knowledge about indigenous herbal treatment. All together 12 different diseases could be recorded which may be treated by indigenous ways. But it does not indicate that the common people do not have any idea about herbal medicine. They too can say many things about their indigenous ways of treatment and may mention a number of plant species used for preparing herbal medicine.

Data were also collected from Kalaluwa Deori village, which is more than 100 years old. There are two professional medicine men in the village itself, having sufficient knowledge about herbal medicine. They could mention 17 different types of ailments which may be treated by indigenous ways. However, door-to-door survey in 30 households has revealed that in general only some of the ailments are treated at home, e.g. stomach pain, dysentery, jaundice, gastric, diabetes, fever, cough, etc. As majority of village women have knowledge about the treatment, they immediately prescribe/prepare the medicine which are available in the surrounding areas. In case of serious illness, they go to Assam Medical College or Barbaruah Health Centre. Mobile medical check-up camp regularly held in the village level, normally thrice a year or during epidemic.

Table 3.2 refers some of common medicinal herbs and shrubs used by both the Sonowal Kacharis and the Deoris to treat many of their ailments. They also use many of the above mentioned herbs and shrubs in their day to day menu. The common people are not aware about the medicinal value, but use it in preparing many dishes. Though both the communities are living in the same environmental condition, yet some of the herbs are more frequently referred by one community than the other. This may possibly be due to the inherent traditional knowledge of a particular community who are conversant about its use from time immemorial. The study clearly indicates that both the Sonowal Kacharis and the Deoris have elaborate knowledge of herbs and shrubs. Of course, some of the herbs are more frequently referred by the Deoris, while some are confined within the Sonowal Kacharis.

The present study also reveals that the Deoris believe in supernatural forces for disease cousation and seek remedies through magico-religious practices. They perform elaborate rituals to please those spirits and deities. There are malevolent spirits such as ghosts, demons, etc. who may harm the people. There are also several deities to give them protection from the mischievous acts of those malevolents spirits. These deities reside in the jungles, trees, rivers, streams, etc. So, to get their blessings, to get security, they always propitiate all those deities who reside in the natural environment or objects. It is believed that if they are displeased, they withdraw their support and leave the people in a state of insecurity.

Table 3.2: Plants and their parts used in day-to-day menu and their Health Benefits

Sr. No.	*Parts*	*Parts used*	*Health Benefit*
1.	Bamboo shoot	Cut into small pieces/ grind	Rich in nutrients
2.	Brahmi sak (*Herpestis monnieria*)	Young leaves/shoots. Cooked/steamed	Helpful in nerve problems
3.	Dhekia (*Diplazium esculantum*)	Tender fronds are cooked/steamed	Rich in iron
4.	Duamali (*Jasminum Sambac Ait*)	Young leaves/buds fried/steamed	Asthma/prevention from respiratory problems
5.	Duranban (*Leucas linifolia spreng*)	Young buds cooked by frying/steamed	Controls blood pressure/cough/sinus
6.	Jilmil sak (*Chenopodium am brosiodesL*)	Young leaves are fried/ steamed	Rich in calorie/ nutrients
7.	Kasu sak (*Colocasia esculenta*)	Tender leaves & tubers are prepared as curry/ roasted wrapping in banana leaves)	Rich in iron, preventive capability from disease
8.	Khutara (*Amarenthus viridis* L)	Young leaves are fried with meat dishes	Rich in calorie/protein
9.	Kolmou sak (*Ipomoea acquatica Forsk*)	Tender leaves and young shoots fried & cookes as vegetables)	Rich in minerals and iron
10.	Kotora (*Bauhinia veregata* L)	Tubers steamed/boiled	Control cough and cold
11.	Kuzi thekera (Garcinia kydia Roxb)	Fruits, seeds/tender portion used for preparing sour curry	Help in stomach disorders
12.	Manimuni (*Centella asiatica*)	Tender leaves are added to dal/vegetable curry	Rich in calorie, helpful in stomach disorder
13.	Marisa (*Amaranthus gangeticus Linn*)	Leaves/young shoots, fried/steamed	Rich in calorie/protein

(*Contd.*)

(*Contd.*)

Sr. No.	Parts	Parts used	Health Benefit
14.	Matikaduri (*Alternanthera Sessilis* (L) R.Br)	Tender leaves and shoots are taken as curry	Rich in calorie, protein, beneficial for stomach disorder
15.	Maha neem (*Azadrachta indica*)	Tender leaves fried	Digestive power/ prevention and curative in worms etc.
16.	Motakuli (*Femingia Strobilifera* R.B.)	Young buds are cooked/ steamed	Gastric/stomach disorder
17.	Musandari (*Houttuynia Cordata*)	Tender leaves cooked as curry/steamed	Stomach disorder
18.	Naltenga (*Tetrastigma thomsonianum planch*)	Young leaves/shoots are added to curries/steamed	Rich in minerals and vitamins
19.	Nepatu (*Clerodendrum colebrookianum*)	Tender leaves. Boiling/ steaming/roasting)	Control blood pressure
20.	Noroshingha (*Leucas aspera spreng*)	Tender leaves added to dal, vegetables & Fish curry	Rich in calorie, helpful in stomach disorder
21.	Ou-tenga (*Dillenis Indica*)	Sheaths of the fruits are used to prepare specially fish curry	Rich in iron, protein/ calorie
22.	Sengmora (*Lasia spinasa* L)	Flower spadix, young leaves/tubes are cooked as vegetables, added to dal	Helpful in healing internal wounds/ bleeding. Beneficial for various diseases
23.	Simalu (*Silk cotton eri, Bombax Malabaricum* D.C.)	Tubers on the roots. Boil/ steam	Helpful in controlling blood sugar
24.	Tita Bhekuri (*Solanum Indicum Linn*)	Young fruits are boiled/ steamed	Controls blood sugar, rich in calorie
25.	Vadailata (*Paederia foetida Linn*)	Young leaves/shoots used for making curry	Helpful in stomach disorder

The traditional healthcare reflected through several practices indicates that primary healthcare is inbuilt in the socio-cultural system of the rural people. There are folk medicine men/healers who have vast knowledge of indigenous treatment. The traditional healers include herbalists, magico-religious therapists, prediction about future. Religious beliefs and practices are deep rooted in the villager's life. They think that a particular deity is responsible for natural phenomenon that happens in everyday life. So, they try to please the supernatural being by praying and offering.

The traditional healers include's herbal and magico-religious therapists, prediction about future, etc. The traditional healer has a specific name in each culture. He has the authority and respect of his community for his commitment to maintain the well-being of everybody. Among the Sonowal Kacharis, they are called as *Bez* (Barua & Phukan, 1998:51:4). Of course, they are referred as *Bez* in rural Assam, including the Deoris. The traditional practitioners detect and diagnose diseases based on general observations of the patients as well as their personal experience of treating human ailments for a long period of time. In all tribes/communities services of the group of specialists may be specified; whether priest and /or magicians or medicine man are sought after, depending on the cause of the illness. Among the Hos (Roy, 1922) there is the '*Deonwa*' or the spirit doctor. It was observed that the traditional healer in most cases is specialized in one or more diseases. The person may be expert in only herbal treatment or sometimes he may treat with astrological calculation or providing chanted oil. There is another kind of healer commonly referred as devinator (*Mongoloti)*. The *Mongoloti* by doing divination, by calculating numbers or counting rice grain can find out the reason of that particular ailment and suggest curative measures, such as offering, propitiating (in the form of ritual) to the responsible deity or benevolent spirit.

There is another category of healers, who perform their healing function through a form of rituals. Both the Sonowal Kacharis and the Deoris perform elaborate magico religious and spiritual practices as curative as well as preventive measures. The ritual healers suggest measure for protection from the effect of some deities, ghosts and devils. When astrological calculation indicates the causes of diseases, appropriate remedies are also suggested. This type of treatment is commonly known as magico-religious therapy.

In almost all societies, there are ritual specialists and spiritual healers, who treat with devination and therapeutic cult rituals. The ritual specialist enters into a trance before being possessed by the spirit. Possession is a powerful belief system prevalent in many parts of the world. The possession usually occurs during certain specific event. Both the Sonowal Kacharis and the Deoris have faith in the possession. Among the Deoris, it happens during the *Bihu puja* (Barua & Bharali, 2001) and among the Kacharis, during *Kesaikhati Gosani puja* or *Ai puja* (Barua & D. Das, 2004:38) either the priest or any common man from from the gatherings may be possessed by the spirit. During possession, the *Deo* is believed to be capable of predicting about future. He can even say about the causes of illness, maladies and possible remedies also.

Over and above, there are women, whose skills in the use of home remedies are widespread across the world. In the present study, it was also revealed that most of the elderly women have the knowledge of treating common diseases with herbs and plants. They are the first person to prescribe the medicine and the patient gets the initial treatment in the family level itself. Thus, it can be said that the largest uses of medicinal plants in India is the household/family. Women are the key stakeholders in the household users. Folk medicine men form the next group of largest users.

If we look back at the history and development of human civilization, we find that from the days of his origin, man has constantly been trying to adjust himself in accordance with his surroundings. Moreover, many species of plants and animal life are interdependent for their sustenance, growth and development. Such mutually beneficial interdependence is called a symbiotic relationship. Thus, environment plays an important role in the formation and development of society and culture. To maintain his living, man has directly utilized the natural environment for food, clothing, shelter, medicine and relaxation. He has used society as a tool to pass on the knowledge, thought and behaviour about himself to the next generation, in order to live in society happily and usefully. Ecology is intimately related with traditional knowledge. Sound ecological principles have been followed by people from its inception. There are many tribes and communities all over India who particularly conserve the sacred grooves and depend very much on it for procuring the herbs, shrubs or the other plants for preparing their elixirs. North East India is not an exception and many socio-religious beliefs and practices emerged in the process of preserving the sacred grooves.

Rain forest all over the world have rich storehouse of medicinal plants. The Brazilian rainforest is also famous for its natural resources. An African in Zaire, having learnt from his father, crushed the heads of a few soldier termites (white ant) on a patient whose skin was being eaten away by a protozoic infection that had resisted all antibiotics. The skin improved spectacularly, apparently under the influence of the mandibular gland secretions of the termite soldiers. Various secretions from ants and termites not only act as pheromones but check bacterial and fungal attack (Lindon, 1991, cited from Brahmachary, 1995). The indigenous knowledge is inextricably linked with bio-diversity of the region, especially in the case of their medical system. The knowledge of ethnomedicine (traditional medical system) is deep rooted in the ecology and culture. The flora and fauna has a significant place in the lives of the tribal people. The adaptive mechanism with the existing environmental condition of the respective area and the knowledge of utilizing the natural resources is the key factor for the survival of human society. Many of the health hazards and certain diseases are due to particular environmental condition. The ecologists put forward an attractive hypothesis which viewed from the health aspect is a dynamic equilibrium between man and his environment and disease as a maladjustment of human organism to environment. Impact of environment on health and disease cannot be ignored. May (1960) mention's that before Second World War in China, some of the villagers were seriously affected by heavy infestation of hookworm. Investigation showed that hookworm patients were rice growers, and others were engaged in silkworm farming. The rice cultivators worked in mud mixed with night soil, while the silkworm farmers spent their working days on ladders tending mulberry leaves (*see* Honigman, 1973:1035). Here disease boundaries and cultural distinctions virtually coincided.

Elwyn (1954) has noted that myths build around trees and animals are considered sacred because of their economic utility, e.g. most tribal believe that the banyan tree is the abode of gods and ensures good health. The peepal tree is the abode of goddesses, the mango tree protect village community and ensure health and prosperity. Plants being the earliest form of life, it is believed that all other living organisms, including man are dependent on them directly or indirectly (referred Barua, 2009:42).

Many of the plants and orchid have medicinal values, and early men were aware about it. From the Vedic age, orchid was described for its beauty and medicinal value. All over the world various parts of orchid, e.g. leave, root and rysome are used for its different medicinal properties. In India, juice extracted from the roots of orchid known as *Cyprepedium elegans* are used for senselessness, hysteria, mental disease and rheumatism. The powder extracted from the seeds of *Dendrobium nobile* (another variety of orchid) is used for immediate relief from cut or burn. The Monpas use the leaves of *Cleisostome Williamson* orchid for the treatment of bone fracture. In Meghalaya, juice extracted from the leaves of *Dendrobium moschatum* orchid are used for relief from pain on ear. The indigenous population of Australia uses the seed of *Cymbidium madidum* orchid for oral contraceptive (Devi, 1991:17). Thus the medicinal properties of different parts of orchids are recognized and utilized for treatment of various diseases in different parts of North East India.

Though many of the orchids and plants are fast disappearing due to ecological imbalance, yet the tribal people have in many cases shouldered the responsibility of germ plasm conservation through their age long rich cultural practices. "The sacred blue orchid (*Vanda coerulea*) although very rare has not become extinct since they are sustained by the Wanchoo tribes in Tirap district of Arunachal Pradesh for use in worship and festival" (Mukherjee & Mukherjee, 1995:71).

Medicinal plants used by the herbalists or the common people are widely grown in natural environmental conditions. Thus, different tribes and communities of Assam use the same varieties for preventive and curative measures. However, the therapeutic use of the plants varies from tribe to tribe. Though the Sonowal Kacharis and the Deoris, i.e. the studied population, are living in same ecological condition, yet variation of using the plants are noticeable. Normally a single plant or combinations of various plant parts are used for a particular ailment. But due to non-availability of all the plants they use the plants which are available in their immediate surroundings. *Aloevera Linn*, *Bombax Malabaricum DC* and *Carica papaya Linn* are used by the Sonowal Kacharis as remedy for burns, fever, diabetes and constipation are also used by the Lotha Nagas for treating burns, cuts and wounds, abdominal pain and eczema, respectively (Jair *et al.*, 2010).

It has been reported (Barua and Sonowal, 2011) that *Terminalia chebula Retz,* as one of the items used for curing tonsillitis by the Sonowal Kacharis. Apatani tribe of Arunachal Pradesh uses this for treatment of cough (Kala, 2005). In the same way leaves of *Stephania hernandifolia* Walp, in combination with certain other items, is used by the Sonowal Kacharis as a remedy for Jaundice and the same is also used by the Lepcha tribe of Dzongu valley in Sikkim to prevent bird flu (Pradhan and Badola, 2003).

It may be noted that the preparation and processing techniques for preparing the medicine differ from community to community.

Such minor variation of using the plant by the tribals in different environmental condition is universal. The tribal's unmediated dependence on natural resources is closely related to their peerless ecological knowledge and their cultural ties to their local environments and thus predisposing those to guard, conserve the plant and animal lives of their traditional habitats and resource bases. For them nature seems to be a set of agencies, simultaneously natural and human like...; that their world...is a cosmic system of sharing which embraces both human to human and human to nature sharing" (Bird, Devid, 1992). The streams, rivers, meadows, valley and the hillside of the tribal traditional territory are considered as the "living pages of our unwritten history", treasure house of vast indigenous knowledge and belief system. The tribal in their traditional environments utilize natural resources to meet all their needs and have been living in this fashion over generations in the process of evolving cultural traditions of the prudent resource use. There should not be any doubt that the ethno medicines, an inherent component of traditional wisdom of rural communities or people's knowledge have been acquired over generation of environmental adaptation. David Alle, an economist who has studied African indigenous knowledge system explains, "It is an unwritten body of knowledge. There is no systematic record to describe what it is, what it does, how it does it."

In almost all the studied villages, there is health sub-centre where facilities of treatment for minor diseases are available. Although, the village sub-centre is not well-equipped, there is the hospital in nearby Borbaruah area, where better facility of treatment is available. For major or critical cases, Assam Medical College is within their reach, only 28 km away from the village.

The people, as a whole, are not totally ignorant about the effect of modern medical treatment, but the traditional medical beliefs still provide a ready frame of reference. So, whenever someone suffers from illness, first they take folk precaution or start treatment prescribed by folk medicine man or perform the traditional ritual of the family. Such beliefs and practices are handed down from generation to generation. At the same time, in serious cases they take the patient to the hospital. It is not that they do not prefer to take help from modern medical treatment, but the point is that indigenous treatments are less costly and readily available to the rural poor. Moreover, they still have a firm belief that deities and spirits are responsible for particular disease. If properly worshipped; they may get the desired result. So they continue to perform the traditional rites and rituals to overcome the effect of such deities. It is also a fact that the prevalence of indigenous medical beliefs has not prevented the utilization of modern medicine where its effectiveness has been shown. This fact has been particularly emphasized by Erasmus (1961) as part of his theory of culture change. Erasmus has stressed that traditions are not blinders that keep individuals from seeing advantages in changing their behaviour. In his words: "*...even uneducated and illiterate people are not simple tradition bound puppets of their culture. Given adequate opportunity to measure the advantages of a new alternative, they act to maximize their expectations.*"

But various intensive studies reflect that despite the increasing reduction in morbidity and mortality, traditional medical system still persists and exert a significant influence on the state of health. The present study also reflects their beliefs and dependency on traditional rites and rituals, whenever someone suffers from illness. There are many beliefs and restrictions associated with health and welfare of the people which are strictly followed by them. As people are emotionally attached to it; a fear psychosis develops that violation of the traditional beliefs and practices may adversely affect them.

Today 80 per cent of the world's population rely predominately on plants and plant extracts for healthcare. According to data released by WHO, ethno medicine has maintained its popularity in all regions of the developing world. In China, traditional herbal preparations amount to 30-50 per cent of the total medicinal consumption. In Ghana, Mali, Nigeria and Zambia, the first line of treatment for 60 per cent of children with malaria is the use of herbal medicine. In San Francisco, London and South Africa 70 per cent of people living with HIV/AID use traditional medicine. Today, the annual global market for herbal medicine stands at over US $560 million (Internet source).

Taylor (1976) has estimated that the organized health services in India provide only about 10 per cent of medical care and the remaining portion is split between home remedies and indigenous practitioners.

4

Indigenous Food Habits and Geographical Settings

In human history, food, shelter and clothing are considered as the basic needs of human life. But on the basis of necessity and from the perspective of survival, their importance varies. It is argued that an individual can live a life time without shelter and cloth, but denial of food means certain death. Wherever man lives he has to adapt himself to his surroundings in order to get two fundamental necessities, i.e. food and shelter. A group of people can only prosper, increase and grow powerful, when their environment supplies them adequate amount of food and other necessary things of life. The nature and the content of food supply are in fact one of the closest tie between men and his environment. The length of residence in one place depends upon whether the springs of its food supply are perennial or intermittent, while the abundance of their flow determines how large a population a given piece of land can support.

Food is man's first biological necessity. Directly or indirectly he gets all from plants or through the animals. Food being the elementary want of man, there is no other fundamental alternative for the growth of human population than the required quantity of food supply. "In every human society food is important from two points of view, i.e. nutritional; satisfying the energy requirements and biological needs of human being; and the sociological, as a means of expressing and maintaining social relationship" (Firth, 1941:45). The overall volume of food production in various parts of the world is determined by the abundance or scarcity of arable land in relation to population, fertility of the soil, climatic conditions and the level of agricultural development and techniques. The interrelationship between men and his food, the animals and plant which produce food and the physical environment which ultimately decides what kind of quality food is available, is really intricate and fascinating. Human beings and all others obtain the body energy and nutrients from food. If food supply is scarce and lacking, the human engine runs down and in the end, it stops working altogether. In this context, it may also be noted that food habit of a group of people sometimes shows situational changes. Thus, in a community there are special types of food meant for ritual use, illness, pregnancy and some other occasions. Moreover, the preparation of food items, preferences and prohibitions, serving and religious offerings are mostly determined by the cultural factors. Thus, food as an item is regulated by complex social factors and only after analyzing the entire network of relations, it is possible to understand the food habit of a particular cultural group.

Human beings from their early stage have acquired indigenous knowledge and techniques for getting food. They also have well developed technology for food, nutrition and preservation. Australian tribes, "have an extensive natural lore. They know the habits, markings, breeding grounds and seasonal fluctuations of all the edible animals, fish and birds of their hunting grounds" (Firth, 1941:44). They are also aware of many indigenous treatments. Because of their harsh natural habitats, they frequently suffer from cut and other injuries, "They know how to make fire, how to apply heat to relieve pain and stop bleeding" (Firth, 1941:44). Moreover, they know how to keep the flesh food from decomposition or "to delay the putrefaction of flesh food." More important is their observation, without any written documents, simply by observing about the movement of sun, moon and tide they could predict about its effect on the earth.

In seasonal scarcities and droughts, they have developed various measures by changing their food habit and moving from one area to another and from one water-hole to another. "In addition they make an intelligent and economical use of the by-products of animals killed for food. The flesh of a kangaroo is eaten; the leg bones are used as fabrication for stone tools and as pins; the sinews become spear bindings; the claws are set into necklaces with wax and fibre, the fat is combined with red ochre as a cosmetic, and the blood is mixed with charcoal as paint" (Firth 1941:45).

The total environment provides man with the raw stuff of experience and we should keep in mind that habitat is an integral and constant element in this environment. He cannot survive unless he meets the challenges of his habitat. M. and S. L. Fortes record from the Talleensi of Gold Coast reveal that, "the Bemba, food supplies are at their lowest in the rainy season at the time of greatest agricultural labour. But these people produce a great deal, and have excellent receptacles for storing food, and know how to utilize them. They could live sparingly during the dry season when there is less work to be done, and keep their major crop for the wet season, to sustain them in their harder labour" (Firth, 1941:46). There are no social and religious values behind such action and it is a fact that their habits develop due to economic and nutritional necessity.

The technique of coping with the difficult habitat used by a people having but the crudest equipment is also illustrated by the pygmy Bushman of South Africa. The need of this people for water is paramount as they are living in one of the most inhospitable desert, i.e. the Kalahari Desert. "They fill ostrich egg shells during the short season when the water holes are not dry, or use their intimate knowledge of the country to find the roots, bulbs and melon like fruits that contain moisture or store up liquids" (Herskovits, 1955:96). Not even the most stagnant pool daunts them, for in such cases, they place grass filters at the bottom of the hollow reeds they use in suckling up water.

An indigenous method of obtaining subsidiary water is used by the central Australians. "This consists in digging out from dry river beds and swamps a species of large frog, which have previously filled itself with water in the rainy season, and draining these unfortunate creatures of their fluid reserve" (Firth, 1941:48). Many agricultural tribes who live largely on grain or root crops have a high proportion of carbohydrate in their diet, but seem to lack adequate amounts of other essential constituents. But knowingly or unknowingly the diet of the people is usually supplemented by a number of subsidiary foods. "The diet of the Bemba, who lives largely on millets, is strikingly deficient in fat and low in animal protein. And though the supply of Vitamin C is short, green vegetables are never eaten raw. "Thus the Bemba, who have little meat, eat caterpillars, locust and flying ants, the first being quite an important item of their diet, and containing a high proportion of phosphorus and iron" (Firth, 1941:49). It has been also revealed that as with many African tribes, the native beer is probably a source of Vitamin C; it also contains a considerable amount of Vitamin B. The relishes eaten by many agricultural people again, provide fat and mineral salts, which help to balance their consumption.

The simple food gathering and hunting economies require considerable technical competence. They must not only have knowledge and ideas of terrain, but of the most favourable times and the best conditions under which to obtain these foods, because most of the tribes do not have a well developed means of preservation. This may best be illustrated by the wild rice gatherers of the upper Great Lakes during March, April and May. These Indians live principally on the maple sugar they made and then they ate early berries, and later green corn. In the autumn and later, the wild rice that was stored for early winter use is consumed. During the spring and summer they supplement their diet with the wild fowl to be found in rice fields. In the late winter they subsist on the meat of the animals they hunted and pemmican, a compound of dried meat and berries (Herskovits, 1955:125).

In time of hunger people often enlarge the range of their food stuffs to take in many substances ordinarily disregarded. "One of the most striking practices is the eating of earth, which occurs in Australia, South-east Papua, Central America, the Congo and parts of East Africa" (Firth, 1941:49). This eating of earth is not simply a means of filling the belly. The Australians of the Daly River dig it out from underneath the slopes of the river bank. They also eat the dry earth of the termite ant-hills, a practice followed also in parts of West Africa. Edible earth contains a high proportion of mineral salts and the people obtain essential constituents for bodily health. In the same way, apparently similar food stuff by two different environments may contain different nutrients. In this context Firth (1941:50) recorded "Kikuyu of Kenya, who live largely on white millet and maize, was deficient in calcium. But the finger millet of the Bemba contains about sixteen times as much calcium as the white millet of the Kikuyu, and bone deformations among the Bemba are much less probable."

It has also been reported by many scholars from North-East India that pregnant women occasionally prefer to eat earth/ashes, etc. It was reported by Firth (1941) that the tribe such as the Bemba, earth eating is practiced mainly by pregnant women and young children.

Sometime, traditional labours and restrictions that exist in a particular tribe directly or indirectly help in the preservation and protection of certain types of animal or birds, though they could easily do so; the Tikopia do not eat many kinds of birds, or eels, for religious reasons, though their Polynesian cousins; the Maori, eat both freely and prize the flesh and fat that they yield" (Firth, 1941:51). Moreover, the different types of attitudes that exist towards diverse animals affect the amount of animal fat and protein consumed. The women of Tallensi of West Africa never cook or eat domestic fowls and dogs, which are common. Hyenas, though killed by young men are spurned by them as filthy things which dig up and devour corpses. It is also a fact that meat is a great delicacy among the Tallensi and a medium sized guinea-fowl may last a family of seven about a week. But the reservations of women of cooking domestic fowls affect their nutritional aspects. In the same way, various beliefs and practices affect the food habits of a particular group. It has been reported by the scholars that woman of Raysi of Gujrat milk the cattle only once a day. It is believed that selling of milk is selling of a son. Due to this there is no scope of developing dairy farming as an occupation. Instead they keep herds of cows and buffaloes of good breed and earn their livelihood by the sale of these cattle (Vidyarthi & Rai, 1976:135). More or less similar beliefs exist in many districts of Ceylon. They do not milk their cows, but keep them for breeding cart bulls, the manure they produce for the fields, and the price they fetch from the butcher. Such type of analysis may help in describing the relation of diets to local customs. The analysis of food problems/habits have shown that they have considerable knowledge of their natural environment, that they have developed ingenious techniques for solving their problems, and that they have a material apparatus, however, simple through which this knowledge and techniques is applied.

The simple people all over the world had to develop their own ways and means for cultivation. "The Indians of USA who planted their maize in hills put a fish in each hill as fertilizer. These Indians also practiced multiple planting. In each hill, squash and bean seeds were placed, so that the bean plants might climb the corn stalks and the squash vines run along the ground. The same principle is operating in West Africa, where gourds take the place of Squash (Herskovits, 1955:125). Multiple crops planting is no doubt is followed by most of the tribes and communities to increase the production. In recent years more emphasis is given by the development agencies in this sphere. Notable techniques in growing crops are irrigation and terracing, "An outstanding example of irrigation is found in the American Southwest, where it has been practiced since early pre-Spanish times" (Herskovits, 1955:126). In this way there are lots of examples all over the world where different communities follow diverse indigenous ways for their survival and security.

The collected data have been arranged community-wise as below.

1. The Sonowal Kacharis

The Sonowal Kacharis have various indigenous beliefs and practices with regard to all aspects of food.

Agriculture is the main occupation of the Sonowal Kacharis. They cultivate mainly two varieties of paddy, i.e. *Ahu* and *Sali*. However, in rare cases, they go for *Bao* rice. At least one granary is seen in every house. They are also good horticulturists. They cultivate banana, pine-apple, guava, lemon, etc. and sell these articles in the weekly market.

The Sonowal Kacharis have their own method and techniques for cultivation. "In carrying out agricultural works, the Kacharis show both application and skill, so much so, that failing some very overwhelming convulsion of Nature, it would seem to be hardly possible that a famine could take place in the Kachari Duaras" (Endle, 1911:12). Moreover, the people are especially skilful in the construction of irrigation canals and earthwork embankments for diverting water from river-beds into their rice-fields. Their efforts in this direction are very largely aided by their closely clannish organization. Each able bodied man clear's the jungles and help's in making canals. In this way it will be obvious that the Kacharis have a highly efficient and very inexpensive "Public Works Department" of their own. Earlier the joint efforts of kin and community members were seen during harvesting and plantation, which is referred as *Hwari* (community help and co-operation). But now-a-days, the money economy has replaced such social system.

Though they could no longer continue many of their traditional techniques, yet indigenous ways of pesticide and insecticide are prevalent among the Kacharis till today.

As regards foods, the Kacharis as a rule have by no means any limitation and restrictions. With the exception of beef, he denies himself of nothing. His great delicacy is pork; and every Kachari village swarms with pigs in almost every possible stages of growth. There is, however, one common article of food, which orthodox old fashioned Kachari will never touch, i.e. milk (Endle, 1911:15). When questioned as to the ground of his objection to milk as an article of food, he usually says that he is unwilling to deprive the calf of its natural support, though the real reason is probably of another character. This prejudice is shared by all section of the Kacharis. As reported about the Dimasa Kachari social life, it is found "the people neither drink milk nor do they milk the she buffaloes for commercial purposes" (Bordoloi *et al.*, 1987:49). Such prohibition is also found among the Garos and other members of the Mongolian race.

As agriculture is the main source of livelihood for the people, quality of cultivable land possessed by the families is a major factor which decides their economic conditions to a great extent. It has already been mentioned that Paroliguri and Nahoroni are forest villages. After being rehabilitated, they had to clear the marginal forest land for cultivation. As per their original record in the forest beat office there were very few families who were allotted land above 15 *bighas* of land. The original record was not updated till today.

On the basis of the present survey the distribution of families in the village according to their possession of land has been presented in Table 4.1.

Table 4.1: Distribution of Families according to pattern of landholding: Paroliguri and Nahoroni

Sl. No.	*Range of land in Bighas*	*No. of Families*	*Percentage*
1	1 – 5	6	6.59
2	6 – 10	37	40.65
3	11 – 15	33	36.26
4	16 - 20	15	16.48
	Total	91	99.98

The above Table highlights that the highest number of families, i.e. 37 (40.65%) possess land within the range of 6-10 *bighas*. 33 families (36.26%) have land within the range of 11-15 *bighas*. Significant number of families, i.e. 15 (16.48%) are found to possess land within 16-20 *bighas*. There are only 6 families (6.59%) who have land within 1-5 *bighas*. Not a single family is recorded who have land above 20 *bighas* of land.

Most of the inhabitants of the village are agriculturists and they devote most of their time in agricultural activities. Generally, the men folk plough their field and the sowing and harvesting is done by both males and females. There are 11 females who have taken service as their primary source of income. On the other hand, there are only a few families, who depend on petty business. Thus, depending upon the nature of livelihood, the daily activities of the people vary from season to season and from person to person.

An effort has also been made to describe to pattern of land holding in the village Duliagaon, in Table 4.2.

Table indicates that in Duliagaon out of total 11C families as many as 48 (43.64%) families possess land within the ıange of 6-10 *bighas*. A significant number of families, i.e. 47 (42.72%) hold up to 5 *bighas* of land. There are 10 families, who possess land within 11-15 *bighas*. Number of families having more than 15 *bighas* of land is not significant. Only 4 families have land within 16-20 *bighas* and there is only 1 family who possess land above 21 *bighas*.

Table 4.2: Distribution of families according to pattern of landholding: Duliagaon

Sl. No.	*Range of land in Bighas*	*No. of families*	*Percentage*
1	1 – 5	47	42.72
2	6 – 10	48	43.64
3	11 – 15	10	9.09
4	16 – 20	4	3.64
5	21 - 25	1	0.91
	Total	110	100

Agriculture is still the main source of living. But a good number of villagers, i.e. 40 have taken service as their primary source of income. The number of persons who have opted for business is also significant. There are 80 individuals who have taken business as their primary source of income.

The only differences between the forest and the revenue villages is that in the revenue villages the people has the authority to sell or transfer their land in emergency, whereas the forest villager has only right of occupancy.

At the time of sowing and plantation the villagers follow their traditional means. Majority of the villagers plough their land using bullock, and only in rare cases, in very low land, they hire buffaloes from nearby villages. They use cow-dung as manure in rice field but that too not very frequently. They have various means of pesticides and insecticides. Some of their indigenous techniques of insecticides are still used by the Sonowal Kacharis of their villages.

To get rid of insects, the Sonowal Kacharis still practice different means of controlling insects. During the plantation of the rice sapling, a type of insect locally called as *Nara puk* infect the seedling. The insects infect the root of the saplings and as a result, the entire sapling become dry and red in colour and finally, the plant dies. As a remedy, branches along with the leaves of *Paspotia goss, Chaste tree* [*Vitex negundo Linn* (*Verbencaseae*)] are just put in the water packed rice fields. The insects die as the said plant species is poisonous to them.

During harvesting season, insect (*Pipoli Khuwapuk*) infects the rice field. They make their way inside the soft tissue of the rice plant and eat up the leaves. The insects also lay eggs inside the soft tissue. Thus, the plant dies before it becomes fully mature. As a remedy, the people use the leaves of *Gossmahudi* (*Croton Joufra*) as an insecticide. The leaves are cut into small pieces and scattered all over the agricultural field. Since the leaves causes some amount of irritation and a burning sensation, the insects being unable to bear the smell comes above the rice plant. Bamboo sticks are placed at several places of agricultural field. The insects in order to get rid of the situation climb those sticks and are eaten by the birds.

They also have another way of controlling the insect. In most of the cases, they use the branches of *Mahudi lota,* [Croton *caudatus Geisel* (*Euphorbiaceae*)]. They cut the branches into small pieces and put it in the rice field. The rotten branches start emiting a foul smell, which cannot be tolerated by the insects. To get rid of the smell, the insects fly in the air and become the delicacy for the birds. Thus, it is found that *Paspotia goss* (*Vitex negun Linn*), *Gossmahudi* (*Croton joufra*) and *Mahudi lota* (*Croton caudatus Geisel*) are used extensively by the Sonowal Kacharis for controlling the insects. Various parts of these plants are used differently in different contextual situation. Sometimes, the leaves of *Passpotia goss* are powdered in the traditional husking lever (*Dhenki*) and scattered in the agricultural field as insecticide. Alternatively, it is also used after ploughing the agricultural fields. The Sonowal Kacharis keep the harvested paddy in the granary. They keep bunches of paddy layer after layer in the granary giving high pressur. It is believed that if they keep the paddy tightly in layers, the rat may get little chance to destroy the paddy stored in the granary. Sometimes, some good and perfect bunches of paddy are preserved/kept separately inside the granary for next year's sowing. They also keep the grain separately in a bucket made of straw and bamboo. For threshing the paddy/mustard, the Sonowal Kacharis never use bullock but do it by foot. The Karbis, the Tiwas also do not use bullock for threshing. They are of opinion that as they consider paddy as *Lakshmi,* so, they never use bullock for threshing. On the other hand after prayers, they start to remove the grains from the stalk by crushing the rice bundle with legs.

Smoking, Roasting and Boiling are the three methods popularly used by the the Sonowal Kacharis for preparing fish and meat dishes. Fishing always played an important role in their socio-economic life. Dried fish, i.e. the very small fish left on the surface of inundated land after the water has subsided. The small fishes are simply dried in the sun and "are carried northward to the Kachari Duars, where it is exchanged for rice and silk (*eri*), etc." (Endle, *1911*:5). The dried fishes is an all time favourite for the Sonowal Kacharis and locally known as *Sukati.* Sometimes, fishes are dried and kept intact, whereas sometimes, these dried fishes are powdered and preserved for future use. Thus, from very early stages fishes are used as an item for barter or used as a good substitute for subsistence living.

Different communities use food items differently. "The Malayan fishermen of Kelantan even "during the difficult period of the monsoon", live above the subsistence level." "It seems probable" we are informed" that the fisherman's family enjoys a diet which at most of the year is sufficient for the energy needs of the people, not too "unvaried and *prima facie*, not badly balanced" (Firth, 1943: 136). Seasonal varieties may cause differences in diet at different periods of the year, rather than a cycle of plenty and want.

During fieldwork, it was reported that among the Sonowal Kacharis also fish is considered as a delicious item in their diet and may be used as subsitute. In the year 2011 due to flood, the villagers could not get a good harvest. But abundant fishes found in the nearby water sources helped them to maintain a sustainable living. Fish became an alternative food item for them. Moreover, during summer and flood, fishes are available in all the water sources. By selling fishes, they could procure the minimum necessity for living. In normal time, they do not sell fishes as they are not permitted to take it as a profession. But in emergency or in difficult period they could survive from starvation due to the availability of fishes.

Community fishing is also common among the Kacharis as a whole and people of these villages go for community fishing mainly during the month of *Magh-Fagun* (January-February). When the date of fishing is commonly agreed by, responsibility is given to a section of members to communicate it. Information is communicated to the villagers by shouting the date and time from the village path. The willing villagers may participate in such community fishing.

Various folk beliefs and practices are associated with the entire process of fishing. They keep their fishing implements with reverence. It is believed that if the fishing implements are touched by others, then they would not be successful in getting fishes. The insects and ants which are trapped on spiders net on Tuesday and Saturday is considered auspicious for fishing. If one can get a chance to attach such insects in their fishing implements, then one can expect to get enough fishes. Just before starting the fishing on pond, river or *beel*, they spit three times with a belief that nobody would cast an evil eyes on them.

Certain fishes are very common in these areas, e.g., *Goroi (Channa punctatum), Chengali (Channa gachu),* etc. Folk songs represent the availability of such fishes. "*Bokare goroi mash bukate ghurile Dal pai ghurili beng. Hohoje dhoriboloi bhal.*"

"As *Goroi* fishes are moving in the mud, the frog jumps around the reeds. It is easy to catch the fishes in that position." The singer here is trying to draw an analogy between the abundant '*Goroi*' fishes and the beauty of Nature in that part of the year.

Similarly, *Chengali* fish (*Channa gachua*) is also necessary while performing a feast commonly referred as *Chengali masher bhoj* (feast). After completing cultivation, this feast is organized in the *Namghar*. During that period the villagers relatively remain free from hard labour and get time for relaxation. In this feast, only *Chengali* fishes are required because it is believed that goddess Lakshmi hides herself in sea. If fishes are caught in running/flowing river there is every possibility that the goddess might be caught unintentionally. So, they catch fishes from such water sources which do not have any connection with river. As *Goroi* and *Chengli* fishes are found only in the muddy water, such fishes are preferred for arranging the feast. Moreover, during cultivation, people lose their energy and strength. The *Goroi* and *Chengli* fishes are considered as one of the nutritious fish, so such fishes are used to regain their health status.

The villagers collect ferns and fishes from the surrounding environment which becomes a delicious substitute on their diet. Many folk songs are composed describing the surrounding environment.

Outala(r) dhekiya, kenha tala(r) butiy Jogibilo(r) kandhuli mash, Bhalkoi sijale Kaboloi bhal. Man brings easily available vegetables like fern and least favoured fish called '*Butiya*'(*Lepidocephalus gunitea*) and the most spiked fish like '*Kanduli*' which are nobody's choice. But if properly cooked, it becomes very tasty after hard labour. Various folk songs also reflect such natural situation. There is a popular folk song where the village youth laments that though he has collected the available fishes and ferns yet his wife is unable to prepare the dish properly. So he states that it would be good to remain a bachelor.

Another kind of fish, i.e. '*Patimutura*' is considered useful in certain diseases. It was reported that when a child continued to wet bed, even after 5 years of age, then a curry is prepared with "*Patimutura*" fish (a kind of fish). It is believed that if the child is fed with such curry, then he/she may be able to control the bladder. The Sonowal Kacharis consider fishes as a symbol of fertility and wealth.

Both men and women take part in fishing either independently or in group. Women normally go for fishing in the shallow water with fishing basket. They get *Puthi* (*Puntius sp*), *Khalihana (Colisa fasciata), Goroi (Channa punctatum), Chengali (Chana gachuai), Singi, Doricana* (*Rasbora bonensis*), etc. which are found in shallow water.

Food Habits

Every human group has some uniqueness with regards to its food habits. The Sonowal Kacharis also maintain certain unique characteristics with regard to food items and preparation. Rice is their staple food and they take rice with different varieties of locally available vegetables. They rarely use *dal* in their daily menu. Meat is preferred and wild boar, deer, *dawak* are found in the forest. They also rear pigs, ducks, chickens, etc. in their independent household. But meat is used occasionally in the day-to-day family diet. Most of the families take fish in all the seasons. They have unique way of preserving fishes which are considered both as nutritious and delicious.

They get vegetables from the agricultural field and cultivate gourd, cucumber, bean, etc. in the highland. Cabbages, cauliflowers are occasionally cultivated, whereas squash are cultivated extensively both in the forest villages and the other villages inhabited by the

Sonowal Kacharis. They also collect edible wild leaves and shoots from nearby forest areas or which are grown in marshy land near the river.

Earlier hunting played an important role in their living. "Their *Hagra* dance is no doubt a symbol of their hunting life" (Sonowal, 2001: 124). In celebrating "*Baithu puja*" boar is essential. In the past the Sonowal Kacharis used to go to the forest in search of boar. How they searched for boar and after catching how it was sacrificed in the altar of '*Baithu*'. The whole process is reflected in the "*Hagra dance*". Now hunting is not a regular feature among the Sonowal Kacharis. Few years back deer was available, but now hunting is almost absent.

But collecting/collection as a way of life is still very much prevalent among the Sonowal Kacharis. As they are living in the forest villages, they collect firewood from the periphery of the forest. The wild herbs and shrubs are collected by the women folk and they prepare curry from these wild herbs, which no doubt have medicinal value. The women have wide range of knowledge about the forest products available in different seasons.

Wild plants play an important role in the life of the Sonowal Kacharis, as they directly depend on various wild plants as vegetable stuff in their day-to-day life.

The people generally take three meals in a day at an unequal interval. The entire family does not eat together. The womenfolk take their meals after their male members have finished. Their three meals consist's of morning, mid-day and evening meals. Usually, in the morning they take either black tea or tea with milk and biscuit or *Chira* (flattened rice). In their mid-day meal, people take rice with vegetables, and rarely do they take dry fish. The evening meal is more elaborate and delicious. They prefer to include a fish curry in their meal and sometime the male member bring's vegetables from the market and it becomes a delicious item. Deer's meat is a delicacy for them. They eat fowls, pigs, ducks, goats and sometimes buffaloes. The people take their evening meal and generally finish it around 7:30 to 8:00 PM and retire to bed as early as possible. Consumption of oil, mustard, milk and coffee are very rare among them.

Rice is the only cereal used by the people which are the source of carbohydrates that provides energy. Potato and different edible roots also supply them with carbohydrates to some extent. The vegetables, wild shoots and leaves also provide them some amount of energy.

They get most of their edible food stuff from forest areas or marshy land on the bank of river. But knowingly/unknowingly, they are getting their nutrition from different food stuff. In their day-to-day menu, they rarely use *dal* but prepare a curry with the available herbs like *Matikaduri* (*Alternanthera sessilis*), *Khutura* (*Amaranthus viridi Linn*), etc. which are rich in vitamins. These herbs are not cultivated consciously, but grow in the homestead land. So, the villagers get their required vitamin from these herbs. However, they cultivate *Marisha (Amaranthus gangeticus Linn)* and *Lai* (a kind of mustard) in their kitchen garden. They prepare these herbs as separate curry or sometimes these are added mostly in preparation of meat curry.

It has already been mentioned, how and wherefrom they collect these herbs "*Outal(r) dhekia, kenha tala(r) mash*", though least precious, forms a delicious item in their menu. These items are easily available in the vicinity of all the villages and paddy fields or near the village path and muddy areas. *Dhekia* (Diplazium esculentum), *Ou tenga* (*Dillenis Indica*) is rich in protein and calorie. Moreover, the curry prepared with *Ou tenga* and fish is very delicious and it increases the hunger and taste. During summer, after heavy agricultural works, curry prepared with *Ou tenga* and ferns are relished by most of the people. Wild herbs and roots provide them sufficient requirement from nutritious point of view. That is why although it seems that they are not taking rich diet from common man's point of view, yet these are considered as sufficient to maintain a good health and capacity for hard work. Of course, this is not specific for Sonowal Kacharis alone, all the rural people of Assam largely depend upon similar food item or preparation because natural environment largely determine the dependence on specific types of food.

Food Preparation and Preservation

Tribal women of Northeastern region have a wide range of variability in the ethnic food made of bamboo, leafy vegetables, different varieties of herbs collected from nearby forest. The Sonowal Kachari women have their traditional indigenous ways of preparing and preserving the various food items.

Rice is prepared in a normal way and cooked in water. Sometimes extra water is strained. But in most cases, the amount of water put in the container is measured in such a way that when the rice is properly boiled, there does not remain any extra water to be strained.

To entertain the special guests or in rare ceremonial occasions, they prepare steam rice and *Bora bhat*. For preparation of steam rice commonly referred as (*Sewa bhat*) two pots are necessary. At first, *Bora rice* [traditional glutinous rice (*Oryzaglutinosa Lour. Poacea*) a kind of gum emitting rice] is kept in a smaller pot made of brass, wood or cane, which has a lid and some tiny holes at the bottom. After closing the lid tightly or covering the container with *Koupat* (*Phrvnium imbrrcatum*) it is placed in the mouth of the bigger pot. Between the mouth of the bigger pot and the bottom of the smaller one, one wet cloth is tightly fixed so that the vapour does not come out. The water inside the smaller pot is thus steamed and it becomes ready for consumption. This kind of rice preparation is common among the Tai Ahoms (Barua, 1978:47), Tai Turungs (Barua, 2001:26).

For preparing *Chunga chawul* or *Bora bhat*, they put the *Bora* rice in a bamboo tube, adding required water for boiling. Then these tubes are burnt in fire for sufficient time. Sometimes, they put banana leaf inside the bamboo tube and put the rice in it so that it can easily be taken out.

Though the Sonowal Kacharis know various preparations of meat and fish, yet vegetables are common to their diet. They do not use much oil and spice in vegetables. Vegetables and herbs are boiled in water and if required onion and garlic are added.

Khar (Alkali) is taken by them very frequently. The Sonowal Kacharis prepare *Khar* from various items, e.g. *Matimah,* a kind of pulse (*Phaseolus radiantus*), *Kol-khar*, plaintain (*Musa sapientum*) and *Kher* (thatching paddy straw). In case of *Matimah,* first the husks are separated from the pulses and then it is burnt in fire. In case of *Khol khar*, bark of *Bhimkol* is burnt on fire. They normally burn the bark when it is needed. Sometimes, the ashes are kept in jar or bottle by adding water to it. In case of *Khe*r (paddy straw) the ashes, after burning, is kept as it is or after mixing to water preserved in a bottle.

In most cases, the *Alkali* is stored in bottles or jars. Usually a spoonfull of it is added during the preparation of curry. In preparing curry with *Duranban* (*Lecas aspera*), *Sewali* flower (*Nyctanthe*s *arbor-tristis Linn*), *Pasala* (a sprout of the plantain tree dressed for food) they prefer to add alkali to make it tasty. While preparing a curry from the bud of banana (*Musa paradisiacal*) or curry prepared from bamboo shoot also, they add alkali. This indicates that *Khar* is one of the most preferred items to make any food preparation delicious.

They use various items for preparing sour (*Tenga*) curry. Normally some fish curry is a must in their daily diet. They use *Naltenga* (*Tetrastigma thomsonianum planch*), *Tengamora* (*Hrbiscus sabdariffa Linn*), *Ou tenga* (*Dillenis Indica*) extensively in preparing *Tenga* curry. Lime is also used for preparation of such dishes.

Fishes are normally used to prepare curry and dried fish (*Sukati*) is used extensively. For preparing *Sukati*, small fishes are collected in large quantities from ditch or shallow water. After washing and cleaning, these are dried in sun. Then fishes are grinded in traditional husking lever (*Dhenki*) and stored in bamboo tube and the mouth is tightly sealed or corked with *Kher* (paddy straw).

For preparation, normally a small portion of grinded fishes are wrapped in banana tree and tightly bounded with cane string. Then the packet is roasted in fire. It is also mixed with vegetables to make it tasty. It becomes tastier, when mixed with arum leaf or edible colocasia species leaf.

Different fermented foods are used in various combinations with traditional vegetables to meet the food and nutritional security.

Bamboo shoot fermentation process is done during May-June, when new shoots are formed. Young and tender bamboo shoots are collected; the sheaths are removed and properly washed before peeling and chopping down. Normally, after making small slices, the bamboo shoot pieces are kept in a bamboo cylinder and made airtight with *Nora* (paddy straw). The cylinder full of bamboo shoots is left for fermentation and is then ready for use. Sometime, salt and turmeric is used in the sliced bamboo shoots and are kept intact for a few days. These are then preserved in bottle for future use.

There are various ways/methods of preparation. Sometimes pounded or sliced bamboo shoots are kept in a perforated cane or metal container. Such a container is used for draining the juice. The bamboo shoots get fermented within 7-10 days. After that, it is preserved either in bamboo tubes or jars. The fermentation done in bamboo tube is consumed within a short period. Jars are used for fermentation when the shoots are to be used for a longer period. In certain occasions, pieces of bamboo shoots are dried in the sun. Then it is grinded and it produces a different aroma. These are then preserved in bottles or bamboo tubes. When preserved bamboo shoots are added to meat or fish curry it becomes very delicious.

The Sonowal Kacharis prepare meat items in various ways. Pork, chicken, mutton area delicacy, but these are not included in their usual daily menu. They prefer roast or smoked meat. Besides meat of chicken, duck, pigeon, wild birds and animals also constitute their occasional delicacy.

Duck meat is considered a special diet of the Sonowal Kacharis. They prepare duck meat with bamboo shoots and gourd, and this is considered a delicious item.

A curry is prepared from the bud of banana (*Musa paradisiaca*) and the meat of pigeon. It is preferred by all sections of population and also used as a nutritious diet for the patient suffering from anaemia or common weakness.

They also prepare chicken dishes with above mentioned method. But to make it tastier, they add crushed rice in the meat of chicken and pigeon. A leafy vegetable, i.e. *Lai sak* is also used in preparing chicken dishes. They do not add much oil in preparing chicken curry but add ginger and garlic in enough water.

Pork is a very favourite and extensively prepared as curry by the Sonowal Kacharis. Dry pork meat is prepared by adding *Lai-sak* and smoked pork meat is also preferred by them. They occasionally prepare a curry from brinjal and the meat of wild bird *Darik*. Earlier it was used extensively but now these are not used frequently as the common people are also influenced by the call for protection of wild animals and birds.

Over the hearth in the kitchen, there are two bamboo shelves/ rakes suspended one over the other. In the upper layer, pitchers of rice-beer and the materials used for preparing rice-beer are kept. In the lower rack, they keep potatoes, pumpkin, bottle gourd, bitter gourd, etc. for future consumption. Fish and meat are smoked over the family hearth and preserved on the platform above the hearth.

Potatoes and arum of different varieties are grown everywhere. During the lean periods of the year, these are used as important alternative items. So, they take measures to preserve it for future use. Harvested potatoes are cleaned and dried in the sun. These are then kept in the shelf above the hearth.

It was commonly believed that *Arum* is not very beneficial to health. But now it is confirmed that it contains all the nutrients, i.e. carbohydrate, protein, vitamin and mineral. In case of liver disease, it acts as a preventive and curative medicine also. Harvested arums are cleaned in water and these are then dried in the sun for a few days. After that it is preserved in the *Chang* (bamboo shelf). Matured pumpkins, gourd of different varieties are also stored in the *Chang*.

Harvested *turmeric* is washed and sliced into small pieces. These are then dried in the sun for a few days. When fully dried, they are preserved/stored in a pot. Sometimes, the dried turmeric is grinded and stored in a pot. Besides the normal food items, there are also some other food items which are very much preferred by the Sonowal Kacharis. Different varieties of insects are considered as delicacy by the Sonowal Kacharis wherefrom they get the required protein. Some of the insects are mentioned here.

Amroli ant/red ant (*Oecophyla Smaragdin*a), *Wisiringa* (*Acheta Domestica*), *Jebangkori* (*Lethocerun Grandis), Ari polu* (*Philosomia ricini*), *Muga Polu* (*Antheraea Assamensis*) and *Pat Polu* (*Bombynimari*), *Bees* (*Apis Indica*) *and Baral* (*Wasp vespa sp*) are eaten by the Sonowal Kacharis, depending on the availability of the insects.

The Sonowal Kacharis also prepare varieties of dishes from crabs and frogs. Most of the tribes of North eastern states prefer to eat these insects which are prepared in various ways.

The Sonowal Kacharis have been found to observe some prescriptions and prohibition in their food items. In case of illness also, they follow their own indigenous belief and practices.

The Sonowal Kacharis invariably avoid taking bitter items during night. In no cases, do they prepare curry with *Borali* fish and *Kordoi* (*Averroa carambola*). It is believed that combination of these item make the curry poisonous.

There is also prohibition that they should not take egg preparation with rice-beer. Though the common people are not aware about the real cause, but a good majority of the people can explain the fact that one would become more intoxicated if he/she would drink rice-beer with egg preparation.

The Sonowal Kacharis prepare a curry with arum leaf or edible colocasia species leaf. It is considered a delicious item in their diet. But in preparing the curry they are not supposed to put oil for cooking. There is a folk belief associated with it. It is believed that if they do it, women would not be able to bear children and their lineage (*Bansha*) would come to an end. It is also said that if it is fried, mother's milk would run dry.

Similarly, in case of illness also, they observe certain restrictions. If there is a cut injury, they avoid sour items like lemon, tamarind, etc. It is believed that it would delay the healing process. Sour and sweet foods are also avoided during cough and fever.

They are advised to avoid brinjal during skin diseases. It is believed that the intake of this item not only delays the healing process, but also sometimes aggravates the ailment. It is also said that bitter items should not be used as food item with fish and chicken curry.

Man eats a variety of both plant and animal food. They are in general not selective about it and are not aware about the nutritional value of the food they take. They eat only those vegetables which they get from their immediate environment.

Almost all the tribes of Northeast India have their own indigenous ways of preparing and preserving ethnic food. In each community, the processing method of these foods is somewhat different based on culture, variability in the materials used in the food and overall knowledge of processing and preparation. The foods used in their dietary system were found to be nutritionally rich and culturally unique in various festivals and religious ceremonies.

An analysis of dietary habits of Sonowal Kacharis reveals that they may not be aware about the food value and nutrition. But they get carbohydrate from rice, potatoes and edible roots of various plants. Protein is derived mostly from fish, egg and meat which, however, are occasional/seasonal delicacies of the people. Fat is also derived mostly from fish and meat as they use minimum oil in cooking. Vitamins and other nutrients are obtained from leafy vegetables and locally available fruits.

The availability of materials found in their environment no doubt provides them with sufficient requirements for their living.

2. The Deoris

Agriculture is the main source of livelihood among the Deoris and rice is their staple food. They cultivate different varieties of paddy according to the suitability of their cultivable land. As they mostly live in flood prone areas, their lands are not suitable for *Sali* paddy cultivation. The cultivable lands, particularly in the forest village Modhupur are very low and regular flood during the rainy season badly affected their cultivation. They extensively cultivate *Ahu* paddy and relish it very much. *Bao* rice is also suitable for their land and it is grown widely.

Traditional glutinous rice (*Oryzaglutinosa Lour: Poaceae*) belonging to japonica variety called *Bora* rice is cultivated extensively. These are used for varieties of rice preparation besides making rice cakes. The people of rural Assam have a special preference for *Bora* rice, and the Deoris are not an exception. The Deoris practice plough cultivation with bullocks like the other peasant communities of Assam. Land holding per family in the Modhupur Deori forest village is not satisfactory. They were allotted land according to the rules of the forest department. Thus, there is hardly any scope of extending their plot of land. They use cow-dung as manure in rice field but that too not very frequently. With the influence of modern cultivation they use fertilizer and insecticide in their paddy field. In spite of it, they still follow some traditional indigenous techniques of insecticides, which are still used by the Deoris of Modhupur village.

To get rid of insects, particularly *Gandhipuk* (one kind of beetle) they follow a different way to control the insects (This problem occurs normally when the paddy sapling just comes out). They pick up crabs in a bamboo stick and place them in the water packed rice fields. As it emits a bad smell, it cannot be tolerated by the insects. The result is that the insects fly away from that area.

In certain cases, the Deori women perform rituals to get rid of the insects or when the paddy does not grow properly. They offer rice powder (*Pithaguri*) and banana in the name of *Ai-matri* (mother earth) and *Lakshmi* (Goddess of wealth). They sing *Ai-nam* to please the mother goddess so that they can overcome the difficulty.

The Deoris are entirely dependent on cultivation and various folk beliefs and practices are associated with it. It has already been mentioned that they have a special passion for *Ahu* rice and it is cultivated in large scale. The village youth play *Ghila* (*Ghila*—a heart shaped seed of a type of creeping plant used by children as wheel/ marble, etc.) and enjoy it very much. It is believed that if they do not play *Ghila* during *Bihu* festival then the *Ahu* paddy sampling will not sprout (Deori, 1964:368). Similarly, they use paddy straw for various purposes. Sometimes straws are burnt for preparing alkali (*Khar*). But they never burn the seedling straw on fire. It is believed that if they put seedling straw on fire, then seedling would turn red like the burning charcoal (Deori, 1964:372).

All the members of the household extend their helping hand towards different economic activities. Women take active part in economic activities both inside and outside the family. From morning till night they remain busy in cooking, household activities, weaving, looking after their children, etc. Kitchen garden is mostly maintained by the housewives. Occasionally, they go for collecting firewood from nearby forest. When the necessity arises they use axe for cutting the firewood. "There is a traditional custom in Deori society that the newly wed bride has to go to the forest and ceremoniously cut wood and bring firewood to home" (Barua, 1994:59). Such type of activity indicates that except tilling, the women are to take part in all economic activities.

The women folk are the actual knowledge-holders, who are actively involved in the preparation of food items using their native knowledge of food preparation technology. As such, cooking is customarily done by the daughters-in-law, daughters and mothers. It is a custom among the Deoris that they are to serve the male members first and the female members of the family eat afterwards. They discuss and extend their opinions regarding various matters relating to their household during the time of taking meal. It is a good opportunity to meet all the family members together. Food is normally served in bell-metal dishes and bowls.

From childhood itself, the boys and girls take their food separately in group. This is distinctly apparent in their community feast and festivals. This relationship among the girls is very strong. "It is a common scene during festivals, marriages and ceremonies where the friends sit in a circular fashion and enjoy the feast from a single plate" (Barua, 2011:80).

The Deoris follow various ways in preparing the rice. Normally bell-metal utensils are used for preparing rice. The Deoris prefer to take hot rice. So, rice is prepared just before serving. They cook rice in water and when the rice is properly boiled, the excess water is drained.

Sometimes they put the water, measuring it in such a way that when the rice is properly boiled, there does not remain any extra water to be drained. In this way, the total starch content of the rice is preserved. Most of the tribes including Ao Nagas follow this type of preparation (Barua & Barua, 2009:313). The Deoris particularly prepare *Bora* rice following these principles.

Sewa Bhat is specially prepared by the Deoris when guests or new relatives visit their home. It is the steamed sticky rice preferred by the Deoris. Here, two different rice pots, one is bigger in size and the other is smaller in size is used. The sticky rice is soaked in cold water overnight for 2 to 3 hours. At the time of preparation the soaked rice is placed in the small pot which has tiny holes in it. This allows the steam from the pot to pass through it. The sponge of dried vegetables is placed at the bottom of the pot. Sometimes bamboo sieve/iron sieve is also placed to prevent the rice from falling down through it. In between the two vessels, a wet cloth is tightly fixed in the joint to prevent the steam from leaking.

The Deoris prepare different varieties of rice cakes during ceremonies and festivals. Rice is soaked in water for 2-3 hours. Then the water is drained and rice is grinded in a husking lever (*Dhenki*). The rice powder is kept in a vessel with tiny holes and it is covered with a cloth, so that moisture remains intact. They may give different shape and sometimes it is fried in oil and sometimes it is steamed.

The Deoris use *Bora* rice for preparing *Korai.* At first rice is washed and fried on the frying pan without any oil. The rice is fried deeply until it became red in colour and increase in volume (swelled). The fried rice is coarsely ground in a *Dhenki.* While preparing the meat dishes, particularly duck and chicken; they add this rice just before the completion of the curry. It makes the curry thick like corn flour and taste differently.

Fish is one of the favourite items of the Deoris. Smoking, roasting and boiling are ancient methods of cooking and it is still followed by most of the tribal people.

Hearth (fire place) plays an important role in smoking and roasting. In every Deori household two or three hanging bamboo platforms are found over the hearth. The platform immediately above the hearth is known as *Gisong.* Above it, there is another platform known as *Lueng.* Sometimes, a big bamboo platform is found above these two platforms.

Sukoti mas (dry fish) are a very favourite preparation of the Deoris. During the rainy season, when fishes are found abundantly, people collect small fresh water fishes. After removing the scale of the fishes, these are cleaned and washed properly. They keep the fishes in large bamboo sieves and are dried in *Gisong.* It is generally kept in this way for nearly two weeks. The dried fishes are then ground in husking lever (*Dheki*). The stem of *Barkachu* (*Colocasia esculenta arum*) are dried and mixed with the ground fish. Sometimes leaves of *Siju-gas* (*Euphorbia neriifolia Linn*) may also be dried and mixed along with the fishes. The entire mixture is grounded together and put inside the bamboo tube (*Chunga).* The tube is either of *Kako bah* (*Dendrocalamus hamiltonii Nees & Arn*) or *Bhaluka bah* (*Bambusa balcooa Roxb)* bamboo. Care is taken to put as much fish as it can absorb, so that there is no chance of air leakage. Then the mouth of the *Chunga* is tightly closed with banana leaves or hay, so that it is not infected or infested with insects. To keep the fish fresh, the tube is kept near the hearth. It becomes tastier if it is opened after fifteen days. But, it would be much tastier if it is kept for a longer period of time. "Sometimes, it may be infested by fungus or bacteria, so the priests of the Deoris are not allowed to take *Sukati mas*" (Deori, 1964:371).

Normally small fresh water fish varieties like *Puthi* (*Puntius sp),* *Singora* (*Myctus vittatus*), and *Donikona* (*Rasbora bonensis*), and *Kholihona* (*Colisa fasciata)* are commonly used by the people for preparing *Sukati mas*. During scarcity of fishes a little bit of *Sukati* may be boiled in water by adding ginger and garlic. It may also be consumed with boiled potatoes or alone.

Though the people prepare *Sukati* to meet their needs in scarcity, yet it has some medicinal values. Such types of fish preparation are considered as one of the way of preventing from malaria. Similarly, the stem of *Borkachu* (*Colocasia esculenta arum*) make the fish mixture solid and the leaves of *Siju* tree (*Euphorbia nerrifolia Linn*) prevent the mixture from being infected by insects. Thus, consciously/ unconsciously they are taking such an edible food which acts as a prevention of a dreaded disease like malaria. Because of some medicinal value; there exists a popular belief among the Deoris that if the women take curry prepared with *Sukati mas* then there would be a good flow of mother's milk.

The fishes may also be dried in sun. After cleaning the fishes, these are spread on a broad bamboo sieve by adding some salt. The fishes dried in sun or smoked in the *Gisang* have slightly different taste. Thus any one method is followed to dry a batch of fishes.

Roasted fish is very much preferred by both the Sonowal Kacharis and the Deoris. Solid and hard fresh water fishes like *Goroi* (*Channa punctatus*), *Cheng mas* (*Channa gachua*), *and Sal mas* (a variety of common fish) are collected. After initial cleaning, the fishes are fixed in iron/bamboo stick puncturing the fishes from tail end and protruding it from the head. A little bit of salt and turmeric are added to it. Then the fishes are slowly roasted over the charcoal rotating the stick by holding two ends. It may be taken immediately with boiled rice or can be preserved keeping that way above the hearth.

Boiling is another way of preparing fish items. In their day-to-day food habit, they prepare the fish dishes boiling it with different vegetables. They specially prepare fishes with *Ou tenga* (*Dillenis indica*). First, they boil water in a container then add *Ou tenga* (*Dillenis indica*) in it. In the mean time they add salt and turmeric powder in the fishes. When *Ou tenga* (*Dillenis indica)* is par boiled, they add fishes in it and boil it for some time till the curry is prepared. Fish curry is also prepared by adding different leafy vegetables.

Fishes are also prepared by wrapping it in banana leaves and roasted in charcoal. Sometimes, they steam it for preparation. In their day-to-day life, they use very little oil for preparation of any item. Smoking, Roasting and Boiling are the three ways of preparing fish dishes. The Deoris prepare and preserve meat dishes more or less like the fish item.

Smoked Meat *is* one of the preferred items. Pork is one of the most preferred dishes of the Deoris as well as Sonowal Kacharis. Earlier wild boar, deer were available in the forest. First, they cut the meat into small square pieces. Then it is boiled in water and when it is half boiled, they add a pinch of salt and turmeric. The water is then drained and the meat pieces are kept in a broad bamboo sieve and smoked in *Gisong*. In this way, it may be used for 2-3 month and it is one of the most preferred items.

Meat is also roasted and normally it is taken along with rice-beer. They prefer to entertain the guests and relatives with the roasted meat. But in their day-to-day life they prefer to prepare the meat dishes by boiling with vegetables, herbs and shrubs and these are very favourite item for them. Moreover, most of the available vegetables like gourd, pumpkin, etc. are added to the meat dishes to make it tastier. Especially they prepare a meat curry adding leafy vegetables like *Lai-sak*.

Bamboo shoot is prepared in a variety of ways by the tribes of North-east India. Consumption of bamboo shoots is extensively spread in the whole of South-East Asia, including North-East India. In India bamboo shoots are consumed both as a fermented and vegetable food. But regionwise, the preparation including the way of cutting into pieces also varies.

Among the Deoris, first the bamboo shoots are collected; sheats are removed and properly washed before peeling and chopping them down. Then the shoots are ground in husking lever (*Dheki*). Water is then added to the ground shoots and normally preserved in earthen pot. After 2 to 3 days it becomes ready for immediate home consumption.

Ground bamboo shoots are also preserved for longer period by adding salt and turmeric. Sometime's salt and turmeric are mixed with the sliced bamboo shoots and dried in sunlight. Such type of bamboo shoots may be preserved for a year. Both the earthen pots and bamboo tube (*Chunga*) are used for keeping the shoots. But they take special precaution to airtight the container so that it is tightly closed. The Deoris mostly prefer to keep it in earthen pots for using it for a longer period. Preserved bamboo shoots are added to meat/fish curry to make it tastier. It may also take as a *Chatni* (pickle).

Indigenous Food Preservation and Storage

The technique of food storage and preservation play an important role in the survival and development of human society. Different crops and vegetables are grown in different seasons. Herbs and shrubs which substitute's food also grow in a particular seasons. In the same way, roots and tubes are collected from the forest. Collection and gathering is no doubt the first stage of economic development. In course of development of civilization, human beings developed new technologies. But some indigenous methods still proves fruitful.

Rice Grain

The Deoris are agriculturist and rice is the main crop. After harvesting, the paddy along with stalk is stored in the granary (*Bhoral*). The granary is constructed on a high post, i.e. platform type. The floor is made of wooden planks or bamboo mat. They observe a small ritual while harvesting the first branches of paddy. On the first day of harvesting, ½ *muthi* (handful of paddy) of paddy is brought to the house preferably by the eldest women or whose star is favourable during that period. They keep the paddy bunch in the granary. In the middle of the bunch, a wild variety of leaves, normally *Neem* (*Azadiracha Indica*) leaves are kept. It is believed that the bunch remain intact for the whole year. Different varieties of paddy are stored separately. After completion of storing paddy, responsibility is given to a woman member (specially the wife of head of the family) to bring paddy when necessary. There is an extension on one side of the granary. Normally, they keep hay stacks on this open platform. Sometimes, the harvested paddy is also kept. Rice is kept in *Guloi*, i.e. a wooden round basket. The length of the basket is 2 ft.

The hearth commonly referred as *Tipai Hal* plays an important part in preservation. There are two hanging bamboo *Changs* above the hearth. The platform/*Chang* immediately above the hearth is known as *Gisong*. Immediately above the *Gisong*, there is another hanging platform known as *Lueng*.

For smoking the fishes, they keep the fishes on bamboo sieve and put on the *Gisong*. The pounded fishes preserved on bamboo tube (*Chunga*) are also kept on the *Gisong*. Meats are also occasionally stored in this way for a very short period of time. They also store potatoes, pumpkins, peer gourds, etc. in the *Lueng*. Harvested potatoes are dried in the sun. These are then spread on a bamboo sieve and put on the *Chang*. They keep leaves of guava in the *Chang* for purpose of drying potatoes. In this way they are able to preserve it for 5 to 6 months. For preservation of shorter period, i.e. 6 to 7 days they store potatoes, green vegetables like cabbage, cauliflowers, brinjal, etc. in a basket made of bamboos. The basket is kept in one corner of the kitchen.

Harvested turmeric are washed and cut into two halves. These are then dried in the sunshine. After being fully dried, it is kept stored in bamboo baskets and placed in the *Lueng*. Sometimes dried turmeric is pounded and kept in the shell of water gourd.

Chillies are normally dried in sunshine or kept in a bamboo sieve and put in the *Lueng*. Chilli powder after being ground is put into the shell of water gourd. Matured ginger are harvested and dried in sunlight for 4 to 5 days. Then it is wrapped in a clean cloth and kept on G*isong* for 3 to 4 months. Sometimes a little bit of salt is mixed with ginger while drying in sunshine. It helps in preservation.

Bananas, particularly *Bhimkal*, are sliced and placed in a broad bamboo sieve. These are dried on fire and after drying, kept on *Lueng* in a bamboo container. In this way it can be preserved for 2 to 3 years. It may be used as folk medicine for cough and cold. Sometimes small tablets are made from banana and dried over the hearth.

Leafy vegetables like *Lai sak* are dried in sunshine for 2/3 days. Then it is kept on earthen pot or thick bamboo container near the *Tipai* for 20 to 25 days.

The Pulses like (*Magu & Matimah*) are fried. After cleaning, it may be preserved in a bamboo container. The plant parts of the black gram are burnt after threshing and are used for preparing alkali (*Khar*). The remaining parts (ashes) are preserved for use as (*Kha*r) alkali.

The Deoris also preserve pulses in different ways. Pulses are threshed thoroughly and only the pulse portions are kept in gunny bags. To prevent from fungus and bacteria, the gunny bags, after sewing the open ends, are used as door mats. People walk over the bags and the airy disturbances prevent the pulses from the infestation of the micro-organism, especially in black grams.

Tobacco leaves are dried in sunlight for 3 to 4 days. Then it is cut into small pieces and again dried in sunlight. After properly drying, these are kept in bamboo tubes with tiny holes on it. It is then kept on *Gisong*. When the bamboo tube is fully dried, it is assumed that tobacco is ready for use. It may take 6 to 7 days to complete the process.

Harvested arums are cleaned in water and first dried in the sunshine. Then it is stored in *Lueng*. Lemons of different kinds, *Amlokhi* (*Emblica officinalis*), *Amora* (*Spondian mangifera Wild*) are kept on salt for preservation.

The matured *Kath-alu* (white yam), *Ronga lau* (*Cucurbita moschanta Duch*), *Moa alu* (a kind of sweet yam) are kept in damp earthen floor and preserved for longer period. The vegetables which are used in their day-to-day life are commonly preserved for a shorter period after drying it in sunshine.

The people of the hills and the plains, including the Deoris prefer to preserve food by smoking. It is considered as one of the earliest method of preservation. Red chilli, gourd, *Mahaneem* (*Azadirachta indica* A. Juss), *Tejpat* (bay leaves), etc. are kept over the platform of the hearth. Salt is another means used for food preservation.

Prescription and Prohibitions

Like most communities of rural Assam, the Deoris also observe some prohibition in their food intake. The Deoris do not take curry prepared with pulses (mainly black gram) on Tuesday and Saturday. Similarly, bitter fruits and vegetables are also not taken on Tuesday and Saturday. Various beliefs and superstitious also exist in their society. It is believed that if they take radish (*Mula*) in the month of *Magh* (January-February), the person would suffer badly from cough. If *Urahi* (*Dolicho lablab* Linn) is taken in the month of *Chat* (March-April) the person would suffer from severe headache.

Discussion (Food)

Food is one of the important aspects of life. Every human group has some uniqueness with regard to its food habit. Dietary habits in different region of the world have been determined by various factors like geographical condition, food cropping pattern and local availability of food resources. The study of food habits of a particular community provides a unique opportunity to look into their customs and trace their social and economic history. Besides ecology, cultural/ racial factor also plays an important role in determining the food habits of a particular community.

The Sonowal Kacharis and the Deoris are both living in the same environmental condition and following more or less the same procedure in cultivating their products. Agriculture is the main source of livelihood among them and rice is their staple food. But a good number of villagers have taken service/business as a source of their livelihood. Majority of them plough their land using bullock, and only in rare cases, they hire buffaloes from the nearby villages to plough the very low land. They use cowdung as manure in rice field but that too not very frequently. Both the communities have their own indigenous techniques of insecticides. In comparison to the Deoris, the Sonowal Kacharis have more elaborate knowledge/ways of insecticide, and are in a position to explain the controlling process.

They cultivate different varieties of paddy according to the suitability of their cultivable land. Among the Deoris, *Ahu* and *Bao* rice is widely grown, whereas the Kacharis prefer to cultivate *Sali* paddy. All the members of the household extend their helping hands towards different economic activities. The Deori women are more hard working and except ploughing they take part in all economic activities. Rice is their staple food and they take rice with different varieties of locally available vegetables. Rice plays a special role in the ritual and ideological life of the Sonowal Kacharis and the Deoris. They are wet rice cultivators. From the time of preparing the seed bed, planting, maturation and harvesting, various rituals are performed. No ceremony or celebration is complete without rice. In the process of cultivation they maintain the division of labour; transplantation and weeding are traditionally the work of the women folk, while ploughing, threshing and carrying paddy bundles are done by the menfolk. For keeping the variety of rice as seed, grains are removed from stalk by crushing the rice bundle with legs so that one variety is not mixed with the other in the threshing ground. Sun drying of grains was performed by the respondents for milling and storage. This is done by spreading the grains on the floor under the sun. Their day-to-day meal consists of rice, *dal* and vegetable curry. Fish and meat are their favourite food items. However, these are taken only as delicacies and are not included in their daily menu.

Traditional glutinous rice (*Oryza glutinosa Lour; Poaceae*) belonging to japonica variety known as *Bora* rice is cultivated extensively. The people of rural Assam have a special preference for *Bora* rice and the Sonowal Kacharis and the Deoris are not an exception. They have a special passion for preparing steam rice commonly referred as (*Sewa bhat*). The procedure of preparation of steam rice is almost same in both the communities. Minor variation may be noticed in the utensils used; sometimes they use bamboo container and rarely use metal utensil for steaming. To entertain the special guests or in rare ceremonial occasion, they prepare steam rice. It is served with duck meat/pork meat. Besides steaming *Bora* rice is also prepared in bamboo tube, popularly referred as *Chunga chawal*. Most of the tribes of North East India prepare both the dishes in their own way.

All the Tai groups, i.e. the Khamyangs, the Turungs, and the Phakey prepare rice packet (*Tupula bhat*) in all the ceremonies and festivals. An amount of cooked rice packed in *Kau pat* (a kind of plaintain leaves) or banana leaves is named as *Tupula bhat* (Barua, 1998:160). The Tai Kamyangs also prepare *Tupula bhat* (steamed rice balls) nicely wrapped in freshly collected broad plantain leaves (*Pyrnium pubinerve BI: Marantaceae*) called as *Tong-sing* and *Kau pat* in Tai and Assamese respectively. Moreover, they prepare varieties of rice cakes in festivals and ceremonies (Sonowal & Barua, 2012:40).

Fish is one of the favourite items of the Sonowal Kacharis and the Deoris. Both individual and community fishing are practiced by both the communities and they have their own ways of fishing technique. They enjoy fish catching in the field and nearby water bodies and also rear fish in the ponds. They know various preparations of fish and meat, but still vegetables are common to their diet. They do not use much oil and spice in vegetables. Vegetables and herbs are boiled in water and if desired, onion and garlic are added.

Smoking, roasting and boiling are the ancient methods of cooking and it is still followed by most of the tribal people. Hearth (fire place) plays an important role in smoking and roasting. In every household two/three layers of hanging bamboo platforms are found over the hearth. The number and size of platform varies from community to community.

They eat both fresh and dry fish. Fresh fishes are roasted or prepared as curry with different vegetables and herbs. When the fishes are available in plenty, they dry or smoke it. For preparation of dry fish, they remove the entrails of the fish and keep it on the bamboo sieve over the plateform. Dried fish (*Sukati*) is used extensively by both the communities. The fishes are dried both in the platform over the hearth or in the sun. The fishes dried in sun or smoked over the hearth have slightly different taste. For drying fishes any one method is used for a batch of fishes. The Sonowal Kacharis prefer to dry the fishes in sun. Roasting is another way of preparing fish and meat. In their day-to-day food habit, they prepare the fish dishes boiling it with different vegetables. Leafy vegetables, e.g. *Lai sak*, leaves of mustard are also added to prepare a fish dish. For preparing fish curry, they extensively use *Ou-tenga* (*Dillenis Indica*). They also use *Naltenga* (*Tetrastigma thomsonianum planch*) and *Tengamora* (*Hrbiscus sabdariffa Linn*) for preparing fish curry. These are the mouth watering dishes and during hot summer it gives a shoothing effect. The water sources of the paddy field and the canals or rivulets provide enough scope for catching fishes. It is a common scene that after plantation, the women catch fishes that are available in the water sources. Wet rice fields all over the world provide the same opportunity of catching fishes. Two popular saying current among the Laos and Vietnamese people are: "there are fishes in rivers and paddy rice in fields" (*Nao nam mipla nau na mi khao*) and "have meals, drink liquor and drink tea" (*kin khao kin lau kin cha*). Men and women go out in separate groups for fishing in the nearby river, brook, forlorn water ways, marsh, boggy, ditches and rice field with various fishing implements. Women can also catch fishes with their bare hands in the muddy paddy fields.

The Dimacha Kacharis have a specific method of preserving fishes for a longer period. At first the fishes which are caught in large number are washed nicely. The fishes are then wrapped with banana leaves into a bundle. Some holes are dug in the ground over which some bamboo sticks are put in such a way that they make a platform. The bundles of fishes are kept on these platforms and nicely covered with earth for nearly one week. The water which remains inside the fishes are slowly drained of through the banana leaves to the ground and the perforated platform makes it easy to drain the water. The earth gives pressure to the fish, which squeezes out the watery juice from the fishes. After one week these are taken out and kept in the sun on a sieve for one day. The fishes become completely dried and then it is preserved in the bamboo tube (*Chunga*). This type of fishes can be preserved for a longer period of time in comparison to other dried fishes. Such example clearly indicates that different communities have their own indigenous ways which they have developed in course of their living in a particular locality..

In case of preparing and processing meat, they follow more or less the same procedure as fish. Dried fish and meat are preserved for future use. It was reported that the Sonowal Kacharis and the Deoris do not sell fishes as they are not permitted to take it as a profession. But during crisis/emergency they have to depend on selling fishes. An incident was narrated where it was revealed that the villagers could not get a good harvest in the year 2011 due to heavy flood. On the otherhand, during summer and flood, fishes were available in all the water sources. By selling fishes they could procure minimum necessity for living. Different tribes of North East India follow different ways to prepare fish dishes. Ao Naga prepares a fish dish known as *Bangtangsen.* In a bamboo tube, the cut pieces of fish are put with a mixture of chilli, salt, and bamboo shoot. Then the mouth of the tube is corked by leaves (preferably banana) and the tube is kept in the hearth of the fire till it becomes ready to be served (Barua & Barua, 2009:313).

Wild herbs and plants play an important role in the life of the tribal and peasant communities as they directly depend on various wild plants as vegetable stuff. The present study reveals that the villagers get vegetables, wild shoots and leaves and other edible stuffs from forest areas or marshy land on the bank of the river. But knowingly/unknowingly, they are getting their nutrition from different food stuffs. In their day-to-day menu, they rarely use *dal* but prepare a curry with available herbs like *Matikaduri* (*Alternanthera Sessilis*), *Khutura* (*Amaranthus viridi Linn*), *Jilmil* (*Chenopodium album Linn*), etc. *Matikaduri* contains 82 per cent calorie, 5 per cent protein, 1.1 per cent fat and 13 per cent carbohydrates, whereas, *khutura* contains 64 per cent calorie, 4.7 per cent protein, 0.5 per cent fat and 4.7 per cent carbohydrates. These herbs are not cultivated, but grow in the natural surrounding areas of the homestead land. So, the villagers get their required vitamin from these herbs. On the otherhand they cultivate *Marisha* (*Amaranthus gangeticus Linn*) and *Lai* (a kind of mustard) in their kitchen garden. *Marisha* contains 39 per cent calorie, 3.9 per cent protein, 0.4 per cent fat and 3 per cent carbohydrates. *Dhekia* (Diplazium esculentum) available in the surrounding areas contains calorie about 14 per cent, protein 5 per cent and carbohydrates

3.2 per cent. Similarly, *Ou tenga* (*Dillenis Indica*) is rich in protein and calorie. Various folk songs were also evolved out of these available herbs, e.g. *Outala* (r) *dhekia, kenha tala* (r) *butiya, jogibilo* (r) *kandhuli mas* though nobody's choice, yet if prepared properly becomes a delicious meal. Folk songs are normally composed on the basis of their day-to-day incidents and most of the tribal as well as rural populations are rich in their folk songs.

It has also been reported that the Tai Khamyangs take various herbs and plants as vegetables, e.g. *Ketury* (wild turmeric), *Musandari* (*Houttuynia cordata thumb*), *Mehundi lata* (*Croton caudatus Geisel euphorbiaceae*), *Mishmi teeta* is a kind of bitter medicinal plant root brought down by the tribe *Mishmis* (captis teeta). Besides *Keheru* (a kind of esculent root, scipus kysoor) contains a very favourite item in their diet. Some other common shrubs taken by the Tai Khamyangs are *Mesaki-goch* (*Sarcochlamys pulcherrima Gaud* (*Urticaceae)* Eng. *Duggal fibre* tree, *Mejenga* [*Zanthoxylum oxyphyllum*, *Medeluwa pat* (*cassia sophera linn*)], *Tikonia Barua* (*Byttneria grandiflora*), *Lehati sak,* etc. They normally collect these plants from the nearby reserve forest during the *Chang Kyan* festival, when the roots came out during monsoon. All have medicinal values and the people are aware about their preventive capacity against many common ailments (Barua, 1998:318). They take special care to preserve the particular area, where these herbs and shrubs grow naturally and never totally uproot the plants. Thus the herbs and shrubs that are collected get naturally replenished during the following season. The preservation of natural resources and its restrictive uses rest on the shoulders of women, which help in sustainable living. Because of the important role played by the women, tribal economy has often been called "female economy" (Boserup, 1970).

The primal people were very conscious about the harmful effect of over extraction of plants. They showed sufficient ecological wisdom in collecting the plants from the nature. Their collection is always limited to meet the day-to-day need only. They live not only for them, but live for the future generation. Because of their indigenous knowledge and wisdom, they have contributed in their own way for the development of human culture and civilization.

All the forest dweller tribes follow a unique way of collecting and preserving the commodities from forest. The collection of roots and tubes are the main economy of Kadars of Kerela. "They excavate the roots in a particular fashion. They dig up the earth up to 2m in length and 10 cm in breadth with the help of an iron implement locally called *Purakole*. After taking out the *Titam,* the ditch is left for further growth" (Vidyarthy & Rai, 1976:121).

Indigenous tribes from the very early stage took care of preservation. Ojibway Indians who depend on wild rice followed more or less same procedure of preservation. They took care to preserve and protect the area where wild paddy grows naturally. When it matures, it is collected, consumed and distributed among their fellow beings. They take special care of the plot so that they would get the desired return in the next year. Though wild, the entire process projects the main principle's of economic structure, e.g. production and consumption, and distribution pattern.

There are various examples where wild herbs, shrubs and paddy play an important role in the process of cultivation. The Tiwas of Assam require a special variety of paddy which grows naturally in the midst of stones; since the shape of place is almost like a *Jakoi,* i.e. fishing basket and is commonly known as *Jakoi Sila Dhan*. During *Lakhmi puja* they select a few pre-puberscent girls, who are given the task of collecting the wild paddy from the hills. In the meantime, the villagers collect a handful of grains from each household and gather it in a common place. Then the wild grains which are collected from the hills are mixed with it. These grains are again distributed among the families, who then preserve the grains for the next year's cultivation. It is believed that this act will give a good product to each household. As they are aware about the significance of the paddy, they take special care for the growth and preservation of this wild paddy in the forest. Such incident naturally reminds us the man-nature relationship (Barua & Dutta Das, 2006:25) or one way of transforming the wild paddy for permanent cultivation. Moreover, it reflects the wisdom of indigenous population about the ways of preservation.

Most of the tribes of North-East India use more or less same food materials, but the processing and preparation of food item vary from tribe to tribe. The whole of South East Asia is rich in bamboo and the Mongoloid culture is invariably referred as "bamboo culture". Fermented bamboo shoots are a popular dish among all the tribes of North East India. Normal method of processing among the Sonowal Kacharis and the Deoris is that the young and tender shoots are cut into small slices. These are then kept in a bamboo cylinder and made airtight with *Nora* (paddy straw). The shoots are also ground in husking lever (*Dhenki).* After adding water it is preserved either in the earthen pot or in glass jars. Ground bamboo shoots are also preserved for longer period by adding salt and turmeric. Sometimes, dried bamboo shoots are ground and preserved in powdered form. It is normally consumed as *chutney*. Bamboo shoots are mixed in meat/ fish dishes to make it tastier.

Different schalars from time to time explain the nutritious values of bamboo shoots. "The juvenile shoots are not only delicious but are rich in nutritents components, mainly proteins, carbohydrates, mineral and fibres and low in fat and sugar. In addition, they contain phytosterols and a high amount fibre that can be labelled as nutracenticals or natural medicine" (Chongtham *et al.,* 2011). However, there is a belief among the rural communities of Assam including the various tribes that if bamboo shoots are taken excessively, the chronic diseases may be revived. Controversial opinion also exists among the scholars about the presence of cyanide in bamboo shoots and its harmful effect (Dutta, 2014). However, repeated washing and the preparation method might have reduced this harmful effect. In case of insect bite like *baral* (wasp, vespa sp), bees (Apic Indica) the *kharisa* (preferably 1-2 years old) works wonder when it is applied in the affected area and the person gets relief. Each ethnic group has their own indigenous way of preparing bamboo shoots based on experience. When there is scarcity of bamboo shoots it mostly taken as side dish. It is also used as one of the ingredients for preparing a variety of dishes which includes fish/meat/vegetables, etc.

Majority of the tribes of North East India make the bamboo shoots into small pieces and keep it into small and large bamboo basket. Sometimes the whole basket is covered tightly with banana leaves or mud and left for 6 to 8 days for fermentation. The *Adi* women (Padam sub-tribe) after processing the bamboo shoots make the semi-fermented shoots into small packet. It is tightly wrapped in *Ekkam* leaves. These packets are then pressed under the stones near the water stream falling from the top of the hills, for several months (3-4 months) to reduce the bitterness. These have many medicinal values (Singh *et al.*, 2007:86). It is also emphasized that it helps in reducing the cyanogenic glycoside content due to the activity of yeast and bacteria such as *Lactobacillus lactis*, which causes major deseases related to nervous system, goiter and miscarriage.

It was also reported that in the hilly areas of Manipur, use fermented bamboo shoots (*Soibum*) along with fermented fish

(*Singiamis*) against plague disease. For preparing fermented fish, required amount of fishes are kept in an earthen pot making it airtight and left for over 2 to 3 months for fermentation. When it is required for using, the earthen pot is opened and the fermented fish is mixed with bamboo shoots and other leafy vegetables (Singh *et al.*, 2007:87). In this way same materials are processed, prepared and preserved in a variety of ways. The entire process is largely depended on cultural tradition.

Fermentation of plants and vegetables as a method of food preparation and preservation are practiced by many tribes and communities of North East India. The Bhutias of Sikkim put the green leaves (*Lai Sak*) in a tin. The tin container is kept in a pit covered with soil. After one month the fermentation is complete. After that the fermented *Lai Sak* is dried in the sun and can be preserved for two years. It is refered as *Gundruk* (Sing, *et al.*, 2007).

Raddish (*Mula*) are fermented by the Gurung tribe of Sikkim. After properly cutting into small pieces the raddish are dried in the sun for 3-4 days. The dried pieces are kept in polythene and placed inside a pit covered with cowdung and soil paste. The fermentation is completed within 15 days. These are used for making soup. It is found to be very effective in curing diarrhoea, stomach pain and consumed mostly during the lean period (*Ibid.,* 2007).

Thus, it may be said that the fermentation of vegetables and plant materials no doudt reflect the wisdom of indigenous population. It is not simply used as food items but has required medicinal properties also.

Khar (Alkali) is a favourite item for them. They prepare *Khar* from various items, e.g. *Matimah*, a kind of pulse (*Phaseolus radiantus*) *Kal-khar* (banana leaves) plantain (*Musa sapientum*) and *Kher* (thatching paddy straw). Normally, alkali is stored in bottles or jars. A spoon is added to any preparation and it becomes a delicious side dish.

Besides the normal food items, most of the tribes of North-eastern states prefer to eat insects, which are prepared in various ways. Some of them have rich medicinal values.

Amroli ant/red ant (*Oecophyla smarandina*) and *Wisiring* (*Acheta Domestica*) are favourite dishes of the Sonowal Kacharis and the Deoris. Almost all the tribes of North East India have their own method of preparation. The people of rural Assam invariably take this item during *Bohag Bihu* (Assamese New Year). It is believed that it would prevent them from various diseases. Eggs and larva of the red ants are collected from the nest of ants. Usually it is fried in onion and chilly.

Wisiringa (Acheta Domestica): At first, they try to identify or locate the ditches and canals where these insects are found. After collecting, their feathers are removed. Then it is prepared by either frying or roasting in fire.

Bees (*Apis Indica*) and *Baral* (*wasp, vespa* sp) are another delicious dish. Eggs and larva of the bees (*Apis Indica*) and *Baral* (*Wasp, Vespa sp)* are also taken by the Sonowal Kacharis, Boros and some other tribes of Assam. It is believed that this act as medicine in case of kidney disorder, rheumatism and eye trouble.

Ari polu (*Philosiomia ricini*), ***Muga polu*** (*Antheraca Assamensis*) and ***Pat polu*** *(Bombynimani)* are considered very delicious by the Tai Ahoms, the Mishings, the Sonowal Kacharis, and the Deoris. Larva and eggs are boiled and then fried in onion, as done in the preparation of eggs.

Besides these insects, there are various other insects which are consumed by most of the tribes of North East India.

White ant (*Odontotermes obesus*) is taken by some of the tribes of North East India. These are roasted in fire either with feathers or featherless. During summer, after a heavy shower in the evening, it is considered as the favourable time for mating by the white ants. A bucket of water and a lighted candle/earthen lamp are kept outside. The light attracts the ants that fall into the water. Their feathers become soft in water and the ants cannot fly. When fried, feathers are automatically removed from the body. These are then grinded with onion and garlic and become delicious *chutney*.

***Lingkori (Agabetes acuductus or hydrochora ricksecker*i)**: This is another popular delicacy among all section of the Boros, including Sonowal Kacharis and the Mishings. Insects are collected from ponds and prepared after roasting or frying in oil.

Heiroglyphus banian, commonly referred as *Pharing* is consumed particularly by the Tiwas of Assam. After removing the feathers it is either roasted in fire or fried in oil.

The Ao Nagas of Nagaland prepare a special dish known as *Chonglong*. It is made from insects which are found in *Naga badam* (Almond) tree and other dry/putrefied trees or logs. At first, the collected insects are washed in hot water and then it is boiled with bamboo shoot (*Bastenga*) till the water is soaked. After this, these are kept in an airtight container. At the time of using, these are slightly warmed and are taken with rice. It is also used as sauce by mixing it with chilli and salt. They also use it as mouth freshner at the time of fever (Barua & Barua, 2009:314). The Ao Nagas also consume some insects (viz. *Grass hopper, Mantis,* etc.). All these substances also fulfil the need of protein and fat in their body.

Most of the insects taken by different tribes are rich in protein and the tribal people get the required nutitions from the least costly materials available in their vicinity.

Jebangkori (*Lethocerum Grandis*) locally known as *Niangprah* among the people of Manipur is one of the delicious items prepared from the insects. These are either roasted or fried in oil. Approximately 20 different varieties of insects are taken by the people of Manipur.

Crabs and snails are their favourite dishes. All section of the Kacharis eats only one kind of snail. They boil the snail and take out the meat portion out of it. It is then fried in mustard oil. Sometimes they prepare curry with boiled snails and rice powder. In this way, knowingly or unknowingly the diet of the people is usually supplemented by a number of subsidiary foods. "The Bemba, for instance, who has little meat, eats caterpillars, locusts and flying ants, the first being quite an important item of their diet, and containing a high proportion of phosphorus and iron" (Firth, 1941:49).

In the family level, they adapt various measures to preserve their foodstuff for future use. The people are very much aware about the security of their food. Each community has developed different ways and means to satisfy the community need. In the Nocte (Naga) village, there is common granary where they store the grains. After every harvest, the village youth collect paddy from each household and store paddy in the common granary. The amount of paddy collected depends upon the harvest of the farmer. The needy villagers may take paddy from this granary, which they have to return in the next year. At the end of every year, the surplus in the granary is sold in the market and the amount, so collected, is used for the improvement of village libray, school building, approach road, etc. (Barua, 2009:41). Among the Tiwas also, there is a provision of common granary where each family have to contribute about thirty five kg of paddy after the harvest. In time of crisis, the individual family may borrow paddy from this granary, but they will have to return it with an additional amount of seventeen kg per thirty kg of paddy (*Ibid.*, 2009:43).

The Karbis have traditionally maintained grain bank, called *Kerung Amei.* They maintained three types of grain banks. In the first type all the families, irrespectives of their social status have to contribute 5 kg of paddy after the annual harvest to the grain bank. During the lean month of the next year, the poor and needy families are given paddy on loan with the condition that the principal amount along with 50 per cent interest in kind must be returned after the harvest (Bordoloi *et al.*, 1987:66). In the second and third type, a plot is assigned to the youth and the aged respectively and after the harvest; the product is kept in the granary. During lean months, paddy is given as loan to the needy Karbi families to be repaid with 50 per cent interest after the harvest. The excess may be sold to the Karbi families at 10 per cent less than the prevailing market price. The third bank serves as the co-operative credit society. Paddy of the bank is sold when the price goes up and the sale proceeds are given to the needy families as loan to be repaid with cent per cent interest.

In most of the villages there is a common pond at the centre of the village or in some suitable spot. Fishes are available in the ponds, but the villagers are not allowed to fish in such ponds. Fishing in the village ponds is allowed only during *Bihus* or community ceremonies.

The existence of such community based voluntary organizations is universal in human society and is perhaps a survival trait from the stages of primodial social formation. If we look back to history, there seems to be little doubt that the presence of a natural crop of barley on the banks of the Nile in Upper Egypt was the pre-disposing factor in the starting the vast revolution in the affairs of mankind which prepared the way for the creation of civilization. This may tentatively be estimated at 4000 BC and settled life began. Since then a settled life with an assured supply of food was favourable to a rapid increase of population and to the cultivation of arts and crafts. The attempts to store animal food led to the discovery of drying and salting as means of preserving fish. The traditional knowledge which passed on from one generation to the next no doubt carries the seeds of various indigenous knowledges and helps in the development of human civilization.

The tribal people all over the world are abandoning their indigenous foodstuff due to many unavoidable reasons, the most acute may be considered as urbanization/industrialization. This has happened with the indigenous people of British Columbia—and all across Canada. As a result both their food sovereignty and food security have been undermined. The arrival of a colonial power and their new attitudes prevented the indigenous people to depend on their earlier roots and shrubs. Because these new arrivals imported livestock, and these took their toll on the root-digging ground. The pigs and cattle started to destroy roots and shrubs by digging the ground. Along with the loss of food itself, perhaps even more serious is the loss of cultural knowledge relating to the production, harvesting, processing and use of the food–the knowledge that has sustained generation of people in their home territories for thousands of years (Deur & Turner, 2005, cited from Turner & Turner, 2008). It was also reported that, of the approximately 100 species of plant food that were harvested traditionally by indigenous people of British Columbia, the majority are no longer used, and many are not even known to the younger generation (*Ibid.*).

In NE India due to deforestation various plants and shrubs are shranking. "Going by current figures, approximately 1-1.5 per cent of forest cover is lost every year in the North-eastern region due to deforestation. With the increase in population pressure, the need for firewood is expected to increase, which means cutting down trees faster than they grow" (Pandey, 2000:25).

The interests of the new generation for tea plantation have also reduced the earlier homestead garden or pheriphery of forest where many herbs and shrubs used to grow naturally. Industrialization also adversely affected the production. The study among the Tai Khamyangs reveals that waste from Oil fields badly affects the soil. According to the villagers, production decreases up to ¼ of the earlier products (Barua, 1998:324). It not only affects their economy, but directly or indirectly makes an impact on food habits.

As the indigenous people are living at the mercy of nature, they are to take various measures to conserve the nature for the security of their own community. Depending on environment and cultural values, the procedures of utilization vary from community to community, but it is also a universal fact that human beings are always aware of balancing ecosystem and maintaining harmony with nature. There are lots of examples cited by scholars about the relationship between ecology, subsistence pattern and culture. Roy A. Rappaport in his book "Pigs for Ancestors", narrated about pigs and rituals in highland New Guinea. It stated, like many other highland peoples, the Tsembaga are horticulturists who also keep pigs. About once every 15 years something mysterious happens. They slaughter nearly all their pigs and after a huge party, they go to war against their neighbours. This they claim is something they do out of deference to their ancestors. But Rappaport interpreted the entire incident in a different way. He found that pigs consume the same food as humans in their environment and thus need surplus food. Pigs are, therefore, slaughtered for bride price and feasting at the end of the war. So, the pigs must be kept at exactly the right number. Moreover, after a few years of slash and burn cultivation, the soil become impoverished. When the pigs are slaughtered and the Tsembaga go to war, followed by building a new village in a new location, they do so for ecological reasons. They gain access to new land and can again begin raising pigs in modest numbers. Rappaport's explanation was not just ecological, but functional too.

What this kind of study may tell us is perhaps not so much how ecology affects society, but about societal flexibility in managing the relationship with the ecological surroundings. Human responces to the environment is important. As Herald Eidheim once said, "cultural ecology may not tell us a lot about ecology, but it definitely teaches us something about culture" (Erikson, 2008:130).

5

Transmission of Indigenous Knowledge Through Socialization

In the present chapter, an effort has been made to focus on how indigenous knowledge of a particular ethnic group is transmitted through the process of socialization/culturalization. To understand the entire process of transmission various parameters have been considered. Moreover, transmission process differs from culture to culture, population to population in various environmental conditions. Each community has its own process of transmitting the traditional knowledge from one generation to another. The parameters considered in this study are: reproductive health, child rearing practices, beliefs, values, and attitudes associated with the entire process.

Health of women and children has always been a major concern for the Anthropologists and Social Scientists. Health of a child depends very much on the care given to the mother during pregnancy and child birth. Various beliefs and superstition normally determine the entire process. The Reproductive and Child Health (RCH) programme was launched in India on October 15, 1997 inspired by action plans and approaches emerging out of the International Conference on Population and Development (ICPD) in Cairo during 1994 and the Beijing Conference in 1995. It reflects not only the vulnerability inherent in the biological and behavioural aspects of reproduction, growth, development and malnutrition but also the social, cultural and historical situation of societies. Reproductive health can be defined as a state in which people have the ability to reproduce and regulate the fertility. The fertility period of women begins on the onset of menarche and ends with menopause. Repeated child bearing, short birth intervals and pregnancy at an early age cause high risk to the health of a woman. It is observed that too many, too close, too early and too late pregnancies are the major causes of maternal, fatal infant and childhood morbidity and mortality (Mexico City Conference 1984). Overall biological, social and cultural factors are responsible for the women's reproductive health.

Child rearing practices play a dominant role in the transmission of values relevant in a particular culture. Child care process generally refers to all the interaction between parents and their children. These interactions include the parent's expression of attitudes, values, interest and beliefs, as well as their care taking and behavioural training modes. Most of the social scientists and psychologists agree on the point that childhood experiences play a very dominant role in the development of individual's life. The child is a living growing organism. He grows in a family which belongs to a group. Thus, the child starts with a biological foundation and grows up in social environment. Since the child lives and grows in a social context, the people in his environment, particularly the parents and the other members of the family earlier, and the teachers and his fellow pupils in the school later, they are very significant in determining the ways in which the child develops. To learn to be human takes time, and that is why the young of human kind are characterized by the longest dependency period in the whole kingdom of nature.

The term child rearing or training is often employed as synonyms to socialization. How to rear children so that they will become adequate adult members of a society is an old and pervasive problem in human life. Almost all the earlier monographs focused on this aspects under the heading "The Life-Cycle of an individual", "From birth to puberty", etc. many different terms were also used. Kuckhohn preferred 'culturalization' and Herskovits proposed 'enculturation'. Although an interest in child rearing is as old as man himself, yet the term 'socialization' was the daring choice of the 1967 conference of association of Social Anthropology held at the University of Birmingham. After that conference it became popular among the Anthropologist. The child socialization has been a topic of interest among Sociologists, Anthropologists and Educationists.

Socialization, in its narrow sense, tends to be confined to the social learning of the children, to the process whereby, they acquire the values of adult society, so as to participate fully within it. In the broader sense, it may be extended to adults, whereby they join a new social group and are expected to acquire a new set of values before participating fully within it. In any culture, it is through the process of socialization that the child acquires the attitudes and values of that culture and develops into an individual with culturally appropriate behaviour pattern. In the course of development, the child goes through two major developmental process simultaneously, individualization and socialization. Elkin and Handel (1972) define socialization as the process by which one learns the ways of a given society so that one can function within it. During the process, many of the interactions occur between the child and other members, particularly between parents and children. Some of these interactions arise out of care taking, feeding, cleaning and protecting. Some are expressions of love or annoyance-reaction, which may not have direct impact on the child's future, but they have significant influence on the growth and development of children's behaviour.

If the term socialization is restricted to the learning of social roles only, then it normally exclude's the transmission of beliefs, values and other cognitive aspects of culture. In reality, socialization covers various dimensions of culture. Socialization is a lifelong development process and does not cease its importance after childhood. Child rearing practices or many of the ideas has changed along with the changing social conditions. However, many of our cultural values continue to exert influence on our life which is transmitted through the process of child rearing itself. It is well known that all parents consciously or un-consciously transmit their specific life style to their offspring. It was considered as an essential part of their social process. Later on, it formed the ground work for civilization. Anthropologists have made us aware that the socialization process and its mechanism have an important role in transmission and survival of any culture. Considering the importance of the process, Albert (1965) has said, "Universal failure in socialization would mean extinction of a society".

An individual's cultural heritage provides the child with certain norms and values which are internalized in the individual's super-ego during the course of development. The super-ego constitutes the categorial conscience which represents the rights and wrongs, the prohibitions and mores of a given social milieu. It "becomes the vehicles which have been handed down in their way from generation to generation" (Freud, 1933 referred from, Norton, 1973:67). It is assumed that different pattern of child rearing will lead to differences of behaviour and thus differences in adult roles. Individual children may be given different chores or tasks of various kinds and analysis of pattern of child socialization may be made from their behaviour in games and recreational activities, ritual and ceremonial life or beliefs about supernatural. Children in large and busy cities may be taught to watch out for automobiles, while children in remote hilly region might be taught to watch out for dangerous animals. In both the cases, the aim is to train the child for safety and survival. Thus, it can be said that ecology, economy, social and political organization are by and large parameters for the behaviour of the agent of socialization. Besides, by learning stories, folk tales also, they learn many things about their culture.

The usual contention is that the ecology of an area determines the maintaining system which includes the basic economy and the most elementary variable of social structure. These basic economic conditions determine in parts the arrangement of people in space, the type of houses and household composition. These in turn, set the parameters for child rearing practices. It is obvious that ecology does more than to set gross parameters for social structure. Within these parameters, the nature and composition of household, neighbourhood and other social groups will make differentiation in child socialization, e.g. Whether or not a grand mother lives in the house or whether other close relatives are at hand will influence a mother's behaviour towards her child. The mechanism of socialization refers to the methods and practices which directs the social learning.

Cultural Anthropologists have described the child rearing processes as a part of enculturation or a mechanism of the transmission of culture. Culture traits are natural, yet they are not a part of the nature. These traits are specific influence and pattern of response in similar situation. This influence is mainly apparent in the early years when a child is physically and emotionally dependent on the mother. The status of women is also considered as an important dimension because according to it, the rearing of male/female child varies. In fact, social learning theorists assert that socializing process or socializing agents are of significant importance on the life of an individual.

A number of studies have appeared in which family structure variables are examined in relation to socialization outcome of children. Strocttbeck's study of the influence of family interaction in Jewish and Italian families (1958) on their son's achievement values and Yarrow's (1962) study of child rearing in families of working and non-working mothers reflect the trend towards the consideration of social system and/or social role variables.

Physical and social environment, formal and casual institutions play an important role in child socialization. Environment is one of the basic factors that relates to education and its progress and development. It provides the base as well as means of learning. It is the environment alone which gives external as well as internal stimulus to all-round development of the child. The growth and development of the child, his pace of progress, quality and pattern of development are all dependent on interaction between his heredity potential, environment and the self factors. Heredity provides the basic elements for development which are acquired by the child from his parents. Environment helps the child to grow and develop out of his hereditary potential. Through interaction between heredity and environment, the child begins to grow and develop. Most of the social scientists and psychologists agree on the point that childhood experiences play a very dominant role in the development of individual's life. Family, which is the smallest unit of society, plays an important role in the socialization of children. The family trains the child in social values, norms and customs and to a certain extent in the tradition of society. It has been mentioned, "all the socialization techniques employed by the adults are probably, less effective in the modification of the children behaviour than the observation and intimation through which the children gradually absorb the skills, customs and values of the group" (Minturn & Hitchock, 1963:331). Slowly in the process of upbringing, the child experiences different customs, rituals, beliefs, prejudices and acquire's its folkways and mores. Most of the training in early childhood is not conscious training. The unconscious training and learning makes him understand his own culture. Each family in every culture has a set of expectations and relationship which influence the eventual development of social skills, behaviour and attitudes. Social contact is necessary for normal development of the infant and child. When children are isolated and brought up with minimum social contact, particularly up to six years, they will show few human responses, like the "wolf children". Thus, family plays an important role in introducing children to their culture.

But there exists a period before the formal institution, which also play an important role in socialization process, i.e. the reproductive health of the mother. Reproductive health can be defined as a state in which people have the ability to reproduce and regulate the fertility.

The fertility period of a woman begins on the onset of menarche and ends with menopause. Besides biological factor, various social and cultural aspects are equally responsible in the child rearing/ socialization process.

All the communities have certain indigenous beliefs and practices, preference and prohibition which directly or indirectly influence the socialization process. It has already been mentioned that each culture has its own way to transmit the values and customs. In the present project two major indigenous communities, i.e. the Sonowal Kacharis and Deoris have been studied. Child rearing practices of each community have been described followed by a detailed discussion on child rearing practices as a whole.

A. Sonowal Kacharis

The Sonowal Kacharis shares a strong desire to have children. The fertility of women qualifies as well as quantifies her social status in the community. The Sonowal Kacharis observe each stage of development by performing elaborate rituals.

Menarche is a biological phenomenon which gets expression in women and is an important stage of life cycle. Each stage of biological change is always associated with rites and rituals and prohibitions and superstitions. "Initiation ceremonies, which marks, the stages of growth, particularly the transition from childhood to adult life, are far more common, among the males than corresponding rites for females" (Piddington, 1963:176). Of course, it does not mean that this stage is not ritually marked among the women. In almost all human societies, this physiological change among the women is ceremonially marked with a slight variation from culture to culture. According to the reports of various investigations, the age at menarche is found to vary from population to population and depends on various factors like environment, society, economic condition, nutrition and heredity. The mean menarcheal age among the Kachari is 12.77 years (Deka, 1975). A study undertaken among the Sonowal Kacharis (Barua, 1996:7) reveals that they observe the puberty ritual very elaborately.

The Sonowal Kacharis celebrate puberty rite in a colourful way than the actual marriage. It is also considered as a status symbol for the family. When a girl first gets the indication of menarche, she informs it to her mother, who immediately sends the message to her friends and invites some of the elderly women. The girl has to follow some rules and regulations during this period. She is lodged in a room and kept away from male person. A sickle is kept just below her bed and she is to carry it whenever she goes out. She is assumed to be very tender during these days and it is believed that she might be affected by bad omen. In the meantime, the father consults an astrologer informing him of the time and day of menstruation. After calculation the astrologer finds out the type of restrictions to be observed by the girl till the day of ceremony. She is allowed to take only uncooked food and fruits for three days.

On the fourth day a small ritual is observed to which only women and girls are invited. A bathing place is prepared placing four banana plants at the four corners. The girl is then given a ceremonial bath. After bath, she is dressed in a new set of *Mekhela chaddar* and takes her seat in the midst of her friends and invitees. In the meantime women folk prepare *Dulani* and *Kalochi* and keep this in front of her. *Dulani* is a small bamboo basket containing half a kg of rice, two *Kaldil* (plantain spike), and one tender banana leaf, a pair of betel nut, one knife, looking glass, one comb, one earthen lamp and one bottle of mustard oil. *Kalochi* is a small earthen pitcher filled with water, fastening its neck with raw white thread. The guests are entertained only with *Pithaguri* (rice-powder) and milk. The girl bows before the gathering and seeks their blessings. From that day, the girl is allowed to take rice only once a day, normally with potato and salt just before sun set. The rice is cooked in a *Mola* (earthen pot) by one of the pre-pubescent girl or by her mother.

In the mean time, preparation is made for the final ceremony, which is to be observed either on the 5th or 7th or 9th day according to the astrological prescription. Before the ceremonial day, the girl takes her bath in the evening and is dressed with new clothes. Her friends stay with her for the whole night. A small ritual, i.e. *Murat-tel-diya* is performed by the elderly women, where they pour mustard oil on her head by keeping a betel nut on a golden ring. While singing the *Biya nam* (wedding song) they offer various advices to the girl. Her friends remain busy in preparing for the ceremony. Some make garlands of mango leaves and hang them on the door frame, while others grind rice and make everything ready.

On the ceremonial day, early in the morning, arrangements are made for a ceremonial bath of the girl. Three pre-puberscent girls are invited to perform specific roles. One of them is to carry the *Dulani*, the other is to carry the *Kalochi* and the third is to sprinkle *Shanti-*

pani (purificatory water). Along with the other elderly women, they proceed towards the river side. First, they clean a side by the river or pond and keep nine banana leaves and two pair of betel nut and leaves. Some amount of rice is put on each leaf. In the front end of each leaf, they keep one burning *salita* (lamp wick). Finally, they perform the ritual act of *Panikata*, i.e. by inserting the knife into water. They symbolically cut the water. It is believed that this act purifies the water from the effect of the evil spirits. This is done four times and the purified water is collected in the pitcher. After completing this ritual, they return home. The girl is then taken out of the room, covering her with a *Chaddar*. At the door step, they observe the *Daiyan-diya,* i.e. one of the female relations after having dipped the betel leaves in curd touches her cheeks, arms, and feet with those leaves so moistened. The girl is then brought to the *Bey* (temporary platform for giving bath). Before taking seat, she is moved around the *bey* three times. At first her mother gives her ceremonial bath with a paste of *Mah-haladhi* (turmeric and gram paste). A small banana plant is placed in one corner of the *Bey*, facing either towards east or west. The banana plant is symbolically considered as her husband and it is anticipated that her future husband would reside in that direction. The mother also gives a ceremonial bath to the plant. After that the *Dulonidhara, Kalachi dhara* and other invitees repeat the same. It is considered as a good sign if the banana plant produces fruit in time. (These are then distributed among the cowherds.) When the ceremonial bath is over, she is dressed in a new set of *Mekhela chaddar* and brought to the main *Pandal* in the courtyard. The colour of the dress is normally determined by the astrologer. The womenfolk sing *Biyanam* and wish and bless her offering various presents. They also make fun by rubbing dry rice-powder on each other's face.

As she is also assigned a status of full grown girl from that period, elderly woman perform a small rite known as doll play or *Kaina lowa*. They make a doll with the help of a *gamosa* and beads. The doll is symbolically considered as a baby who is placed on the girls lap. The girl is to return it after fondling it. This is repeated three times. On certain occasion, a small child is placed on her lap and it is believed that if a male child is fondled on that day then she would bear male child in future. The whole process of this doll play is nothing but a symbolic rite of fertility of women. The girl bows before the gathering who offers certain advices as she retains an important stage of life.

The puberty ritual is observed in the same manner by other rural Assamese people. The caste Hindus have gradually abandoned this rite, while the Sonowal Kacharis are very particular about it. When enquired about the reason for elaborate performance of this ritual most of them are of the opinion that generally conjugal marriage is performed by process of elopement so they do not get the opportunity to celebrate it. Secondly, it may be a way of announcement that the girl has attained proper time for conjugal marriage. The present study also reveals that the marriage by elopement dominates among the Sonowal Kacharis. The data collected from Jakai Harak Pathar during 1991 reveals that the Sonowal Kacharis got married at an early age. Most of the marriages took place within the age of 16 to 30 years in case of males and in case of females it is within 16 to 25 years. Regarding the type of marriages, 44 were by way of elopement, 30 by simple negotiation and one was performed through extensive negotiation out of a total sample size of 76. The data collected from Lepetkata Kachari village during 1993 also focuses that the frequency of marriage was highest within the age group of 25 to 30 years for males and 15 to 19 years for females. Elopement marriage is also higher among them.

It has already been mentioned in *Chapter* 2; that the Sonowal Kacharis perform their marriage ceremony through four different ways, depending on the socio-economic condition. A couple generally expects a child after one year of their marriage. But if it goes beyond two years, it worries them and they try to find ways and means for having baby and seek advice from both modern and traditional practices.

Pregnancy after marriage is a matter of pride and a childless mother is not considered as a complete woman. She is debarred from taking active part in some religious activities. There exist various beliefs and practices relating to pregnancy and birth of a new born. When the family members know about the pregnancy, the elderly women offer various suggestions to the expectant mothers about what to do and what not to do. As a whole they are not worried about pregnancy as they consider it as a natural phenomenon in their life. And there are no restrictions on any type of work. She handles her household duties till her health does allow. They continue all laborious household works up to 5 to 6 months of pregnancy. Taboos, restrictions and preferences are marked practically in all the Indian tribes in one form or the other.

Majority of women take normal diet as they cannot afford extra nutritive diet due to their poor economic conditions. But there is a general belief that pregnant woman should be fed with her desired dishes to ensure the birth of a healthy baby. Though there are no strict rule of avoidance during pregnancy, yet the pregnant woman never touches any cooked items which are sent from a family where death had occurred recently. Similarly, the husband is not allowed to attend the funeral ceremony and the rituals that are performed later on. The pregnant women are not allowed to stitch any torn cloth and majority of them keep mustard seeds with them. They are not allowed to sit or stand at the eaves during evening. More or less same types of restrictions are noticeable among the Boro Kacharis. "A pregnant woman is advised not to stand at the eaves or cut anything during the eclipse" (Barua & Barua, 2009:137). It is believed that such activities would bring harmful effect on the baby.

During pregnancy period, both the husband and the wife are not supposed to kill any animals. It is believed that it will be harmful for the foetus if one kills any living animals before delivery. The husband is advised not to fix handles of axe, knife, etc. It is believed that such act would make delivery painful. The husband is also not allowed to go for fishing or hunting during this period. Various beliefs and superstitions exist among different communities which reflect their indigenous ways of thinking and acting. Among the Sonowal Kacharis uses of amulet is popular. Normally, they do not use this, but in certain unusual case, the pregnant women go for it. The women are encouraged to do such work as grinding the paddy in *Dhenki* (husking lever). It is believed that such activities would make the delivery easy. They are allowed to take part in all activities relating to cultivation. But effort is made to avoid heavy work and it is considered that heavy work may lead to miscarriage.

Restrictions of diet of the pregnant women are a universal feature and it varies from culture to culture. A pregnant woman should not eat twin banana or any other pair of fruits or vegetables because it is believed that in such cases she will have twin baby. Eating of any edible pair of things is strictly prohibited for all males and females for fear of twin birth. However, men and women who have crossed the reproductive stage do not observe such a taboo. They are also not allowed to take alkaline food like papaya (*Carica papaya*), *brinjal, and silikha* (*Mysoballum*). "An Ao Naga expectant mother avoids eating twin fruits, hot chillies and tortoise; she avoids the sight of dying animals, monkeys, big snakes lest blindness should afflict her baby" (Vidyarthi & Rai, 1986:293).

The Sonowal Kacharis believe that the mother is solely responsible for the upbringing of children in early stage and it is assumed that they may form certain ideas regarding the ideal size of a family. An attempt has been made to find out the expected number of children from each family in the forest villages of Paroliguri and Nahoroni. In the absence of mother sometimes opinions are collected from the father. As they suggested diverse versions, 7 categories of opinions were found.

Table 5.1: Expected Number of Children per family in Paroliguri and Nahoroni

Categories	*Number of Children*
1 son, 1 daughter	43
2 sons 1 daughter	26
2 sons, 2 daughters	14
1 son, 2 daughters	3
1 son	2
3 sons, 1 daughter	1
Any two	2

From Table 5.1 it is clear that there are 2 women who prefer single child, i.e. a son in the household. Health centre are 43 families where preference is given to 1 son and 1 daughter. Next higher percentage is found, i.e. 26 where they prefer 2 sons and 1 daughter. There are 14 families who prefer 2 sons and 2 daughters. It is interesting to note that in this category, one family has 3 daughters. Of course, there are differences between real and expected number of children in a family. There are 3 families, where the preference is 1 son and 2 daughters. There is only 1 family who has made their preferences on 3 sons and 1 daughter. And two mothers expressed that 2 children are enough for a family. She did not mention about the sex of a child.

The family is the most important asset of any community. And to have an ideal family is the preference of all human society. In every society, the couple has an opinion regarding the ideal size of a family, gap between two children, and their attitude towards family planning, care during pregnancy, etc. Overall, being a patriarchal society, the Sonowal Kacharis have preference for son. At the same time all are concerned about the training that should be given during the early years. Family welfare is a broader concept and includes both economic and social welfare of the family. Economic programmes and social education can make valuable contribution towards the promotion of family welfare. To find out the attitude towards family planning, a study was conducted where 25 Sonowal Kacharis women were interviewed (Barua & Gogoi, 1978: 108). The study revealed that 9 (36%) out of 25 respondents have been practicing family planning. Among these, it is found that weak health of the mother is the main reason of adoption of family planning method. It was also found that adoption of family planning of respondents having two children showed favourable attitudes towards the family planning programme. The study also revealed that majority of those who have not adopted family planning expressed that they want more male child. Overall, there is a difference between attitude and real picture and planning method was closely related to the number of children a couple already had. Fifty per cent of respondents having two children showed favourable attitude towards the family planning programme. The study also revealed that majority of those who have not adopted family planning expressed that they want more male child. Overall, there is difference between attidude and real picture.

A discussion on reproductive and child health among the Sonowal Kacharis reveal that they have various beliefs and practices relating to reproductive and child birth. The study also focus that as they are emotionally and culturally attached to it majority of them still follow it. An effort has been made to find out children below 5 years of age in the revenue village Duliagaon during the year 2010-11.

From Table 5.2 it is found that there are 48 children below 5 years of age in the present sample of population. Out of 110 families, the number of children within 5 years of age is 48 and the numbers of boys are 24, whereas equal numbers of girls are found, i.e. 24.

Place of delivery in most cases guided by social tradition. Among the Sonowal Kacharis there is no rigid rule regarding the place of delivery, but it is preferred that deliveries should take place at husband's house. Normally, it takes place in usual bed room and it was reported that earlier a separate room was kept for this purpose. To get rid of the spirits, thorny branches or torn fishing nets are hung in the door of the room. They also place a ladder and *Rash* (a weaving instrument) near the door.

Table 5.2: Distribution of children below 5 years of age in Duliagaon

Period	*Male*		*Female*		*Total*	
	No.	*Percentage*	*No.*	*Percentage*	*No.*	*Percentage*
From birth to 1 year	2	8.4	3	12.5	5	10.5
1-2 year	4	16.6	4	16.6	8	16.6
2-3 year	4	16.6	4	16.6	8	16.6
3-4 year	2	8.4	3	12.5	5	10.5
4-5 year	12	50.0	10	41.8	22	45.8
Total	24		24		48	100

Table 5.3 shows the place of birth according to sex. Most of the deliveries took place either at Borbaruah Health Centre or Assam Medical College, Dibrugarh. Maximum numbers (35.41%) of children were born at Assam Medical College, Dibrugarh. Next higher percentage, i.e. 33.33 per cent birth took place at Borbaruah Health Centre. But a significant number, i.e. 31.25 per cent where delivery took place at home.

Table 5.3: Place of Birth according to sex in Duliagaon

Place of Birth	*Male*	*Female*	*Total*	
			No.	*Percentage*
Home	7	8	15	31.25
A.M.C (Medical College)	7	10	17	35.41
Borbaruah Hospital	10	6	16	33.33
Total	24	24	48	100

In case of home delivery, normally the elderly women of the village extend their helping hand, because there is no professional mid-wife in the village. Generally, complicated cases like caesarean and forceps delivery are done at Assam Medical College, Dibrugarh. There are two *Asha Karmis* in the village who keep all the information about the pregnant women of the village. Once in two months, health care camps are held in the primary school of the village. The *Asha Karmis* visited each pregnant woman and advised and pursued them to come for health check up. The *Asha Karmis* get prescribed remuneration per delivery, so they take initiative in doing their work regularly. Moreover, now-a-days the Government has introduced various welfare schemes, where a woman gets money if delivery takes place in Government Hospital. So, the people prefer to take the advantage of delivery at hospital. Moreover, the Borbaruah Health Centre is nearly 2 km away.

Whereas, in another investigation done among the Sonowal Kacharis in Borbaruah area during 1979 revealed that number of home deliveries were significant. The percentage of delivery that took place at Assam Medical College was 38.37. Home delivery and birth at Borbaruah Health Centre are almost equal, i.e. 30.00 per cent and 31.42 per cent, respectively. In case of home delivery, they use a piece of split bamboo, sharpened into a knife to sever the umbilical cord. In case of complicacy, sometimes village medicine man (*bez*) is summoned. He performs certain rites in front of the door of the delivery room by breaking an egg. It is believed that such acts help in having a smooth delivery.

Thus, it is found that within the period sufficient improvement is visible in the Healthcare practices within the same locality. In case of home delivery, it is reported that they announce the birth of a boy by making *Uruli* (a trilling sound uttered by women in concert on any joyful occasion) and in case of girl, it is announced by making sound on the wall of the room. This act no doubt indicates that among the Sonowal Kacharis, preference is given to the birth of a boy. There also exist beliefs among the Sonowal Kacharis, regarding the prediction of sex of unborn child. It is believed that if she feels it on the left side, it is thought to be a male and if on the right, it is a female (Barua & Bora, 1979:336).

With regards to ***Antenatal Care,*** it is revealed that mostly it depends on the economic condition and awareness of the mothers. The present study reveals that the *Asha Karmis* are very active in this village. It has already been mentioned that fishes are available in various water sources. Though no specific care is provided with regards to food but considering the health of pregnant women, they provide the women as far as possible the fish curry prepared from *Magur, Singi,* and *Chengali*, etc. There are two *Asha Karmis* in the village. One of them reported that their main duty is to provide regular information to the expectant mother. They urge the pregnant women to come to Borbaruah Health Centre for regular check up and pursue them to take injections in the Health centre. They also provide to the pregnant woman 100 folic acid iron tablets which are supplied by the Health Department. Thus, it is revealed that pregnant women are getting sufficient information and regular support from the *Asha Karmis*.

After ***Birth*** certain beliefs and practices are followed in every community. Among the Sonowal Kacharis, just after the birth of a child, the placenta, which connect's the baby with the mother, is cut by a doctor in medical hospital. But in case of home delivery it is performed by any elderly experienced woman of the family or from the village. They invariably use a sharp piece of bamboo, which are available in their surroundings for this purpose. And the placenta, locally known as *phool*, is deeply buried in the permanent bed room of the couple. After filling earth, they give high-pressure by foot. This act is to be invariably done by the husband. They never bury it outside, as it is believed that it may be affected by spirits or evil eyes. The belief associated with it varies from culture to culture.

Among the Sonowal Kacharis, the time of removing the umbilical cord varies from child to child. For easy removal of the umbilical cord, they use oil, both coconut and mustard regularly. Gradually this cord get's dried and becomes blackish in colour. "They keep the cord of each child and a cage of cocoon is specially used for keeping this cord. It is believed that the water extracted from this dry cord is very useful for the child in case of certain diseases, like dysentery, fever, etc." (Barua & Bora, 1979:336). It is also believed that in future if any misfortune occurs then "they perform the *Ayu Tula* (bring back the life) by using the dried umbilical cord of the child" (Sonowal 2001:158). In some cases, this cord is put on the child's waist or arm with the help of a thread. It is believed that if a child wears it, he will be healthy and strong. After birth, a fire is kept burning inside the room and occasionally they pour mustard seed, garlic and *Boss* (*Acorus calamus Linn*) plant in the fire. A garland made of garlic and *Boss* is considered as a protection from evil eyes.

With regard to ***Post natal Care*** among the Sonowal Kacharis, it is revealed that, the mother and child are considered polluted for at least 16 days after the birth, though it actually depends on the falling of naval cord. The woman is not expected to attend any household duties during the period. As a result she gets rest for 10–15 days. This period starts from the birth of a child to the ritual of purification. The mothers get sufficient rest during this period. The ritual of purification is locally known as *Sudhi.* Therefore, till that time, a mother is considered as polluted.

The performance of purification ceremony differs on the basis of sex. In case of girl it is performed on 30th day and in case of boy it is performed on 25th days. In certain cases it is performed immediately after the falling of naval cord which sometimes happens on the 7th day. Even though, this time limit of pollution is not strictly adhered to these days, yet care is taken of both the mother and the child by other family members.

After 3 days of birth a curry is prepared with arum leaf, adding sufficient black pepper on it. It is believed that such kind of curry would heal the wound after delivery. They also believe that it would help in increasing the milk of mother. The mother is also given different varieties of curry prepared from *Sukhloti* (*Pogostemon benghalense)*, *Duran phool* (*Leucas linifolia*), etc. Sometimes these leaves are roasted after wrapping it with banana leaves. It is believed that the mother will regain health if she is taken care with such vegetables and curries.

After the falling of naval cord, the Sonowal Kacharis observe various rituals. Immediately after the falling of naval cord, the room where the delivery took place is cleaned and the straws and other related matters were burnt. The baby is also given a bath and they observe a ceremony of sun worship. A few elderly women are invited for the ceremony and a place is cleaned in the courtyard. A low wooden tool (*pira*) is placed where they put a *Gamosa;* a burning earthen *Chaki*; one jar of water, grinding stone. A burning bundle of straw is kept near the tool.

The mother, taking the baby in the lap moves round the tool three times. The mother is to throw four pairs of betel nut and leaf in different directions and the baby is shown towards the sun three times. Then, the baby is placed on the tool. The grinding stone is striked on the tool and it is then lightly put on the navel of the baby. This act is done three times and each time the mother expresses her wishes, i.e. "not to harm by fire, not to die by drowning and be safe from all unexpected troubles". Then a thorny branch (*bagiri jeng*) is thrown away after pulling below the feet of the baby.

The Sonowal Kacharis observe various measures to protect the child from evil eyes. If the mother, after spitting on the mud thrown up by earthworm and put's a spot on the forehead with it, then it is believed that the baby will be protected from all evil eyes. There is also a belief that "if the torn heddles of thread are wrapped on wrist and feet of the baby then the evil spirit may not harm the baby" (Sonowal, 2001:159). It is also believed that if the mother eats rice taking the baby in her lap, then the baby would be healthy and strong.

Feeding practices differ from culture to culture and are always been a topic of special interest with studies of child rearing practices. There are wide cultural variations regarding the onset of feeding, kind of feeding, length of feeding, introduction of solid food, etc. Mother's milk is considered to be the best for an infant. It has been revealed that the yellowish-lemonish looking fluid known as colostrums, which appears in the mother's breast towards the last month of pregnancy, contains certain antibodies which remain in the colostrums for only eight hours after the birth of the child. This would certainly suggest that the new born should have the opportunity to injest these antibodies at the earliest possible moment.

The Sonowal Kacharis mothers may not be aware of the medical significance and follow some practices which differ from place to place. It was reported that "after cutting the umbilical cord, the tongue of the new born is cleaned with the hair of the mother. Then a few drops of rice-beer are given to baby considering it as *prashad* of god" (Sonowal, 2001:158). But there is no strong prohibition of giving mother's milk immediately after birth. It is reported that onset of breast feeding appears to have cultural influence. "Among the Bodo Kacharis neonatal and infants are usually suckled by the mother and breast feeding usually continue's up to age of two or three years or till the delivery of the next child" (Barua & Barua, 2009:140).

Cultural factors play dominant role in feeding practices. "The Sonowal Kachari's mothers feed their children openly both within the house as well as outside. Except three cases, breast milk were the only food among the sample families" (Barua & Bora, 1979:338).

Weaning is also considered another important step in relation to child rearing practice. Weaning practices refer to the manner in which the infant is weaned from the mother's breast or the bottle. Among the Sonowal Kacharis, the age of weaning varies from family to family and also within the children of same family. The majority of the women tried to wean their children between 1½ years and 2nd year. In some cases, children were weaned before the 3rd month, due to shortage of breast milk.

There are various methods of weaning. Majority of them weaned automatically when they began to take solid food. But in certain cases, they are to use various harsh methods for weaning, e.g. using ashes, bitter objects, chillies, solid food, beating on the mouth of the child.

Beliefs associated with ***Teething*** also varies from culture to culture. Regarding the eruption of teeth, certain beliefs exist in all communities belonging to various cultural groups. "Among the Sonowal Kacharis, it is believed that a child will be greedy, if the first tooth erupts on the upper jaw. There is also a belief that if the child's first tooth erupts on 6th month after birth, it is considered good for the baby" (Barua & Bora, 1979: 340). Child health care refers to care of children from conception to birth and after birth till the age of five. Majority of the sample families kept good health during pregnancy and had safe deliveries. At the same time, abortion and miscarriage were also reported from the village.

Abortion

Abortion is a process by which the underdeveloped embryo can be destructed within the mother's womb before delivery by expert. This process of abortion is also found among the Sonowal Kacharis.

Table 5.4 reveals that there are four abortion cases found in the sample families. Maximum number of abortion cases is reported in the 2nd issue. Economic condition may be considered as one of the main reason behind abortion.

Table 5.4: Number of Abortions

Sequence of issue	*No. of Abortions*	*Percentage*
First Issue	—	—
Second Issue	3	75
Third Issue	1	25
Total	4	100

Miscarriage

It is a case of loss of children due to untimely and abnormal delivery before maturity of giving birth of a dead child. It differs from abortion in the sense that abortion is intentional and miscarriage is accidental. But the majority of women believe that it is due to the effect of evil spirit or black powder.

There are 4 cases of miscarriages reported from sample families

(Table 5.5). The number of miscarriage both in the first and second issue is 2.

Table 5.5: Numbers of Miscarriage

Sequence of Issue	*No. of Miscarriages*	*Parcentage*
First Issue	2	50
Second Issue	2	50
Total	4	100

Medical Facilities and Health Centre

There is no health sub-centre within the village. The villagers have to go to the Borbaruah Health Centre which is about 5 km away. For major and critical cases, Assam Medical College is within the reach of the villagers and is only 20 km away.

The child health is determined by overall living condition of a group of people, generally refers to the housing facilities, availability of drinking water, nature of environmental sanitation and quality of personal hygiene, etc. The children mostly suffer from fever, cough, dysentery, etc. The people of Dulia village usually vaccinate their children as per schedule. Formerly, people used to avoid or intentionally delay to get their children vaccinated. But with the spread of education and compulsion by the health department, people get their children vaccinated. Vaccination against DPT, Polio, BCG, and Typhoid are given appropriately.

Table 5.6 shows that all the children were vaccinated. Only 2 children were not given the last vaccine, because they were too young to be vaccinated. It is also revealed that children are mostly treated at Assam Medical College, at Borbaruah Health Centre and

Table 5.6: Schedule of Vaccination according to the sequence of Issue in Duliagaon

Time Period	*No. of Children (Male)*	*No. of Children (Female)*
Birth to 3 months	—	1
Between 3–6 months	1	—
Between 6–12 months	1	2
All injections completed	22	21
Total	24	24

at home, respectively. The common villagers also have the knowledge of treating the children by herbal medicine. For cough they prepare a mixture of basil leaves, ginger with a drop of honey in it. They also prescribe a paste of guava leaves which are considered effective in certain diseases like dysentery and loose motion. The children normally suffer from fever, cough, measles, asthma, dysentery, fever, etc. They are treated as per convention followed in the community. In minor cases they are treated at home by indigenous ways. In emergency they are taken to the hospital.

There are cases, when medical treatments did not work, they take the help of folk medicine man (*bez)* and according to their calculation perform *Deo puja, Apeswari Sabha*. The Sonowal Kacharis, as a whole believe in ancestral spirit and regularly perform *Pi-Diya, Mritakak diya* to propitiate their deity. Measles is another kind of skin disease common among the children for which they never go for medical treatment. Instead they perform *Ai sabha* by inviting three to five *Gopinis*.

B. The Deoris

The birth of a child is always a happy event among the Deoris like any community in the world. As a patriarchal society, they have a preference for male child, but the girls are not considered as burden. The study indicates that most of the women feel happy if the first born child is a girl. But in most cases, it is not because of any preference, but for the help mothers may receive in rearing the next issue (Barua, 2009, 2011). The children are brought up under the care of family members in usual natural setting.

Age at menarche and socio-cultural aspects associated with first menstruation always play a significant role in understanding the social system/the reproductive system. In almost all communities, each stage of biological change is always associated with rites and rituals, prohibitions and superstitions. Among the Deoris, the puberty ceremony is not associated with elaborate rites and rituals. However, they observe the passage of stages of life in elaborate manner. When a girl crosses childhood, she is to wear/take a cloth on her body which is short and not so broad. This is referred as *Pakani*. But when a girl attains puberty a long *Chaddar/gamusa* is put under the arms and wrapped twice across the breast. This is referred to as *Baiga mora/ gamusa pindhua*. A girl can participate in *Gamusa pindhua* ceremony to recognize herself as a marriageable girl. "It is a traditional practice, where newly matured girls are helped by the elderly girls the way of wearing/putting the *Gamusa*." As it is a group ceremony, it may not be possible for every girl to attend the ceremony immediately after attaining puberty. Sometimes, the girls are to wait for 1-2 years for this formal ritual. But it should be performed before a girl attained 18 years of age (Barua, 2011:79).

There is another group ritual which is performed between the age group of 15 and above and known as *Kakal bandha* a traditional belief that a girl is to take part in this ceremony before the formal marriage. In this ceremony the senior girls help the juniors in the process of wearing *Kakal bandha* at the waist. Moreover, the seniors advise the juniors about the conjugal life and how to live happily in husband's family. Social solidarity and responsibility of Deori women are well reflected through all the group ceremonies and activities. "The rigid age grade system may not be marked among the Deoris, but the stages may be clearly traced through elaborate socio-cultural system" (Barua, 2011:80). Though the ritual part is not so marked, social solidarity is clearly visible through all the ceremonies. Age at Marriage is an important aspect in the reproductive life.

While dicussing about ***Pregnancy*** among the Deoris, it is revealed that the birth of a child is always a happy event and a childless woman is detested by her community. In matters of sex, though they have a strong desire for sons, girls are not considered as a burden, because females shoulder's the maximum responsibility in the household work. The intense desire for a son is partly due to the fact that the Deori is a patriarchal society and a son is needed to continue the family line. The family is the most important asset in any community. In every society, the couple has an opinion regarding the ideal size of a family, gap between two children, and their attitudes towards family planning, care during pregnancy, etc.

The investigation in Modhupur forest village revealed that there is not a single woman, who prefers single child. There are 25 mothers where preference is given to one son and one daughter. Next higher percentage is found where twenty-four mothers prefer two sons and one daughter. There are fourteen families, where preference is given for two sons and two daughters. There is only one family who has made their preference on one son and two daughters.

Earlier an effort was made to trace the expected and real picture of the number of children among the Deoris in the Kalaluwa Deori village (Barua & Bharali, 2000)..Table 5.7 reveals that maximum number of respondents prefer 1 son and one daughter in the family. Next higher percentage is reported where mothers prefer 2 sons and one daughter.

Table 5.7: Expected number of children per family in forest village

Categories	*Number of mothers*
1 son, 1 daughter	25
2 sons, 1 daughter	24
2 sons, 2 daughters	15
1son, 2 daughters	1
1 son	0

From Table 5.8 it is clearly found that there are 67 mothers who prefer four children per family. Next higher percentage is found, where 58 mothers who prefer three children per family. While analyzing the actual picture at the time of survey, it was found that there were 63 mothers who have more than 5 children. Next higher percentage was found where 53 mothers had 4 children. Thus, it is revealed that there is a vast difference between the expected and the real picture of the number of children per family (Barua & Bharali, 2000:34).

Table 5.8: Expectation regarding number of children in Kalaluwa Deori village

Total no. of housewives	*Expected number of children per family*				
	1	21	3	4	5 and above
186	Nil	34	58	67	27
	Real number of children per family				
	Nil	29	41	53	63

The period of pregnancy is not considered unclean or polluting by the Deoris. When a child is born, at least a period of one week or till the falling of naval cord is regarded as polluting period. There is no restriction before and after birth for any kind of work. She handles her household duties till her health permits. Of course, there are beliefs which debars a pregnant woman from doing certain types of activities. During investigation, almost all the women gave the same reply that killing of animals; fishing and crossing the river during that period are not encouraged. The husband is also not allowed to kill any type of animals. "It is believed that if the husband kills any animals, then the expectant mother may give birth to a child having characteristics of that animal" (Barua, 1996:164). Majority of the respondents were aware about these beliefs, while a small section did not go deep into it and simply replied that they are doing these activities as they are asked by the elders or mother-in-law.

Regarding the state of health during pregnancy, it was found that in general they do not take any particular precaution during that period. Normal food was taken along with other members during pregnancy. Of course, if one cannot digest any particular food, then it is avoided. Sour fruits were favoured by most women.

A study among the Deoris of Modhupur village, reveals that "out of 53 cases, in 20 cases the women had suffered from pain, vomiting during first three months of pregnancy" (Barua, 1996:164). Majority of them were in good health during pregnancy. In certain cases, they took medical advice, whereas six cases were reported where they performed a kind of ritual locally known as *Ai Tupula Bandha Sakam,* for early delivery. It is a simple ritual, where three *Gopinis* (elderly women who had attained menopause) are invited. Rice powder, banana, betel nut and leaf are the main items required for the ritual. The expectant mother bows before the *Gopinis*, who bless her for the welfare and normal delivery. As Modhupur forest village is only 28 km away from Dibrugarh, almost in all cases, they took the facility available in Assam Medical College, Dibrugarh. In certain cases they came to Barbaruah Health Centre which is 12 km away. There is a health subcentre situated near the Forest Beat Office which is 1.5 km away from the village. But when delivery takes place at home, it is done in the usual bed room. At home, the mother-in-law or some elderly women, provide's help at the time of delivery. There are no restrictions on the part of women including the mother-in-law to extend a helping hand at the time of delivery. There was no particular woman working as mid-wife in the village.

Period of pollution varies from 3 to 7 days depending upon the falling of navel cord. As soon as the navel cord falls, they perform *Bhajori* ritual. Normally, they invite odd number of women, i.e. 5-7 married women. The family arranges 1 cock, 1 jar of rice-beer, leafy vegetables, i.e. *Kachu sak* (Taru-Yam). When the preparation is completed, the *Gopinis* symbolically offer one portion of the cooked food to the child and give one or two drops of rice beer and *kachu* curry in the mouth of the child. The mother bows before the *Gopinis* who bless her for a happy life. Pollution period is over after this purificatory ritual.

With regard to ***Feeding practices***, it is reported that breast feeding is common among the Deoris. Normally, immediately after an hour of child birth, the baby is given mother's milk. When mother's milk is not sufficient, or if the baby refuses to suckle mother's milk, then to supplement it, cow milk is given to the baby. A study among the Deoris revel that "two cases have been reported where the baby refused to take mother's milk right from the beginning. In these cases, supplementary cow milk was used, and then the next preference was given to tinned milk" (Barua, 1996:166). Among the Deoris, the mothers do not have fixed time to nurse the baby. Most of the mothers reported that if they were busy, they fed the children whenever they cry. If not busy, the baby could be sucked the whole day. But in the initial days, the baby is fed every 3 to 4 hours. This indicates an unscheduled way of breast feeding.

Weaning practices refer especially to the manner in which the infant is weaned from the mother's breast or the bottle. Among the Deoris, it was reported that during the first five to six months, the mother's milk is almost the only food, which the child receives. Then gradually, the child is given supplementary food, besides the mother's milk. A study conducted among the Deoris revealed that "out of 53 cases, in 23 cases it was found that weaning was done a little after two years. On the otherhand, in 13 cases, the children were weaned a little after eight months (Barua, 1996:167). Regarding the method of weaning, in most of the cases, mothers apply bitter/sour substance in the nipple. After weaning, the child is given the same food as the adults take.

Thus, it can be said that among the Deoris, there is no fixed age limit for weaning. It is normally determined by social and cultural events, such as mother's pregnancy or the birth of a younger one. Earlier studies in the forest village Modhupur, three cases were reported where the children continued to suckle up to four years of age" (Barua, 1996:167). After weaning, the child is given the same food as the adults take.

A discussion on the ***Teething practices***; it is reported that in allmost all cultural groups there are certain beliefs regarding the eruption of teeth. Among the Deoris, it was found that in most of the cases, mothers were unaware of such beliefs. In majority of cases, however, they could recall, whether it was erupted in upper or lower jaw. Only a few elderly women could explain that in case of boy, it was a sign of good brain if the tooth first erupted in the upper jaw, and the child would be expert in climbing or swimming, if it erupted on the lower jaw. In the case of a girl, if the tooth erupts on the lower jaw, she might be an expert in depicting flowers on the loom (Barua, 1996:167). This indicates that no prejudices exist among the Deoris regarding the eruption of teeth.

Toilet training is an important aspect of child socialization. Among the Deoris, there is no specific way of toilet training. It was reported by the mothers that they never forced the children in such cases. When children were young, occasionally defecation or urination was done on the hole of the bamboo floor of platform type house. Pigs and dogs below performed the duty of scavengers. Most of the mothers were of opinion that when the child attains the age of two years, they instruct them to go to the backside of the house for defecation and urination. As they rear pigs, mothers or elders have to guard the child. When the child is between 3-4 years of age, he is already aware of the proper place for urination and toilet. There were rare cases, where the child used to wet the bed for up to four years. Mothers were not harsh towards the children but the fathers expressed their disgust and sometimes physically handled the child. But at night, the mothers took the child personally to the courtyard for excretion.

It was found that the children were given bath with a 2 to 3 days interval in the winter season. Of course, during summer, they took bath everyday. It was reported that the child was trained to clean the teeth regularly from three years onward. But this training in all cases was completed at the age of five years. Mostly, they used charcoal for brushing, and only in a few cases, they could identify the brand of tooth-paste.

A discussion on ***Caretaking process*** reveals that after giving birth to a child, a mother takes every possible care according to their living condition. In most cases, mother is the primary care taker of her children. But they seek help from the secondary care takers also. A study among the Deoris of Kalaluwa Deori village revealed that out of 186 mothers, there were 63 cases, where mother was the only care taker in early stage. In such cases, they had to take the children while going for harvesting and sometimes for transplanting also. If situation demands, they are to carry the child to the field even during plantation. In such cases, they keep the baby in high land after making a shed. But at the time of harvesting, they invariably carry the baby to the field and place them on the paddy straw, keeping a cloth over it. But there are 123 mothers who reported that they took the help of secondary care taker and in most cases they were either mother-in-law or husband's sister (Barua & Bharali, 2000:37). Even in nuclear families, they were getting help from kin members, because in rural areas, kin members are always ready to offer help at the time of crisis. The availability and acceptance of modern feeding techniques has freed the mothers from prolonged demand feeding. The mothers usually return to her normal household work immediately after the purification ceremony. While doing regular household work, the baby is kept in a cot so that she would be able to keep an eye on the baby. The child health is considered as one of their prime concern. The Deori mothers follow various measures to keep the child healthy. They are quite aware about medical facilities and almost in all cases; they took special care so that the children were vaccinated in time. Along with the medical treatment, they have full faith on certain traditional beliefs. They put "black spot" on child's forehead. Similarly, tying a black string or *Bagh moni* (big beads) on the waist is a common practice. They do it to protect the child against an evil eye. The children mostly suffer from fever, cough, dysentery, etc. In minor illness, they are treated by home remedies using various herbs and shrubs.

The children are normally brought up in a natural way without much attention from their parents. They follow their elders to the field or kitchen garden and children of 4 to 5 years of age are asked to bring something from the kitchen or pass on household articles from one person to another. When enquired whether they were taught before being admitted to school, in most cases, the reply was in negative. Though the children were not given formal education before 5 years, yet mothers all the time gave training like how to behave towards the elders or junior members of the family. Though a Deori child is normally not forced to do any type of activities, yet some kind of obedience is expected from the children. A study conducted among the Deoris revealed that "out of 186 mother's 38 mothers' emphasized prompt obedience from their children. While there are 148 mothers who casually remarked that they did not give much stress on it. And it depended on the nature and urgency of the request" (Barua & Bharali, 2000:37). By six years, the child is chronologically as well as developmentally ready to go to school and to absorb from a world beyond the family. They also form a play group and normally play marble, *Tang-guti*, *Chor*-police, etc. which are popular among the children. The children are provided with less costly play materials like marble, *Luddu*, etc. Supplying of different types of materials mostly depend on economic condition. Nature also provides enough scope of playing and it is found that the children who reside near the river bank spend a part of their time in swimming, playing in the sand. On the other hand, the children of other part of the village do not know the art of swimming except a few of them. When the daily activities of the children were studied, it has been found that a child of 7 years is normally free from heavy household works like ploughing, carrying crops and harvesting, etc. but he is to perform works like shopping, fishing, cleaning the cowshed and sometimes do the duty of cowherd. During transplanting and harvesting, they are given the task of carrying *jalpan* to the workers in the field. The girls between the age group of 5 to 8 years are also free from any heavy duties. They normally do the works like washing utensils, cleaning the house, etc. Sometimes, they also go for fishing in the nearby village ponds.

Discussion (Socialization)

Child rearing/child socialization play an important part in the transmission of indigenous knowledge. In the present study two large Scheduled Tribe communities, i.e. the Sonowal Kacharis and the Deoris were studied. Field data were collected from two settings, i.e. the forest villages and revenue villages.

The family is often called the basic social institution, because of its important functions of procreation and socialization. To an individual, family means his first school and next best security after his mother's womb. Worldwide it is the family tie that may be considered the most important and significant tie. Whenever a child is born into a family, he is also born into a culture. There are already prescribed values and pattern in the culture. It is through the process of socialization that the child acquires the attributes and values of that culture. In other words, simply he is to put it, as it were his "cultural spectacles" and sees and interprets situation and conditions as defined by his culture. Socio-cultural influences reach the child through his every perception and experience, but in early childhood these are likely to involve the members of his own community. In fact, the learning process starts in the family and the child learns through the process of limitations and suggestions within the family. The family trains the child in social values, norms and customs and to a certain extent in the tradition of society. It has been mentioned that "all the socialization techniques employed by the adults are probably, less effective in the modification of the children behaviour than the observation and imitation through which the children gradually absorb the skills, customs and values of their group (Minturn & Hitchock, 1963:331). Most of the training in early childhood is not the conscious training. The unconscious training and learning makes him understand his own culture. The social anthropologists emphasize the importance of cultural factors in socialization process. One of the main problems of human life is the preservation and continuity of culture. And socialization may be considered the ideal way of preserving one's own culture. Moreover, social contact is necessary for normal development of the infant and child. When children are isolated and brought up with minimum social contact, particularly up to six years, they will show few human responses, like the "wolf children". Thus, family plays an important role in introducing children to their culture.

In all human societies, each stage of biological change is always associated with rites and rituals, prohibitions and superstitions. On the basis of biological change, distinct age-set system also develops in the community. The available literature no doubt emphasized "Initiation ceremonies, which mark the stages of growth, particularly the transition from childhood to adult life, are far more common among the males than corresponding rites for females" (Piddington, 1963:176). Of course, it does not mean that this stage is not ritually marked among the women. In almost all human societies, this physiological change among the women is ceremonially marked with a slight variation from culture to culture.

The Sonowal Kacharis and Deoris both observe this stage ceremoniously. The Sonowal Kacharis celebrate puberty rite in a more colourful way than the actual marriage. "They symbolically perform and carry out all the activities which are done in actual marriage" (Barua, 1996:67). When enquired about the reason for elaborate performance of this ritual, most of them are of opinion that generally conjugal marriage is performed through elopement. So, they prefer to observe the puberty ritual in an elaborate way. The Deoris also observe the puberty stage ceremoniously. Though the ritual part is not so marked, yet social solidarity is clearly visible through all the three stages which are observed after attainment of puberty. These social ceremonies on the other hand also focus on the fact that the girls have become ready for marriage. Child marriage is absent in both the communities.

Though all these communities do not observe it ritually, yet the restriction or prohibition during the first menstruation as well as in subsequent period are observed by most of these communities. In no case they are allowed to visit religious places or take part in religious ceremonies. They are not allowed to pluck vegetables or flowers during the period and it is believed that their touch will destroy the plants. Both among the Sonowal Kacharis and the Deoris, the girl is debarred from touching any article needed for preparing rice beer. They are also not allowed to touch or feed silk worm during that period (Barua, 1996:69).

It is difficult to confirm whether such prohibitions have any scientific meaning or not. But many social restrictions have physiological reasons behind them. Anything she may have touched during catamenia must either be destroyed or purified. In the Old Testament also such types or expression of beliefs and practices are found. The Roman view points are also described in this way on the approach of a woman in this state, which are touched by her becomes sterile, grafts wither away, and garden plants are parched up. A swarm of bees if looked upon by her will die immediately; brass and iron will instantly emit an offensive odour (referred from Montague, 1957:195). These are for the most part nothing but ravings which we may term superstition. But, it is also fact that large number of beliefs that are described may still be found persisting today in many parts of the world.

One of the oldest belief concerning menstruation is that the touch of a woman is capable of causing flowers and plants destroy is widely prevalent. "In many parts of Europe, menstruous women are excluded from certain occupations. In the Great French Perfumeries, for example, women are not permitted to work during the time of their menstruation; nor are they allowed to pick mushrooms in those regions in which their growth is a profitable industry. In the south of France at such times they are not allowed to tend silk worms and in various wine districts of France and also of the Rhine, women are debarred from approaching or handling the vessels in which fermentation takes place for the reason that should their course begins, fermentation would be accelerated and wine spoilt" (Montague, 1957:195). It was also reported that many "beauticians" advised against a visit to the beauty shop during the menstrual period, because during that period, so called permanent hair wave will not take place as compared to the intermenstrual period. It is difficult to give any definite conclusion, yet it is said that as the bio-electric potential of the body differs from normal conditions during menstruation and their hair becomes more firmly fixed in the skin and that the force required to epilate hair is greater at this time than any other" (Montague, 1957:197). Though the reason may be different, yet it is reported from rural Assam that earlier women were debarred from using cosmetic or fine hair do during the period (Barua, 1996:70).

The restrictions and prohibitions which are almost universally associated with menstruation create various interpretations. It was possible that primitive man, who was extremely good observer noted that certain deleterious changes produced in living beings were associated with the presence of menstruous women. This observation may have been made once or independently by different groups at different times. As the inference was drawn, that women in their periods were responsible for these undesirable effects, a prohibition was put upon women during this period. The simple people, who lived under natural conditions, are to make a close observation of every aspect of their economic activities. The observance of certain association might have developed various prohibitions in the activities of people.

Pregnancy

After marriage, pregnancy is a matter of pride. A childless mother is not considered as a complete woman. She is debarred from taking part in some religious activities. The fertility of a woman qualifies as well as quatifies her social status in the community. A couple generally expects a child after one year of their marriage. If it goes beyond two years, they first approach the local medicine man (*bez*) or perform various rituals to appease the supernatural. To cure barrenness, "a Juang husband worship the *Sujna* tree and the paste made of *Sujna* flowers or simply *Sujna* seeds are given to the wife to eat; one seed is supposed to bring a boy, half a seed a girl" (Vidyarthi & Rai, 1985: 291). It was found that a pregnant woman is not subjected to any restrictions on any type of work, of course, pre-natal care finds less significant in most of the tribal people. She is allowed to handle all her domestic work as long as she can manage. Majority of the women take normal diet, but if some particular food does not suits her, she may avoid it. But there is a general belief both among the Sonowal Kacharis and the Deoris that a pregnant woman should fed with her desired dishes to ensure the birth of a healthy baby. Taboos, restrictions and preferences are marked in practically all the Indian tribes in one form or other. "Among the Sonowal Kacharis, the pregnant woman never touches any cooked food items which are sent from a family where death occurred recently" (Barua & Bora, 1979:334). They are also not allowed to stitch any torn cloth and majority of them keep a knife or mustard seeds with them. "Among the Deoris, killing of animals, fishing and crossing a river during pregnancy are not encouraged (Barua, 1996:164). The husband is also not allowed to kill any type of animals. It is believed that if the husband kills any animals, then the expected mother may give birth to a child having characteristics of that animal (Barua, 1996:164). Among the Boro Kacharis during pregnancy the mother keeps a knife with her, particularly when she goes outside the house. She also keeps mustard seeds with her all the time. She is also advised not to sit near the fire place or warm the hand and body on fire. She is also asked not to stand at the eaves or cut anything during the eclipse. It is believed that such activities would bring harmful effect on the baby (Barua, 2009:137). Superstition relating to eclipse seems to exist in different communities of India. Among the Mavchis "during a solar eclipse pregnant woman do not cut vegetables or cook food. They are not allowed to look at the eclipse for fear that the child will be born with a cleft palate or some other congenital deformation" (Tomar & Tribhuwan, 2005:44). It is also believed by the Mavchis that a pregnant woman must not interact with an infertile woman; she is a bad omen for both the pregnant woman and her child. Among the Tai Khamyangs and Tai Turungs, both the husband and wife are not allowed to kill animal (Barua, 1998:156). There is a common belief among the Tai Turungs that they should not kill a serpent during pregnancy. If such act is done, then the child may frequently exhibit the tongue (*ibid.*). Among the Tai Phake, another Tai Buddhist Community, a pregnant woman should not eat *Kakila* fish or crab. It is believed that if she eats such prohibited fish or crab, then her child would smell very bad (Sharma Thakur, 1982:90). Over and above these restrictions, there is a prohibition among the Tai Turungs that during pregnancy, the members of the family are not supposed to repair or fix handles of axe, knife, etc. It is believed that such an act make delivery painful (Barua, 1998:156). Among the Sonowal Kacharis, the pregnant women are not allowed to stitch any torn cloth and majority of them keep a knife or mustard seed with them (Barua & Bora, 1979:335). An Ao Naga expectant mother avoids eating twin fruits, hot chillies and tortoise; she avoids the sight of dying animals, monkeys, big snakes, lest blindness should afflict her baby (Vidyarthi & Rai, 1986:293).

Different types of prohibitions are there and most common being the prohibition against seeing or attending a funeral and touching the crops as a precaution to protect the child in the womb from evil spirits. Moreover, prohibition of eating twin/joint fruits is very common as there is a fear of giving birth to twin. In many tribes including the Tangsa, in case of twin birth, one baby may be killed. The Lepchas believe in stopping fishing with stick to save the child from nose wound (Vidyarthi & Rai, 1986:293). It was also reported that among the Gonds of Chhattisgarh, a woman is supposed to keep away from a horse's shadow to prevent an unduly longer period of pregnancy. They believe the woman would have to carry her pregnancy for a year as a mare does (Vidyarthi & Rai, 1986:293). In middle India, "a Munda expectant mother is not allowed to touch seeds. If this is violated, they would not sprout. And if they did and it grow, half of the plant would either go dry or the field itself would turn barren" (Vidyarthi & Rai, 1986:293). In case of Abuj Maria (live in the Abuj Marh hill tract of Madhya Pradesh) a woman during pregnancy generally avoids going to the forest alone. Child birth in a forest is regarded very badly, as evil eyes are there to harm the newly born baby and its mother (Sarkar & Dasgupta, 2000:59).

Among the *Kumars* (1976:299) during her first pregnancy, a woman should not cross a *Dhenki* (husking lever). If she does it, it is believed that her son will have no skin covering on his glands. She should not cross a plough, or else her child will develop the habit of crying loud in the manner of a man who drives the bullocks yoked to the plough. In rural areas of Bangladesh, "*Mrigel* fish is not given to pregnant woman because it causes epilepsy and *Gaja*r fish is not given because it has ugly eyes and may cause the eyes of the foetus to become ugly" (Maloney *et al.*, 1981:65).

Thus, it is found that different types of prohibitions and restrictions exist among different tribes and communities of India. The main reason behind such prohibitions is to keep the pregnant woman safe and sound. Most of the tribes do not observe any rites of pregnancy invariably, though there are some exceptions.

Place of Delivery

Among the Sonowal Kacharis and Deoris, there is no rigid rule regarding the place of delivery. Normally birth takes place at the husband's house. But at present, they invariably take medical help.

The villages are within the easy reach of medical facilities. But when delivery takes place at home, it is done in the usual bedroom. At home, the mother-in-law, or elderly woman extended help at the time of delivery. But if certain complications arose at the time of delivery, different remedial measures are taken by various communities. Among the Sonowal Kacharis, "in complicacy, sometimes a village medicine man (*bez*) is summoned. He performs certain rites in front of the door of the delivery room by breaking an egg and it is believed that this act may help in having a smooth delivery" (Barua & Bora, 1979: 335). Among the Tai Khamyangs, a piece of stone which has been struck by lightning could be used. This stone should be pulverized and the resulting powder put into water and drunk by women in labour (Terewiel, 1980:29). Among the Tai Phakey, a fly shuttle is sunk in some water and a portion of that water is given to the expecting mother (Sharma Thakur, 1982:91). Whereas, among the Tai Turungs, in complicacies, they immediately remove the wooden handles or nails from the axe, knife, etc. which might have been fixed during the period of pregnancy (Barua, 2001:88). Different types of beliefs exist in various communities. "The Ao Nagas consider presence of the father at the birth of a child" is good for the family (Vidyarthi & Rai, 1976:295). Various superstitions exist among different communities. Among the Gonds, "twin birth is considered a bad omen, as it is believed to be the consequence of cohabitation with a ghost or a breach of menstrual taboo" (Vidyarthi & Rai, 1986:295). Among the Todas an unwanted child, specially, a girl was suffocated at birth and buried like a still born. The twins, sons/daughters, too were killed (Vidyarthi & Rai, 1976:296). The birth of twin is considered to be a worst kind of curse among the Muklom Tangsas. The Muklom Tangsas took various measures to kill the twins. The twins are taken to the jungle where they were strangulated to death with a rope. Then it was kept in a bamboo basket and hung on a tree and the animals and insects consume the dead body" (Barua & Dutta Das, 2007:154). But now infanticide is almost absent. Still born is believed to be a curse among the Tangsas. The child is wrapped in cloths, and then it is covered with flattened bamboo and tied with cane ropes. Then, the child is buried under the ground of the family's residence. On that day the members of the family take frugal meal on banana leaves. "The Angamis resorted to infanticide in case of children of unmarried girls. It was believed that such children would bring misfortune to the village. The girls were sent to the jungle for delivery and there the baby was strangled" (Raaton, 2006:231).

Among the Sonowal Kacharis and the Deoris, there is no midwife in the village. Mother-in-law and elderly women help in such matters. In home delivery, they use a piece of split bamboo, sharpened into a knife to sever the umbilical cord. However, there are some variations with regards to the place of procuring the piece of sharp bamboo. The Tai Khamyangs and the Tai Turungs, during investigation did not specify the place from where the bamboo sliver had to be obtained. "But they are of opinion that it should be from the bamboo framework which upholds the roof" (Barua, 2001:89). Whereas, according to Tai Phakey, the sliver had to be cut from bamboo rack (*Khaa-fai*) above the kitchen fire (Terewiel, 1980:31). Terewiel offering various examples from Thailand emphasized that the using of bamboo sliver is a characteristic feature of the Tai culture. Hank's reporting from central Thailand noticed that the knife had been sliced out of the old bamboo house beam and Pederson states that the instrument is obtained on the spot of bamboo from the house (cited from Terewiel, 1980:30). While not ruling out the fact that using of bamboo sliver is a dominant characteristic of Tais, yet it is very difficult to determine from where the custom originated. Since the whole of South East Asia is rich in bamboo and the Mongoloid culture is invariably referred to as "bamboo culture". Such practices are common among most of the rural communities of Assam including Sonowal Kacharis and the Deoris. Today, however, the villagers do not depend much on such practices and the present study revealed that most of the delivery took place at hospital. In the same way the custom regarding the keeping of a fire in a pot in the delivery room, appears to be of South East Asian origin. It is referred by the Anthropologists as bed-roasting, because a fire is always kept near or under the bed (Hart *et al.*, 1965:65). The present study also reveals that the villagers invariably put mustard seed, garlic and *Bosh* (*Acorus calamus Linn*) plant on the fire. The members, coming from outside, are to warm up their hands in the fire before touching the child. This is done to ward off the affect of evil spirit which might have affected the person on the way. The fire in the delivery room is also used to cauterize the raw navel of new born, which has been cut with a bamboo sliver. If a baby cries much, the elders might advise that the navel may be cauterized again. The practice has the effect of reducing tetanus infection (Maloney *et al.*, 1981:67).

Birth

After birth, the placenta and other matters incidental to child birth are normally buried. But the place of burial differs from community to community. "Among the Sonowal Kacharis, the placenta locally known as *phool* is deeply buried in the usual bed room of the couple. After filling the earth, high pressure is given by foot. This act is done always by the husband. They never bury it outside, as it is believed that it may be affected by spirit or evil eyes" (Barua & Bora, 1979:336). The beliefs associated with it vary from culture to culture. Among the Tai Khamyangs, the placenta is buried within the compound and they never give any pressure on it. "It is believed, if pressed heavily, the new born baby would suffer from pain" (Barua, 1998:157). "Whereas, among the Tai Turungs; they bury such matter in the ground just below the eaves drip, in front of their *Chang-ghar.* In case of male child, these are buried directly opposite to the main "house post" and in case of girls near the *Pari khuta*, i.e. the partner post of the main post" (Barua, 2001:89). They take particular care, so that it may not reach the animals. "Among the Tai Phake it is believed that, if the umbilical cord is taken out by a fox, the child will suffer from nerve disorder" (Sharma Thakur, 1982:92). Among the Tai Khamyangs also there is a belief that "deeper the pit is, larger will be the gap between two issues" (Barua, 1996). More or less, similar beliefs exist among the Sikligars. "After parturition, the placenta is buried underground, where care is taken in burying the placenta deep. They believe that the deeper it is the better it will be for the health of the mother and the child. It is buried with great caution and without any delay. According to their belief if a barren woman happens to have it, she can trouble the baby a lot" (Banerjee, 1987:66).

Among the Tai Ahoms also, such type of beliefs exist. "It was reported that the placenta and other materials must be buried by the father, normally within the compound. It is also believed that if these are buried at a distance, there will be larger gap between the two issues" (Barua, 1978).

It has been recorded that among the Oraons of Chota Nagpur the placenta and naval cord together with a worn out broom and an old winnowing busket are buried. And it is not the depth of the pit for the burial of the afterbirth, but the height to which the digger of the pit raises his spade, that determine the gap between the two issues (Roy, quoted from Ghurye, 1963:121). Thus, the way of disposal of placenta and other related matters reveal that there exist some sorts of ideas regarding the gap between the two issues in every culture which are reflected in such beliefs and practices.

Among the Didyai, a small tribe of Orissa, delivery of a child takes place in corner of the living room which is attended by senior women preferably of the same lineage. After birth, the navel cord is cut by an arrow in case of male issue, while for female issue; it is cut with a knife. The placenta and other things are wrapped with some leaves and buried in the corner of the house, to protect the baby from evil eyes (Sarkar & Dasgupta, 2000:75). Among the Mavchis the cord is buried in the cowshed to prevent it from being used as a magical devise by witches and sorcerers to harm the child (Tomar & Tribhuwan, 2005:44).

It was also reported that the Muslims of Sind with few exceptions dispose of the placenta, whereas Muslims of Upper Sind frontier generally throw it over a nearby thorny fence. "The people who bury the placenta believe that if it is eaten away by any animal, something terrible will happen to the child's mother. Those who throw it away do so, in the hope, that if a dog eats it up the mother will be as fertile as bitch" (Ghurye, 1963:99).

The necessity of gap between the two issues was realized long back by many aborigine tribes. Among the Australian aborigines, a new born baby will be buried alive or exposed should it be born to a mother who already has a one year old and perhaps one or two other children. It is believed that a newborn baby is not, in fact, quite human, and so a human life is not really being taken, and because it is not fair to the older children since the mother cannot pay proper attention to them. Bringing up human beings, the Australian aborigines hold is a full time job. Infanticide is practiced for similar reasons among many other tribes (Montague, 1963:60).

The dried stump of the navel-cord is carefully preserved by most of the communities. "The Sonowal Kacharis, keep the cord of each child. Cage of cocoon is specially used for keeping this cord. It is believed that the water extracted from this dry cord is very useful for the child in certain diseases like dysentery, fever, etc. In some cases, this cord is put on child's waist with the help of a thread. It is believed that if a child wears it, he will be healthy and strong (Barua & Bora, 1979:336). It was reported that "the Marathi-speaking people use it as an antidote against scorpion-bite, it being applied mixed in water, at the spot of bite" (Ghuye, 1996:104). The Gujar caste preserves it most carefully. For them it must be cremated with the corpse of the person to whom it belongs. The custom among the Muslims; is to place it in a rat-hole with the idea of inducing great fecundity like that of the rat" (Ghuye, 1996:104). At Nasik, the stump of the cord is preserved and used as a medicine if the child should have any bowel-complaint or an enlargement.

Period of pollution varies from 3-7 days depending upon the falling of navel cord. Till then the mother is considered as impure. She is not allowed to draw water or take part in cooking and other activities. The family members are not allowed to take part in any religious ceremonies. The period of pollution indirectly helps woman to take rest after delivery.

Feeding

Feeding practices among infants have always been a topic of special interest with studies of child rearing practices. There are wide cultural variations regarding the onset of feeding, kind of feeding, length of feeding, introduction of solid food, etc. Mother's milk is considered to be the best for an infant. It has been revealed that the yellowy-lemonish looking fluid known as colostrums, which appears in the mother's breast towards the last month of pregnancy, contain certain antibodies which remain in the colostrums, only for eight hours after the birth of the child. This would certainly suggest that the new born should have the opportunity to injest these antibodies at the earliest possible moment.

Colostrums are extremely high in protein, containing 8.5 per cent as compared with 1.5 per cent in mature milk. Among other things, colostrums contain one of the most digestible forms of protein for the baby, i.e. whey protein. This is present in the extraordinary proportion of 63 per cent of the total protein, twice as much as mineral salts and half as much fat and carbohydrates as the later milk.

Colostrums might prove to be the best preventive of diarrhoea in human young. The fact that the only known cure for diarrhoea in human infant is breast feeding.

Breast feeding is common both among the Sonowal Kacharis and the Deoris. The mothers may not be aware of the medical significant of immediate breast feeding. But there is no taboo in giving mother's milk immediately after birth. Among the Deoris, immediately after half an hour to one hour of child birth, the baby is given mother's milk. When mother's milk is not sufficient, or if the baby refuses to suckle mother's milk, then to supplement it, cow milk is given to the baby. Most of the plain tribes of Assam do not have any prohibition of giving mother's milk immediately after birth. But certain fallacies existed among many tribes. In the Sioux system of child rearing "the colostrums was generally considered to be poison for the baby, thus the breast milk was not offered to him until there seemed to be good stream of perfect milk" (Erikson, 1963:135). Among the Yurok also, the new born is not breast fed for ten days, but is given a nut soup from a tiny shell. The Yurok have a definite weaning time around the six months. The first solid food is Salmon and deer meat, well salted with sea weed. Salty foods are Yurok's "sweets" (Erikson, 1963:175). But still such beliefs are found to exist among certain tribes and communities. Among the Jat Sikh, "the baby is not put on the breast feeding right after birth". If a child is born in the morning, it may not suckle until evening, but in the meantime, the baby is given water with sugar with the help of a cotton swap or a piece of cloth (Banerjee, 1987:118). It is reported that Mavchis of Namdubar district, in the state of Maharashtra do not breast feed their new born for two or three days after delivery. "Believed impure, the colostrums is squeezed out and discarded. It is feared that the "thick" and "sticky" nature of this first milk will cause the milk to stick to the lining of the newborn's intestines and prevent the baby from passing the stool. As this milk is indigestible, it may lead to diarrhoea or dysentery in the infant. During this period, mothers feed their infants a mixture of honey, cow's milk and water," (Tomar & Tribhuwan, 2005:42). Dave and Tavkar (1985) found among the tribes of Panchmahal district of Gujarat, the child is fed with goat's milk for the first three days after birth followed by breast feeding which usually continue till the next pregnancy. "Among the Bodo Kachari neonatal and infants are usually suckled by the mother and breast feeding usually continue up to the age of two or three years or till the delivery of the next child" (Barua & Borua,

2009:140). Swain (1988) found that among the Santhal of Northern Orissa, women work in the field till the nine month of their pregnancy. Immediately after birth, the child is given honey or jaggery. Soft rice, gruel and pulses form a major supplementary food. In some of the tribal communities like Santhal of Mahurganj district milk is not consumed and is thrown away as it is not good for human consumption (Ray & Roth, 1991).

Many of the studies like Sears (1955) and others reveal that there appears no evidence of different characteristics in breast fed and bottle fed children. Hoefer and Hardy (1929:615) found that artificially fed children were less nourished and started greater susceptibility to illness and were mentally inferior to the babies fed by mothers. It was also reported, children who had been nursed from 4 to 9 months were definitely physically and mentally superior to those who had been nursed less than 4 months (Montague, 1957:20). Sewell and Mussen (1952) quoted from Kuppuswamy (1984:56) made an extensive study of some phases of infantile feeding and found no relationship between the type of feeding in infancy and various oral symptoms like thumb suckling, nail biting and stuttering among five and six years old. But most of the earlier studies give an indication that feeding practices are a phenomenon of wide cultural and economic variation.

Weaning

Weaning practices refer to the manner in which the infant is weaned from the mother's breast or the bottle. According to the psychoanalysis, weaning cause's great frustration and sudden weaning has a traumatic effect. Among the Sonowal Kacharis "majority of women tried to wean their children between one and half to two years and in some cases children were weaned before the third month due to shortage of breast milk" (Barua & Bora, 1979: 338). However, among the Deoris for the first five to six months the mother's milk is almost the only food which the children receive. It was revealed that weaning time varies from eight months to more than three years of age" (Barua, 1996: 167). Regarding the method of weaning, in most of the cases, mothers apply bitter/sour substances in the nipple. After weaning; the child is given the same food as the adult takes. It was referred (Bhogle, 1978:9) that rich mothers adopt the method of gradual weaning. Among the Sonowal Kacharis also, period of breast feeding is shorter among those who were able to supplement or replace breast milk with cows or tinned baby milk powder from 3 to 4 months after delivery. Those women, who continue breast feeding till the next pregnancy or delivery, were mainly from poorer family. In some tribal communities by continuing a longer period of suckling, they try to maintain the gap between the children. As for example, among the Bantu, there is a long period of suckling, which is continued until the second/third year's of infant's life. The mothers usually delay weaning until she is aware that she has conceived again. Sexual intercourse between husband and wife is taboo for the first two years after the birth of a child, so that the period of lactation is nessarily a long one (Piddington, 1963: 259).

Teething

Regarding the eruption of teeth, certain beliefs exist in all culture groups. "Among the Sonowal Kacharis, it is believed that a child will be greedy, if first tooth erupts on the upper jaw. They also believe that if the child's first tooth erupts in the 6th month, it is good for the baby" (Barua & Bora, 1979:340). However, among the Deoris no such prejudices exist. It is believed that "it was a sign of good brain if the tooth first erupted in the upper jaw, and the child may be expert in climbing and swimming, if it erupted on the lower jaw. In case of a girl if the tooth erupts on the lower jaw, she may be expert in depicting flowers on the loom (Barua, 1996:167). Different types of prejudices existed among the different cultural group. Among the Sikligar, when the first tooth erupts in the upper jaw, it is believed to be unlucky for his maternal uncle. This misfortune may be averted if the maternal uncle presents a *Kansal katori* (metal bowl) to the baby" (Banerjee, 1987:69). While among the Bazigar, the child's tooth is gently struck by the maternal uncle with a silver wire or with any article made of silver. The ceremony is known as *Dand thokna* (Banerjee, 1987:97). Among the Jat Sikh, the tooth is struck with a piece of mud clod (*Ibid.*, 121).

Toilet Training

Toilet training is an important aspect of child rearing. Various opinions were forwarded as to when the toilet training should begin. In case of severe and rigid toilet training, there developed different type of characteristics/personality. Ruth Benedict, Margarent Mead has analysed how toilet training had an impact on the child socialization.

The present study revels that both the Sonowal Kacharis and the Deoris do not have any specific way of toilet training. A study among the Sonowal Kacharis reveals that "normally toilet training is completed within one or two and a half years of time period" (Barua & Bora, 1979:339). It was also reported that children had to use gutters or open spaces nearby their house for defecation, till they were 6 to 7 years old. There are certain superstitions among the rural communities of Assam including the Sonowal Kacharis that when a child continued to wet bed, even after 5 years of age, then a curry is prepared with *Patimutuna fish* (a kind of fish). It is believed that if the child is fed with such curry, then the child may be able to control the bladder. It was noticed that generally, children of the maximum families stopped bed wetting by about the 2nd year.

Among the Deoris also children were not forced for toilet training. When children were young, occasionally defecation or urination was done on the hole of the bamboo floor of the platform-type house. Pigs and dogs below performed the duty of scavengers. Most of the mothers were in opinion that when the child attains the age of two years, they instruct them to go to the backside of the house for defecation and urination. By the age of 3-4 years, the children are aware of proper place for urination and toilet.

Freud emphasized the crucial importance of toilet training to the development of child's personality. Erikson (1954) focused that there is the danger of development of shame and guilt if toilet training is too severe and rigid. It was also reported that the later the toilet training began, the quicker the child learnt (Brazelton, 1962:121-28; quoted from Bhogle, 1978:10). The issue is still confusing, however, "clinical reports show the harmful consequences of severe toilet training" (Kuppuswamy, 1984:57).

Care Taker

Among the Sonowal Kacharis and the Deoris, a child is brought up in the natural environment, without much artificial pressure. Till 2-5 years, a child is associated with its mother or with the female members of the family. They follow various measures to keep the child healthy. As the villages are within the easy reach of the modern medical facility women take help of medical check-up during pregnancy. Vaccinations against DPT, Polio, BCG, Typoid, etc. are common among the villagers. Almost in all cases, children were given triple injection.

Only a few cases were reported where they could not provide this, which according to them is due to negligence. Along with the medical treatment, they have full faith on certain traditional beliefs and observe various rituals to appease the deity responsible for a particular disease. Some families also treat the children at home by herbal medicine. It was reported that "When children suffer from fever, occasionally juice is prepared from earth worm (found in the root of big banana tree), pepper and water" (Barua and Bora, 1979:343). Such incident is not a regular feature and reported in rare cases. But the Sonowal Kacharis invariably preserve the dried naval cord and the water extracted from this cord is used in certain diseases like dysentery, fever, etc.

To protect the child from evil spirits they put "black spot" on child's forehead. Similarly, tying a black strings or "*Bagh moni*" (big beads) on the waist is a common practice. They are no doubt aware of the benefit of modern medical facilities. But at the same time, they believe in the effect of spirit or evil eyes. Among the Tai Khamyangs, for the protections of small babies from malevolent spirit, evil eyes, e.g. *Daini, Alokhoni*, are manifested by various means and techniques applied duly from time to time. When a child suffers from stomach pain and cries continuously, it is thought that he is possessed by *Alokhoni* (female spirit). It is believed that such spirit resides in the eaves drip. If a child is taken to such places, either in the morning or in the evening he/she may be possessed by such spirits (Barua, 1998: 319). The adult may also be possessed by *Daini* who are believed to be residing in forest, big trees, ponds, etc. To propitiate *Daini/ Alakhani*, they are advised to perform *Daini puja.*

For performing the *puja*, a big cock is offered for the patient, citing the name of *Daini*. Then the cock is killed and cooked by the priest. In the meantime, a *Tum* (a wicker work basket used for holding grain is made with bamboo stripe *Tongali*). Rice and meat are kept in the *Tum*, which is finally tied by the entrails of the cock, nails and feathers of the cock are also placed inside the *Tum*. The priest offers the *Tum* towards the patient and prays in the name of *Daini*, so that she may leave the patient. The *Tum* is taken to the forest by the priest alone and while keeping the *Tum*, he loudly mentions that, "they are offering a cock as big as an elephant and rice as much as the product of 1 *bigha*". After shouting three times, he puts off the earthen lamp for 5 minutes. As reported, there are occasions, when thet *Tum* is taken away by the *Daini*, during these 5 minutes. Sometimes, ornaments, clothes, etc. are also placed in the *Tum* to appease the

Daini. There are rare occasions, when they perform such ritual (Barua, 1998:319). The study reveals that both modern medical reatment and traditional rituals are performed to keep the child healthy.

By six years, the child is chronologically as well as developmentally ready to go to school and to absorb from a world beyond the family. They also form a play group and play marble, *Tang-guti*, *Chor-police*, etc. Nature also provides enough scope and it was found that the Deori children spend a lot of time in swimming, playing on sand, finding fruits and edible from the nearby forest. As the children are provided with less costly materials, they have to find their own way to spend their leisure. "In many primitive communities games form a part of or are carried on side by side with responsible task. Among the Chaga, for example, young boys when tending cattle organize themselves into play groups, elect one of their member as chief of pasture and carry out battles in imitation of adult warfare" (Piddington, 1963:181). They observe various rituals and festivals which provide enough opportunity of transmission of their knowledge.

The Deoris have a tradition of maintaining youth dormitory system commonly known as *Morang ghar*. Dormitory system is a in-built mechanism for co-ordinating the activities of individuals and other social units for smooth functioning of society. In the absence of a mechanism for transmission of the heritage orally and through living, the continuation of culture would be adversely affected. Its training imparts them the lore and learning necessary to cope with any situation because of the rigorous training through which youth are to go through their formative years. Once they acquire the necessary skills they feel proud in transmitting the same to the next generation. Youth dormitory has been found as an elaborate system among the Trobriand Ilanders, the Australian, the Melanesians and the East and West African tribes. The system is widely found among many tribes of Central and South India and among the tribes of North East India. The traditional function of youth dorminatory among the Deoris was very strong, where the village youth spent their time together at night, learning and training the younger ones about the values and customs of the society. "Though the *Morang ghar* in its traditional form does not exist among the Deoris, yet at present they are involved in solving some of the current problems of the villagers, e.g. electricity, water supply, communication problem, etc." (Barua, 2000:41). In most of the rural communities, there are youth (both boys and girls) associations for performing various collective functions. Such associations fulfils the function of uniting the individuals through collective participation at public rituals and ceremonies. The Tai Khamyangs and the Tai Turungs observe various religious festivals and ceremonies. The youth associations perform a significant role in organization and co-operation. Such community festivals offer a platform for organization, co-operation and an opportunity where each and every member performs her/his role. The villagers perform regular prayers in *Vihar* during the *Varsavara (brata)*. It starts from the day of full moon in the month of *Sawan* (mid-July) to the full moon day in the month of *Ahin* (mid-October). The *Astasheel* holders stay in the *Vihar* during the night also. During such festivals, the youth and young boys and girls look after the comfort of *Astasheel* holders, who take part in *gatha*. The youth organizations (boys/girls) look after the management of the festival.

Generally, in almost all the festivals, the children assemble in the *Vihar*. The *Vante* (religious head) in such occasions tell the stories from *Jataka*, which are full of moral values. The significant events of Lord Buddha are also explained on such occasions. All their religious ceremonies are invariably followed by a feast or different types of merry making. The children and the youth get the opportunity to prepare/serve their traditional dishes. They normally make *Tupula bhat* (rice packet). An amount of cooked rice packed in *Kau pat* (plantain leaf) or banana leaves is named as *Tupula bhat*. They also prepare pickles from some indigenous herbs like *Pofaihem* (Polygonum Oderatum), *Lung pat,* etc. After the prayer all the members partake in the feast. The feast or tea party on the occasion of the festival is jointly arranged by the youth and children. Their joint efforts indicate a sense of oneness among the villagers (Barua, 2001:103). In the words of Firth, "religion rites unite the members of the society in common assembly, under an aegis which cannot be basically disputed and so reaffirm their solidarity and enforce social interaction" (Firth, 1971:239). The children from their infancy accompany their mothers to the *Vihar.* While observing the action of their elder members very closely, they understand the roles and moral values behind it. The ceremonies, major or minor, performed within the circle of family and communities consolidate the child's and adult's beliefs that the family ties are the most moral, durable and reliable of all social relations. Gradual participation and acceptance in the wider world make the children aware about the folkways and mores and they become conscious about their roles and functions. The culture in which the child is born is too vast, too comprehensive, and too diverse to be transmitted entirely, either by the family or other agencies subsequently assisting him. But at the same time it is a fact that such occasions provide enough scope of transmitting the indigenous knowledge to the next generation, and getting scope of learning their culture on their social setting.

To mould the individual and for the continuation of the society, transmission process is considered very significant. Social life is the essence of human life. It develops out of constant patterning of social interactions and relationship among human beings, as such, "A human community is a body of people sharing in common activities and bounded by multiple relationship in such a way that the aim of any individual can be achieved only by participation with others" (Firth, 1961:41). Life in a community means organizations of the interests of the individuals, regulation of their behaviour towards one another, and grouping of them together for common action. The social structure of any community includes the different types of groups which the people form and the institutions in which they take part.

Thus, as a social system in each community there is a systematic arrangement of individuals for fulfilling social functions. A social system may often been defined as a plurality of individuals interacting with each other according to shared cultural norms and meaning. Dictionary of Anthropology mentions, "The social system consists of both a social structure of interrelated institutions, statuses and roles and functioning of that structure in terms of social actions and human interactions" (Chopra, 2005:228). All social organizations/institutions are part of social system as all individuals are to perform specific functions for the continuity of the society. Thus social system may also be defined as a set of social relations which are regularly actualized and thus reproduced as a system through interaction. The groups and institutions in a society are always based on some principles and transmitting process works through such institutions both informal and formal. The frequent interaction with elders and inter- and intra-communal activities leads to learning about indigenous wisdoms and transmitting process starts. The seeds of social relations developed, nurtured and sustained through instructions imparted at family level, institution like village dormitory etc. In the present day the associations of various types fulfil the role of transmitting process in a community, the nature of transmmiting process may be different but in the absence of any such system, the continuity of the cultural values and traditions is not possible.

6
Summary and Conclusion

The present chapter has been devoted entirely to summarize the data presented and discussed in the preceding chapters. To highlight the findings, some concluding remarks have also been incorporated here and there.

The main emphasis of the present study is to explore the indigenous knowledge and belief system among the two major Scheduled Tribes of Assam. Effort has also been made to incorporate the available published data to give a meaningful interpretation of the study. The North East India is the home of diverse tribes and communities. Each has their own traditional knowledge which a particular community acquired in a given environmental condition. Thus, the entire region of North East India is a world of indigenous skill and knowledge. They are applied in different areas of problem solving covering a wide range of day-to-day activities such as, health care, ethno-medicine, environmental protection, agriculture, food security and preservation, etc. There is no written record of such practices, but they are guided by well established unwritten principles, which are transmitted from one generation to the next. These are all time-tested skills.

Ecology or a particular environmental condition plays a significant role in developing the traditional knowledge. This is because traditional knowledge is the local knowledge which has been specially developed to meet the need of a particular community in a specific environmental set-up. These, no doubts, provide a suitable base for the survival of the community. Though, a particular environmental set up may be considered as one of the major factor responsible for developing indigenous knowledge, yet cultural factor contribute equally for the emergent and continuity of indigenous knowledge system. The two tribes living in the same environment may have developed different knowledge system for their survival. Thus, ecology and culture go hand in hand for the continuity and development of indigenous wisdom, which may also be referred as indigenous knowledge. It is also a fact that different communities living in same environment utilize/use the same materials or herbs and shrubs for their survival. Here, comes the question of adaptation. As mentioned by Cohen (1968:48) "every culture has a strategy of adaptation and each represents a unique social design for extracting energy from the habitat." Moreover, people are emotionally attached to their culture/racial origin. And it has always been reflected through their socio-religious beliefs and practices. The uniqueness of a community is reflected through such parameters. So, for understanding the total gamut, a number of issues should be considered.

The traditional knowledge provides us various clues to understand the folk wisdom. It was mentioned by Elwin (1989:290) "the tribes have discovered the secrets of living under hard conditions that the rest of us needed." From earliest stage, men had to develop practical wisdom in dealing with their immediate environment. This they have learnt after a long struggle; sustainability is the end result of their hard and enduring labour. Similarly, in course of migration or movement, the people had to face both favourable/unfavourable environmental conditions. In spite of their unique adaptive mechanism, they are trying to preserve their traditional wisdom and sometimes such situation may adversely affect their adaptive mechanism. In a new situation, they are to acquire/learn new knowledge from their immediate tribes and communities. Thus, when we analyze the indigenous knowledge, in certain sphere we find that all the tribes and communities share similar knowledge system. While in some other spheres we observe differences. Thus, we have to admit that indigenous knowledge is the local knowledge which emerged in a particular situation. We cannot make a rigid watertight compartment of the communities in interpreting the local knowledge. However, beliefs and superstitions are culturally transmitted. In this sphere, ethnic/racial factor may be considered significant. Considering the entire interpretation, indigenous knowledge system encompasses the innovations, technologies, traditions, practices, wisdom and teaching, etc. of certain regional, indigenous or local communities within a particular environmental condition.

For the present study two Scheduled Tribe communities, i.e. the Sonowal Kacharis and the Deoris were considered for intensive study. The Sonowal Kacharis are one of the most ancient Scheduled Tribe (plain) living within the geographical perimeter of Assam. They are a sub-group of the great Kachari tribe of Assam belonging to the Asiatic Mongoloid race of Sino-Tibetan stock.

The Deoris constitute one of the distinct Scheduled Tribe of Assam. Linguistically, they are affiliated to the great Tibeto-Burman group and racially they belong to the Mongoloid stock.

Two major objectives of the study are:

(i) To explore and document the indigenous knowledge and belief system. Its domain includes areas like indigenous health care, reproductive health and child care, food preparation and preservation, natural resource management and host of other activities of the indigenous communities.
(ii) To find out to what extent such knowledge may be utilized in Developmental process. What steps may be taken to preserve the knowledge.

Indigenous knowledge system encompass a number of areas for investigation. Hence, it is humanly not possible to incorporate all the areas under a single study within a stipulated timeframe. Due to this constrain, the present investigation has been conveniently limited to:

(a) Indigenous Health care practices.
(b) Indigenous knowledge relating to food.
(c) Indigenous knowledge and socialization process.

Standard Anthropological method has been used either independently or in combination with others. For studying indigenous skills, the qualitative approach has been adopted. Depending on the nature of data, the techniques have been used either independently or in collaboration. For quantitative data, more emphasis has been put on techniques like observation and collection of concrete cases, etc. On the basis of pilot survey, both open and close-ended schedule has been prepared.

Considering the communities, data have been collected from three Sonowal Kacharis and two Deori villages of Dibrugarh district of Upper Assam. The village is situated 22 to 30 km away from

Dibrugarh town. Villages have been selected from two different settings, e.g. Forest villages and Revenue villages.

Forest villages were selected keeping in mind that indigenous knowledge, beliefs and customs may distinctly be traced in forest villages because there exists a symbiotic relationship between the tribal population and forests. The reservation of forest land in Assam is slightly different from other states of India. Most of the forest villages of Assam were established to rehabilitate the flood affected communities in the initial stage. Their villages were established in the periphery of forest land. They have the right to stay in the forest land but they do not have the right to sell the land even in emergency. They even cannot mortgage the land. Because of it they are not in a position to utilize the benefit of developmental schemes launched by the government. Where there is availability, they are expanding their land for cultivation purposes. They are to abide by rules of Forest Department.

The data generated from the field which were carefully systematized and scientifically analyzed have conveniently been distributed for presentation in six different chapters. The first two chapters are exclusively devoted to include the aims and objectives of the study, research design, methodology, communities and areas of study, the historical background of the communities, their distribution, etc.

A detailed description of micro field, their settlement patterns and demographic variables have been analyzed in the Chapter-2. An analysis of data on demographic variables among the Sonowal Kacharis in two forest villages revealed that the total population of 515 is distributed in 91 households. The average number per household is 5.7. The percentage of male 272 (52.81%) is slightly higher than that of the female, i.e. 243 (47.18%). It has been observed that 16 to 20 age group category has the highest number of individuals, i.e. 54 (10.48%) out of which 25 (4.85%) are males and 29 (5.63%) are females. Again the lowest number of individual which is 4 with a percentage of 0.77 is found in the 71-75 and 75-80 age group categories.

The children (0-5 yrs) constitute approximately 7.76 per cent of the population, whereas the figure in the next higher group (6-10 yrs) stands at 8 per cent, approximately. This may reflect a reducing trend in the birth rate during the last five years.

The revenue village of Duliagaon is homogeneously inhabited by the Sonowal Kachris. For the present study 110 families were considered for intensive socio-demographic study. The demographic trends reflect more or less the same picture in two different settings. In this village also out of total population of 534, it has been found that 270 (50.56%) are males and 264 (49.44%) are females. It indicates that percentage of male is slightly higher than that of the female. It has also been revealed that 21-25 age group categories have the highest number of individuals, i.e. 62 (11.61%). The lowest number of individual which is 1 (0.18%) is found in the 86-90 age group categories comprising a single male member.

The distribution of families according to size in two forest villages and one revenue village reveal that medium-sized family occurs in the highest frequency, i.e. 40 (43.95%) in the forest villages while in the revenue village, small size family occurs in the highest frequency, i.e. 54 (49.1%). The very large family, i.e. 9 and above member is found to be significant in forest villages (15.38%), whereas in revenue village, the number is not that significant, only 6.3 per cent of very big families are recorded. The differences in size of families may be due to location and set up.

A study on type and composition reveals that nuclear family predominates in both type of the villages. The percentage is slightly higher in forest villages (49.45) than the revenue village (47.27). The number of joint family is comparatively higher in revenue village, i.e. 36 (32.72%) than the forest village, i.e. 20 (21.98%).

Among the Sonowal Kacharis, both inter- and intra-village marriages are found, but the study reveals that village endogamy is very common. In the forest villages 55 marriages (34.59%) have taken place within the village. There are only 3 marriages which took place beyond 100 km. More or less same picture is found in the revenue village. There are 92 (60.14%) marriage which have been performed within a spatial distance 0-1 km, i.e. within the same village. There are only 3 marriages (1.96%) which took place beyond 111 km.

The Sonowal Kacharis are endogamous having a number of exogamous clans. Clan exogamy is the most important consideration that the tribe most strictly adheres to. The analysis reveals that in the forest villages, maximum number of marriages, i.e. 128 (80.50%) took place within the same tribe and it is a good example of tribal endogamy. The Sonowal Kachari villages are situated in the midst of other communities and occasionally marriages take place within those communities. Significant number of marriages, i.e. 16 (10.06%) occurred with other backward communities, i.e. the Ahoms, Chutias, etc. There are 7 cases (4.40%) where marriage took place with the Deoris. The Sonowal Kacharis and the Deoris have a congenial relationship from the past.

An analysis of socio-demographic study among the two different settings projects more or less the same picture with a slight variation in certain aspects.

In case of Deoris, intensive study was made in the forest village Modhupur Deorigaon. The village falls under the jurisdiction of Dihingmukh Reserve Forest. The two villages, inhabited by the Sonowal Kacharis are situated adjacent to the Deori village. Thus, it is found that all the three villages are situated in the same environmental condition having same kind of facilities and facing similar problems.

The demographic analyses among the Deoris reveal that the total population of the village is 406 distributed in 62 households, giving the average size of the family as 6.5. The analysis also indicates that the population of female 210 (51.72%) is slightly higher than the male 196 (48.27%). The children (0-5 yrs) constitute approximately 10.09 per cent of the population. It also reveals that the active labour force (16-55 yrs) is 245 (60.34%, of the total population), that is supposed to look after 39.6 per cent dependents, i.e. children and adolescent.

An analysis of the families according to size among the Deoris reveals that medium sized family occurs in the highest frequency, i.e. 28 (45.16%). The trend is more or less same as Sonowal Kacharis of forest villages. The analysis of the type and composition shows that number of nuclear family is found in highest frequency, i.e. 27 (43.54%). It indicates that in both the communities, the trend of nuclear family is apparent.

The Deoris are endogamous, having a number of exogamous clan/*Bansha*. They prefer to confine their marriage within the same tribe, but marriages occasionally take place with other tribes and communities according to the demand of the situation. The study reveals that significant number of marriages, i.e. 80 (77.66%) took place with the other neighbouring tribes and number of marriages which occured with the Sonowal Kacharis, i.e. 12 (11.65%) is significant. The same trend is noticeable among the Sonowal Kacharis where maximum number of marriages took place with the Deoris. Thus, it may be said that inter-community marriages among the Deoris and Sonowal Kacharis are common.

Economy of a group cannot be considered as an independent unit, because it is clearly linked with the total socio-cultural life. Economic activities should not always be considered from survival strategy, because it is equally necessary to find out how it helps in reflecting their culture. Thus, communities living in the same ecological condition may have different ways of technology and belief system. Both the Deoris and the Sonowal Kacharis is agriculturist and agriculture is the primary means of livelihood. They cultivate different types of paddy like *Ahu, Sali* and *Bao* and other improved varieties of paddy according to the condition of their paddy field. The present study also reveals that though they are agriculturist, yet a noticeable percentage of persons have gone for other occupation. As all the forest villages are not far from Dibrugarh town and better communication facilities enable the villagers to utilize the educational facilities of the town. This also helps in increasing the general literacy rate. Among the Sonowal Kacharis the literacy rate is 78.45 per cent and among the Deoris it is approximately 75 per cent. In both the communities, a sizeable number of persons are engaged in professional job, like the Doctor, Engineer, etc.

While analyzing the settlement pattern and house type, it is revealed that all the households among the Deoris are platform type, normally referred as *Chang-ghar*. Though the Sonowal Kacharis and the Deoris are living in the same environmental condition frequently affected by flood, yet not a single platform type of house is visible among the Sonowal Kacharis. Of course, they raise the plinth of the houses slightly higher to protect it from flood water. As the traditional house type of the Deoris is platform type, they continue their tradition in any settlement areas. The impact of culture may be traced in such traits like other tangible cultural heritage of the population.

The present study particularly emphasized the traditional health care system. A study of indigenous/traditional knowledge system among the Sonowal Kacharis and the Deoris reveal that they have a rich tradition of indigenous knowledge, which they have accumulated in course of living in a particular region. Chapter-3 incorporates detailed description of indigenous health care system among the two communities. It deals particularly with ethno medicine and the treatment of diseases. Along with it, an effort has been made to incorporate the data relating to ethno medicine from other communities. The analysis of data in two different settings, i.e. forest village and the revenue village shows slight differences.

A study in two forest villages inhabited by the Sonowal Kacharis reveals that there are very few elderly persons who can describe the indigenous treatment. Though, there is no professional folk medicine man, yet there is an old man who has the knowledge and prescribes the appropriate medicine in time of need. Only 19 different ailments were recorded. On the otherhand, 30 different ailments were reported from the individuals of the revenue village Duliagaon. In the village there is a folk medicine man, commonly referred as *bez,* who treats the patient immediately. Moreover, many of the elderly males/females are conversant with the traditional treatment. They can immediately prescribe the required medicine with the available herbs in the vicinity. As all the prescribed herbs are not always available in the locality, the elderly women starts the treatment with the available herb. In this way, the patient may get some relief. It was reported that the same disease may be treated with maximum of 5 to 6 different ways, using a single herb or combination of many herbs.

The Sonowal Kacharis also believe in supernatural causation of diseases. All through out the year, they observe various religious rites and rituals to propitiate the specific god, responsible for a particular disease.

A study of ethno medicine among the Deoris reveals that in the forest village only 12 different diseases could be recorded which may be treated by indigenous ways. There is no folk medicine man in the village and in emergency they seek the advice of folk medicine man of the nearby villages. This does not indicate that the common people are not aware about their indigenous ways of treatment. They could explain it in their own ways. A study in another Deori village (Revenue) which is more than 100 years old; reveals that they are rich in ethno-medicine. There are two medicine men in the village having sufficient knowledge about herbal medicine. They have treated different types of ailments and in the present study, 17 different types of ailments were recorded. But door to door survey in 30 households reveals that only some of the ailments are treated at home. And in most cases, they prefer to go for medical treatment at hospitals. The study also reveals that the Deoris believe in supernatural forces for disease causation and seek remedies through magico-religious practices. They too perform various socio-religious rites and rituals to propitiate the specific deities responsible for a particular disease.

An analysis of indigenous health care system in two communities situated in different settings reveals slight differences. The settlement of population in revenue village is very old and it could be traced that the village is more than 100 years old. While all the forest villages were established to rehabilitate the flood effected people and it occurred after 1950s earthquake. While analyzing the ethno-medicine, it was found that the people could tell more about their indigenous treatment and in some of the villages, there are traditional folk medicine men. They treat the patient of their own village and also the people who come from the nearby villages for treatment. Most of the household have well maintained kitchen garden and the common jungles in the surrounding areas provide them with the necessary herbs and shrubs for treatment. It is a familiar scene in rural areas of Assam that each village has a common jungle from where they collect firewood, herbs and shrubs, etc. The community organization seemed to be strong or have solid bases in revenue villages.

While the forest villages in the rehabilitated situation projects a different situation. Most of the households do not have well maintained kitchen garden. Of course, they collect some of their requirements from immediate forest land or from the marshy land near the river bank. It seemed that they do not have strong community base and in the absence of it, the indigenous knowledge system may not be properly preserved and transmitted.

In case of food habits of the population, environment and local availability of food resources play an important role. Besides ecology, cultural/racial factor plays an important role in determining the food habits of a particular community.

The Sonowal Kacharis and the Deoris are both living in same environmental condition. They have their own methods of preparations and preservation of food items. Rice is their staple food and they prepare rice in various ways. *Sewa bhat*, *Chunga chawal* is their favourites and they invariably prepare such items to entertain the guests. The people eat three heavy meals a day. They are fond of drinking tea in the morning. During festivals like *Bihu,* they prepare different types of rice cakes and other delicacies. The people drink country liquor prepared from rice. Most of them also offer such drink to their ancestors and use in ceremonies as tradition. After a hard work, or in leisure time, a drink is a must especially for the male members of the communities.

Smoking, roasting and boiling are the ancient methods of cooking and is still followed by most of the tribal people. Hearth (fire place) plays an important role in smoking and roasting. The hanging platform above the hearth is a must in the kitchen, but the number and size of platform varies from community to community. Invariably, fishes are dried both in the platform over the hearth or in the sun. In case of preparing and processing meat, they follow more or les same procedure as fishes. Preservation process mainly deals with fermentation, smoking and sun drying. This may be considered as one of the earliest wisdom of indigenous population as it is done without using any chemicals thereby retaining the nutritious values of the food materials. They use various implements for catching fishes. During plantation, they also collect fishes with bare hands. All over the world, wet cultivators follow such practices in catching fishes in the paddy field.

It is also reported by the villagers that they get vegetables, wild shoots, roots, leaves and other edible stuff from the forest areas or marshy land on the bank of the river. The common villagers as a whole are aware about the benefit of various herbs. During a visit to the village school, the teachers, office staff talked about a wild shrub *Sengmora* [*Lasia Spinosa* (L)]. They narrated how it is beneficial to heal the internal wound of the cattle. One of the members immediately rushed to the nearby forest and collected two saplings. They also reported that it is also prescribed for the individual who suffers from cancer. Such interpretation no doubt made it clear that common people are also aware of the medicinal values of wild herbs and shrubs. In their day-to-day life, they consciously/unconsciously prepare curry from herbs/shrubs which have medicinal value. Different varieties of fish and meat dishes are prepared by them. Bamboo shoots are very popular among them. Besides the normal food items, they are very much fond of insects which are considered as delicacy. They also observe some prescriptions and prohibitions in their food items. In case of illness, they follow their own indigenous beliefs and practices.

Man eats a variety of food derived from both plants and animals. They are in general not selective about it and are not aware about the nutritional part of the food they take. They take only those vegetables that are getting from their immediate environment. But while collecting they have shown ecological wisdom in plant resource utilization and there are various examples from different communities, e.g. Ojibway Indians, Autralians, Melanesians and the studied population including the Tiwas of North East who follow their indigenous wisdom in collecting food materials. This wisdom no doubt evolve from the empirical experience of generations over a period of time. Of course, in recent years, it is observed that commercial foods have become popular among them.

Detailed analysis of ethnic food items may also reveal the migration history of a tribe, to a certain extent. It is well established fact that written history of Assam started with the arrival of Tai Ahoms in the soil of Assam. The Tai Ahoms entered Assam during 12th century A.D. and ruled in Assam for a long six-hundred years. Before the arrival of Tai Ahoms, there were various indigenous tribes in Assam, having independent kingdom. It is said that the Tai Ahoms learnt the art of preparing/eating *Amroli*/red ant (*oecophyla smaragdina*) from Borahi, a section of Kacharis, who were experts in preparing various ethnic foods. History tells us that because of their culinary expertise, they were engaged in charge of royal kitchen.

Kuchia (Hog-fish) is considered as delicious item and works as medicine in piles and stomach trouble. Before the arrival of the Tai Ahoms, the Kacharis did not know how to catch hog fish. They were surprised to observe how the Tai Ahoms could catch it in low muddy earth. They wanted to learn the skill from the Tai Ahoms. The Ahoms inmate replied that it was possible because they possess a special power to see and interpret even the interior of the human body not to speak of fish beneath the earth. The Kacharis were moved by the expertise and strength of the Ahoms and made friendship and started to communicate many of the royal secrets of the Kacharis to the Ahoms. Many of the scholars were in opinion that it might have indirectly helped the Tai Ahoms to conquer the Kachari Kingdom.

Indigenous knowledge/traditional knowledge are to be transmitted from one generation to the next. To understand the transmitting process, it is essential to consider various parameters, i.e. how the children are reared or culturalized. Whenever a child is born into a family, he is also born into a culture. The child acquires the values, attitudes through the process of socialization. The study rightfully incorporates how mothers are treated from conception onward. Various beliefs, prohibitions, preferences emerged among the communities living in different parts of the world. As an example, we may cite the issue of maintaining gap between the two issues. After birth, the placenta and related matters are buried and the process of burial varies from culture to culture. Among the Tai Khamyangs, the placenta is buried within the compound. It is believed that deeper the pit, longer is the gap between two issues (Barua, 1998). Among the Sikligars, it is believed that deeper the pit, the better will be the health of the mother and child (Banerjee, 1987). Among the Oraons of Chota Nagpur, it is not the depth of the pit for the burial of the after birth, but the height to which the digger of the pit raises his spade, that determine the gap between the two issues (Roy quoted from Ghuye, 1963).

Thus, the way of disposal of placenta and related matters reveal that most of the communities believe that gap between the two issues is essential prerequisite for the welfare of the mother and child. The existence of more or less same kind beliefs among the communities residing in two different poles, i.e. North-East, North and West inspire us to think about the evolutionary theory, i.e. the psychic unity of mankind. While emphasizing the uniformity, effort should be made to find out the uniqueness of each community because uniqueness of cultural heritages in different regions of the world is the outcome of indigenous knowledge system.

On the basis of their indigenous beliefs, the planners and developmental scientists may pursue the people to adopt family planning programme. Through the folk songs, folk tales, the children are learning their traditions. Moreover, various socio-religious ceremonies performed in the family and village level provide enough opportunities to observe and learn their traditional culture. The very basis of unity and co-operations are instilled through such activities. The informal organizations and institutions provide enough scope to learn many things about their culture. In their day-to-day life, by observing the making/using of implements and materials, they are learning their technical skills. The proper utilization/preservation of natural resources are also transmitted to the next generations from the observation of the day-to-day activities of the population. The survival strategy is learnt by the children through such processes and it helps in continuation of culture.

No human society is free from problems and it is a common impression that the lives of early men were not so congenial. Of course, compared to modern life, their livelihood patterns were different. From early stage of civilization, the human being is to take measures, develop indigenous ways to deal with problems, both environmental and social. There can be few questions about gathering, hunting and fishing existed long before herding or cultivation. Despite their simplicity, food gathering and hunting economy require considerable technical competence. To find and gather wild roots, nuts, seeds and berries, to trap or hunt the food animals requires knowledge not only of the terrain but of the most favourable times and the best conditions under which to obtain these foods, to say nothing of preserving them for future.This has successfully done by the primal people for their survival.

As the indigenous people are living at the mercy of nature they are to develop various conservative measures for the security of their own community. Depending on environment and cultural values, the procedures of utilization vary from community to community, but it is also a universal fact that human beings are always aware of balancing ecosystem and maintaining harmony with nature. Man lives in variety of ecosystems, warranting both biological and cultural adaptations. The adaptive mechanism and the knowledge of utilization of the natural resources is the key factor for the survival of the human society. The study focuses that the knowledge system or precaution which the indigenous people emphasized is entirely meant for longer social security. The various socio-cultural beliefs and practices, which emerged in course of development of human society, no doubt reflect the unwritten laws for their action. Different communities maintain their indigenous ways to manage the community resources in terms of food, storage, wild herbs and shrubs for their benefit. The sacred conservation practices, superstitions, religion taboos and prohibitions no doubt play an important role in protecting the natural resources and thereby managing the ecosystem. Their knowledge about different aspects and elements from their traditional environment is also reflected in their folk literatures. Thus, to have a greater understanding of the entire process of preservation and management, the various aspects, i.e. cultural, historical and political factors need analysis, what anthropologists refer as holistic approach. It is the responsibility of social scientists and anthropologists to explore the indigenous process, because there rest the basic philosophy of survival mechanism of society. The indigenous people may not be aware of the scientific reasoning behind each action and it is the job of social scientists to put scientific meanings into what may be referred as traditional wisdom. There is no doubt that many of the indigenous beliefs and practices have scientific meaning. On the other hand, there are certain deep seated beliefs which are pure fallacies. There are many communities where mothers do not breast-fed the new born immediately. Colostrums are considered impure and squeezed out, which are pure fallacies.

Special emphasis should be given to trace those beliefs which have scientific reasoning behind it. The social scientists should try to enter the heart of the communities through such existing concepts. At the same time attempt should be given to identify those values and beliefs which are pure fallacies. Stress should be given to convince the people about the adverse effects of such beliefs.

In both the situations, the developmental and social scientists should be very cautious about the cultural background of the communities. While writing the introduction to the book "*Cultural factors in technological change*", Spicer rightly observes that changing people's customs is an even more delicate responsibility than surgery. When a surgeon takes up his instruments, he assumes the responsibility for a human life. On the other hand, when the administrators of a programme seeks to alter a people's way of life, he is dealing not with one individual but with the well-being and happiness of generation of men and women (Spicer, 1952). So, heavier responsibility rests on the shoulder of social scientists and the anthropologists. In such condition it is the responsibility of the social scientists to document the entire indigenous/traditional knowledge of different tribes and communities. The indigenous knowledge, particularly ethno-medicinal practices are gradually disappearing due to various reasons. Thus, documentation of indigenous knowledge/wisdom is an urgent need of hour. Traditional knowledge/local wisdom is invariably link with the culture. Everywhere local wisdom develops on the cultural background. It is equally true that the pattern of culture is deeply embedded in traditional knowledge system. Thus, while analyzing the local wisdom, we may get enough scope to interprete their culture. This on the otherhand encourages the indigenous population the necessity for its revitalization. So, proper measures must be initiated in terms of analysis and documenting the indigenous knowledge system.

The importance of indigenous people and their traditional knowledge was stressed by the independent scholars as well as by various National and International organizations. The Rio Declaration on Environment and Development (in its principle 22; 1992:44) pinpoints the significance of tribals and their close relationship with the ecology. It states, Indigenous people and their communities have a vital role in environmental management and development, because of their knowledge and traditional practices. The practical applicability of indigenous knowledge system no doubt help in formulating alternative development model of sustainable nature. To achieve it we need the basic data from indigenous communities living in various regions. Regionwise variation would help us in interpreting the traditional knowledge system and there lies the seeds of developing alternative model for sustainable living.

Moreover, knowledge and beliefs are always interrelated. Knowledge emerges in course of practical action and beliefs help in continuation of knowledge. So while studying the indigenous knowlesge system, one is to give equal importance to other related matters. The society acts through social action and social interaction so that established norms and order is maintained and thereby stability of society exist. When the anthropologist attempts to describe a social system he necessarily describes a small model of social reality. This model represents in effect the anthropological hypothesis about "how the social system works". The different parts of the model system, therefore, necessarily form a coherent whole. Thus, the study of indigenous knowledge is not an isolated study or there is specific boundary to limit its scope. Various aspects of social life are reflecting through such study. Similarly, to utilize the knowledge systems properly, the combined effort of government, social scientists and researchers are considered essential. All are to play its role in maintaining and preserving the indigenous knowledge system which is fast disappearing due to various factors. The North East India is unique both from the ethic diversity as well as indigenous knowledge of these diverse tribes and communities and there are still enough scope for exploring and interpreting these vast treasure houses of indigenous knowledge.

Bibliography

Banerjee, B.C., 1987. *Child Development and Socialization*. New Delhi, Deep and Deep Publications.

Barua, B.K., 1969. *A Cultural History of Assam*. Guwahati, Dutta Barua & Co.

Barua, I. and A. Bharali, 2000. Mother's View towards Child Socialisation: A case Study among the Deoris of Assam. In *Bulletin of the Department of Anthropology. Dibrugarh University*. Vol. 28.

Barua, I. and A. Bharali, 2001. A Glimpse into Socio-Religious Life of the Deoris of Assam. In *Journal of Human Ecology*.12 (2): 87-94. Delhi, Kamla-Raj Enterprises.

Barua, I. and A. Gogoi, 1978. Attitude towards Family Planning: A Case Study among the Sonowal Kachari Women of Lejai Barua Gaon. In *Bulletin of the Department of Anthropology*, Dibrugarh University, Vol. 7-8.

Barua, I. and P. Barua., 2009. Socio-ecological Dimension of Food: A Study among the Ao Nagas of Nagaland. In *Journal of Indian Anthropological Society*. 44, 307-316.

Barua, I. and P. Bora, 1979. Child care and Motherhood, A Case Study among The Sonowal Kacharis of Assam. In *Man in India*. Vol. 79.

Barua, I. and R. Phukan, 1994. Socio-Cultural Roles of Deori Women. In *Bulletin of the Department of Anthropology, Dibrugarh University*, Vol. 22.

Barua, I. and R. Phukan, 1998. Socio-Religious aspects of Health among Sonowal Kacharis. In *The Eastern Anthropologist*, 51-4.

Barua, I. and R. Sonowal., 2011. Indigenous herbal medicine among the Sonowal Kachari Tribe: A Study in a Forest Village in Dibrugarh, Assam, India. In *NeBIO* 11:4 .

Barua, I., 1978. *Social Relations in an Ahom Village*. New Delhi, Sterling Publications Pvt. Ltd.

Barua, I., 1992. The Tai Turungs of Assam: A Study of Socio-Demographic Profile. In *Man in India*. 72(3), 317-329.

Barua, I., 1998. Family and Socialization Process: A Study among the Tai Buddhist Communities of Assam. In *North-East India Ethno Cultural Perspectives and Processes*. (Eds). A.K. Danda, B. Dasgupta, A. Basu. J. Sarkar., Calcutta, Indian Anthropological Society.

Barua, I., 2001. *The Tai Turungs of Assam*. Allahabad, K.K. Publications.

Barua, I., 2012. Textile and Handloom Weaving: Some Observations. In S. Sengupta (Ed) *Indigenous Knowledge Traditions*. New Delhi, Gyan Publishing House.

Barua, R. and I. Barua, 2009. Boro Kachari Women: A Glimpse into their Social Life. In *Bulletin of the Department of Anthropology*, Dibrugarh University. Vol. 37 .

Bhadra, R.K. and J.B Tirkey, 1997. *Health* Culture Practices in Rural Society: Case Studies of Castes and Tribes of North Bengal, (pp. 79-94). *In Health Studies in Anthropology* (Eds). F.A. Das and R.K. Kar., Department of Anthropology, Dibrugarh University, Dibrugarh.

Bhasin, V., 1997. Medical pluralism and Health Services in Ladakh. In *Journal of Social Science*, 1: 43-69.

Bhasin, V., 1999. *Tribal of Ladakh: Ecology, Human Settlement and Health*. Delhi, Kamla-Raj Enterprises.

Bhasin, V., 2002. Traditional Medicine among Tribal's of Rajasthan. In *J. Soc. Sci.*, 6(3): 153-172.

Bhasin, V., 2007. Medical Anthropology: A Review. In *Studies on Ethno-Medicine*. Delhi, Kamla-Raj Enterprises.

Bhuyan, S.K., 1960. *Assam Buranji*, Guwahati.

Bora, M., 2007. Origin of Deoris. *Assam Tribune*.

Bordoloi, B.M., G.C. Sharma Thakur and M.C. Saikia., 1987. *Tribes of Assam (Part-1)* (Ed.) Tribal Research Institute, Guwahati, Assam.

Boserup, E., 1970. *Women's Role in Economic Development*. London, George Allen & Unwin Limited.

Brahmachary, R.L., 1995. Traditional Knowledge and Modern Ecology. In *Journal of the Indian Anthropological Society*. 30:103-107.

Chongtham, N., M.S. Biht and S. Harongbam, 2011. Nutritional Properties of Bamboo Shoots: Potential and Prospects for Utilization as a Health Food. *Comprehensive Rev. Food Safety*, 10-153-169.

Choudhury, P.C., 1959. *The History of Civilization of the People of Assam to the Twelth Century AD*, Guwahati, Department of Historical and Antiquarian Studies.

Chaudhuri, B., 1986. Social Science, Health and Culture: The Tribal Situation. In *Social Action.* 39.

Chaudhuri, B., (Ed) 1990. *Tribal Health: Socio-Cultural Dimensions.* New Delhi, Inter India Publications.

Cohen, Y.C., 1968. Culture as Adaptation. In *Man in Adaptation: Biosocial Background* (Ed) Y. C. Cohen. Chicago, Aldine Publishing Company.

Darshan, S., 1998. Conserving a Community Resource: Medicinal Plants. In *Communities and Conservation.* (Eds). A. Katari *et al.*, UNESCO. New Delhi, Sage Publications.

Das, A.K. and Hui. Tag., 2006. Ethno-medicinal Studies of the Khamti Tribe of Arunachal Pradesh. In *Indian Journal of Traditional Knowledge.* 5(3)

Das, B.M. 2007. Sonowal Kachari Nigostiya Parichya (pp. 1-3) In M. Sonowal (Ed) *Sonowal Saurav Smarak Granth,* Assam: Sonowal Kachari Sanskritic Mahotsava.

Das, B.M., 1980. *People of Assam*, New Delhi, Gian Publishing House.

Das, F.A., I. Barua. and D.D. Das., 2008. Ethno-Medicinal Practices: A Case Study among the Sonowal Kacharis of Dibrugarh, Assam. In *Ethno-Medicine* 24(1); 33-37.

Dasgupta, S. and A. Sarkar., 2002. *Ethno-Ecology of Indian Tribes.* New Delhi, Rawat Publications.

Dave, P. and N. Tavkar, 1985. People of a Tribal Child of Panchmahal. In *Social Welfare.* 5.

Deka, R., 1976. Menarcheal Age among the Sonowal Kachari Women of Upper Assam. In *Bulletin of the Department of Anthropology,* Dibrugarh University. Vol. 5.

Devi, A. Premila., 2011. Plant Used by Meitei Community of Manipur for the Treatment of Diabetes. In Assam University Journal of Science & Technology (Bio & Envir. Sc.). 7(1)

Devi, J., 1999. Orchidor Arihana. (Assamese). *Prantik*, Vol. 10, Guwahati, Assam.

Devid, Bird., 1992. Beyond the Original Affluent Society, *Current Anthropology*. 33.25-47.

Dutta, A.C., 1985. Dictionary of Economic and Medicinal Plants. Khelmati, Jorhat. Assam.

Dutta, A.K., 2014. Kharisar Apakaritaou Thake. In *Amar Asom.*

Endle, S., 1911. *The Kacharis (Reprint),* New Delhi, Cosmo Publications.

Erasmus, Charles J., 1961. *Man Takes Control.* Minneapolis, University of Minnesota Press.

Eriken, Thomas Hylland, 2008. *What is Anthropology*? New Delhi, Rawat Publications.

Erikson, E.H., 1963. *Childhood and Society*, New York: W.W. Norton and Co.

Firth, R., 1941. *Human Types*. London, Thomas Nelson & Sons Ltd.

Firth, R., 1959. Acculturation in Relation to Concept of Health and Disease. In I. Galdston (Ed) *Medicine and Anthropology*. New York, International University Press.

Firth, R., 1971. *Elements of Social Organization*. London, Tavistock Publication.

Gait, E.A., 1969. *A History of Assam*, Calcutta, Thacker Spink & Co.

Government of India Report, 1994, *Ethnobiology in India. A Status*. New Delhi, Ministry of Environmental and Forest, Government of India.

Government of India, 1946. *Report of Health Survey and Development Committee*, New Delhi, Manager of Publication.

Grierson, G.A., 1966. *Linguistic Survey of India*. Vol. 1. Motilal Banarsi Das.

Guha, A., 1986. Folk medicines of the Boro-Kacharis—A Plain Tribe of Assam, pp. 191-199 B. Choudhuri (Ed) *Tribal Health*. New Delhi, Inter-India Publications.

Hallowell, A. Irving., 1963. Ojibwa World View and Disease. In I. Galdston (Ed) *Medicine and Anthropology*. New York, International University Press.

Herskovits, M.J., 1953. *Cultural Anthropology*. New Delhi, Oxford and IBH Pub. Co.

Honigmann, J.J., (Ed) 1973. *Handbook of Social and Cultural Anthropology*. Chicago, Rand McNally College Publishing Company.

Hughes, C., 1963. Ethno medicine, *International Encyclopedia of the Social Sciences*. New York, Free Press, MacMillan.

Kala, C.P., 2005. Ethno-medicinal Botany of the Apatani in the Eastern Himalayan Region of India. In *Journal of Ethnobiology and Ethnomedicine*. 1:11 doi: 1186/1746-4209 1-11

Kapoor, A.K. and S. Kapoor., (Ed) 1994. *Ecology and Tribals in Central Himalayas*. New Delhi. M.D. Publications.

Kumari, P., 2006. Etiology and healing Practices: A Study in Primitive societies of Jharkhand, (pp. 487-499). In P. Dash Sharma (Ed). *Anthropology of Primitive Tribes in India*. New Delhi, Serial Publications.

Landy, D., (Ed). 1977. *Culture, Disease and Healing: Studies in Medical Anthropology*. London, Macmillan Publishing Co. Ltd.

Lindon, E., 1991. Lost Tribes, Lost Knowledge. *Time Magazine*, September 23.

Linton, R., 1936. *The Study of Man*. New York, Appleton Century.

Lowie, R., 1953, *Primitive Society*. New York, Bony Liverright.

MacIver, R.M., 1924. *Community*. London.

Madan, G.R., 1964. *Changing Patterns of Indian Villages*. New Delhi, S. Chand & Co.

Mahapatra, L.K. and J. Das., 1990. Nutritional Eco-system of Orissa Tribal. In *Cultural and Environmental Dimensions of Health* (Ed) *B. Chaudhuri*. New Delhi, Inter India Publications.

Mahapatra, S., 1990. Cultural Patterns in Health Care: A View from Santal World. In *Cultural and Environmental Dimensions of Health.* (Ed) B. Chaudhuri. New Delhi, Inter India Publications.

Mahapatra, S., 1986. *Modernisation and Ritual Identity and Change in Santal Society.* Calcutta, Oxford University Press.

Maiti, S., 2005. A Study of Ethnomedicine among the Bholias of Chamoli (Uttaranchal). In *Social Dimensions of Health*. (Ed) A.K. Dalal and S. Roy. New Delhi, Rawat Publications.

Mao, Ashiho A. and N. Odyue., 2007. Traditional Fermented Foods of the Naga Tribes of Northeastern India. In *Indian Journal of Traditional Knowledge.* Vol. 6(1) 37-42.

May, Jacques M., 1960. *The Ecology of Human Diseases.* Annals of the New York Academy of Sciences, 84.

Minturn, L. & J.T. Hitchock, 1963. The Rajputs of Kholapur, India. In *Six Cultures* (Ed) B. B. Whiting. New York, John Wiley & Sons.

Misra, P. and A.K. Kapoor, 2003. Ethno-medical practices in a primitive tribe, (Vol. 1). 185-205. S. Sahay and P.K. Singh (Ed.). *Dimensions of Researches in Indian Anthropology*, New Delhi, Serial Publications.

Monghan, J. and Peter Just., 2006. *Social and Cultural Anthropology. A very Short Introduction.* Oxford University Press.

Montague, A., 1957. *Anthropology and Human Nature*. New York, McGraw Hill Book Company.

Nath, M., B.K. Dutta, and P.K. Hajra, 2011. Medicinal Plans used in Major Diseases by Dimasa Tribe of Barak Valley. In *Assam University Journal of Science & Technology.* (Bio & Envir. Sc., 7(1).

Norton, W.W., 1973. *New Introductory Lectures on Psychoanalysis.* New York.

Piddington, R., 1963. *An Introduction to Social Anthropology.* Vol.1. London, Oliver & Boyd Ltd.

Pradhan, B.K. and H.K. Badola., 2008. Ethnomedicinal Plant use by Lepcha Tribe of Dzongu Valley bordering Khangchendzonga Biosphere Reserve in North Sikkim, India. In *Journal of the Ethnobiology and Ethnomedicine* 4:22 doi. 1186/1746-4269-4-22.

Raaton, T., 2006. *History, Religion and Culture of North-East India.* Delhi, ISHA.

Rajguru, S., 1988. *A Medieval Assamese Society*. Asomi. Nowgaon.

Rappaport, R.A., 1967. *Pigs for the Ancestors*. New Haven, Yale University Press.

Rivers, W.H.R., 1924. *Medicine, Magic and Religion*. London, Kegan Paul, Trench Turners & Co.

Sachidananda., 1994. Socio-Cultural Dimensions of Tribal Health. In *Tribal Health in India* (Ed) S. Basu. New Delhi, Manak Publications.

Sahu, C., 2002. *Tribes of North-east India: An Ethnographic Profile*. New Delhi, Sarup & Sers.

Sajem, A. L. and K Gosai., 2010. Ethnobotanical Investigations among the Lusai Tribes in North Cachar Hill District of Assam, North-East India. In *Indian Journal of Traditional Knowledge*. 9(1)

Sarkar, A. and S. Dasgupta., 2000. *Ethno-Ecology of Indian Tribes, Diversity in Cultural Adaptation*. New Delhi, Rawat Publication.

Sarkar, R.M., 2008. *Primitive Tribal Groups in India. Tradition, Development and Transformation*. New Delhi, Serial Publications.

Sengupta, S. 2012. *Indigenous Knowledge Traditions*. New Delhi, Gyan Publishing House.

Sharma Thakur, G.C., 1972. *The Plain Tribes of Lakhimpur. Sibsagar and Nowgong*. Guwahati, Tribal Research Institute.

Singh, A., R.K. Singh and A. Sureja, 2007. Cultural Significance and Diversities of Ethnic Foods of Northeast India. In *Indian Journal of Traditional Knowledge* Vol. 6. (1) 79-94.

Sonowal, C.J., 2000. *Gender System among the Sonowal Kacharis: A plain Tribe of Assam*. Joipur, Raj Publishing House.

Sonowal, C.J., 2007. Demographic Transition of Forest Villages of Assam. In *Studies of Tribes and Tribals*. Vol. 5(1).

Sonowal, H. and G. Sonowal, 2001. Sonowalsokalor Lokodristi. Janma and Mritu In M. Sonowal and G. Sonowal (Ed) *Sonowal Kachariir Samaj and Sanskriti*. Dibrugarh, Printwell.

Sonowal, R. and I. Barua, 2011. Ethnomedical Practices among the Tai-Khamyangs of Assam. *Studies on Ethno-Medicine*, 5(1) 41-50.

Sonowal, R. and I. Barua, 2012. Indigenous Knowledge and Bioresource Utilization Among the Tai-Khamyangs of Assam, North-East India. In *International Research Journal of Biological Sciences*. (197): 38-43.

Sonowal, R. and I. Barua, 2013. Traditional Food Storage-Preservation Technology of the Tai Khamyangs of Assam. In *Bulletin of the Department of Anthropology, Dibrugarh University*. Vol. 41.

Spicer, E.H., 1952. *Human Problems in Technological Change: A Case Book*. New York, Russel Sage Foundation.

Taylor, C.E., 1976. The Place of Indigenous Medical Practitioners in the Modernisation Health Services. In *Asian Medical System: A Comparative Study* (Ed) C. Leslie. U.S.A, California Press.

Modernisation Health Services. In *Asian Medical System: A Comparative Study* (Ed) C. Leslie. U.S.A, California Press.

Tomar, Y.P.S. and R.D. Tribhuwan, 2005. *The Mavchis of Nandurbar: A Lesser Known Tribe* (Report) Pune, Tribal Research and Training Institute.

Vadakumehery, J., 2003. *Tribes and Cultural Ecology in Central India*. New Delhi, Mittal Publications.

Vidyarthi, L.P. and B.K. Rai, 1976. *The Tribal Culture of India*. New Delhi, Concept Publishing Company.

Wadell, L.A., 1901. *The Tribes of Brahmaputra Valley.* New Delhi, Logos Press.

Zhan, Ziaorui, 1994. WHO's Policy and Activities on Traditional Medicine. In *Traditional Health Systems and Public Policy* (Ed). Anwar Islam and Rosina Wiltshre, Ottawa. Canada.

Index